Columba's Iona:
A New History

✠

Columba's Iona:
A New History

✛

Rosalind K. Marshall

SANDSTONEPRESS
HIGHLAND | SCOTLAND

First published in Great Britain
and the USA in 2014 by
Sandstone Press Ltd
One High Street
Dingwall
Ross-shire
IV15 9WJ
Scotland.

www.sandstonepress.com

The publisher acknowledges subsidy from
Creative Scotland towards publication of this volume.

ISBN: 978-1-908737-82-3
ISBN e: 978-1-908737-40-3

Jacket design by Gravemaker + Scott
Typeset in Columcille and Sabon by
Iolaire Typesetting, Newtonmore
Printed and bound by Ozgraf, Poland

Contents

Foreword

by the Very Reverend Dr Finlay A.J. Macdonald,
Chairman of the Iona Cathedral Trust

Columba's Iona: A New History by Rosalind K. Marshall has
been commissioned by the Iona Cathedral Trust to mark the
1450th anniversary of Columba's arrival on Iona at Pentecost,
563. It is the Trust's first initiative under a new charitable purpose 'to advance the education of the public in relation to the
history, culture and heritage of Iona Cathedral and the island
of Iona'.

This new charitable purpose formed part of a reorganisation approved by the Office of the Scottish Charity Regulator
in 2010. Originally the main purpose of the Trust, as set up
by the 8th Duke of Argyll in 1899, was to care for the ancient Abbey and related heritage on Iona. Today this work
is carried out by Historic Scotland under lease arrangements
entered into in 2004 by the Trust, Historic Scotland and the
Iona Community.

The Trustees believe that *Columba's Iona: a New History*
is a valuable and timely contribution to the literature on this
rich seam of Scottish history. In Dr Marshall's experienced
hands the narrative is readily accessible to the general reader.
At the same time those who wish to dig more deeply will find
an absorbing series of endnotes which should more than satisfy
their requirements.

With thanks to the author and to Robert Davidson, Manag-
ing Director of Sandstone Press, I warmly commend *Columba's*

Iona: A New History. I also place on record the Trust's appreciation of the co-operative relationships it enjoys with Historic Scotland and the Iona Community as together we seek to secure this important heritage for future generations.

Finlay A. J. Macdonald
Easter 2013

Acknowledgements

I was delighted when the Iona Cathedral Trust commissioned me to write about the fascinating history of Iona Abbey, and I would particularly like to thank the Very Reverend Dr Finlay A. J. Macdonald, Chairman of the Trust and his colleagues, the Very Reverend Dr Gilleasbuig Macmillan, Minister of St Giles' Cathedral and Sir Ian Diamond, Principal of Aberdeen University. The Reverend Peter Macdonald, Leader of the Iona Community, Raymond Young, and Peter Yeoman, Head of Cultural Heritage, Historic Scotland, spoke to me about the abbey and the Iona Community today, while Graeme Bell, Head of Conservation, Historic Scotland, facilitated my research.

Dr Kenneth Veitch, Research Fellow, Edinburgh University, kindly read and commented on the first three chapters of this book in draft and Dr Janet MacDonald generously gave me a copy of her as yet unpublished 2010 Ph.D. thesis, 'Iona's Local Associations in Argyll and the Isles, *c*.1203-*c*.1575'. I have had very helpful information from Morag Cross, who compiled the catalogue of the Iona Cathedral Trust's archives, now deposited with the Royal Commission on the Ancient and Historical Monuments of Scotland and from Ishbel MacKinnon, Archivist, Inveraray Castle, who arranged access to the Argyll Papers there. I am likewise grateful to Anna Gordon; the Reverend Tom Davidson Kelly; Dr Ian Fisher; Dr Alison Rosie, National Records of Scotland; Olive Geddes and Sally Harrower, Manuscript Curators and Robert James, imaging technician, at the National Library of Scotland; the staff of the Royal Commission on the Ancient and Historical Monuments of Scotland; Denise Cowan, Head of Records Enterprise, National Records of Scotland; Sandra Kramer, Publishing Manager, Wild Goose Publications; Scotsman Publications Ltd and The British Newspaper Archive.

My special thanks go to Peter Backhouse, who went to Iona and took the excellent new photographs which form many of the illustrations. I also thank the copyright owners of the other illustrations: Glasgow Museums; Historic Scotland; National Library of Scotland; National Museums of Scotland; National Portrait Gallery, London; Reginald Bailey Archive; Royal Commission on the Ancient and Historical Monuments of Scotland and Trinity College Library, Dublin. I much appreciated the patient response of their picture librarians, who dealt so efficiently with my requests.

R.K.M.
1 March 2013

List of Illustrations

PICTURE CREDITS

© Peter Backhouse: 1, 2, 3, 6, 8, 10, 11, 12a, 16, 17, 18, 19, 20a, 20b, 20c, 20d, 22, 23 and 24.

© The Board of Trinity College, Dublin: 4

© National Museums of Scotland: 5

© National Library of Scotland: 7

© Crown Copyright Historic Scotland reproduced courtesy of Historic Scotland www.historicscotlandimages.gov.uk): 9, 12b.

© National Portrait Gallery, London: 13

© CSG CIC Glasgow Museums Collection: 14

© RCAHMS. Licensor www.rcahms.gov.uk: 15, 21, 25, 26, 28, 30a, 30b, 31, 32

© Raymond Bailie Archive: 27

© The Iona Community Archive: 29

Chapter 1

✠

Columba: Fox or Dove?

Why is Iona so special? For centuries people have been visiting this small and remote island off the west coast of Scotland, travelling there by land and sea, on foot, on horseback, by coach or train or car, by steamer or by ferry. Some speak of the magnificence of the scenery, the quality of the light and the sense of tranquillity. Others think of themselves as pilgrims, visiting an important early Christian site, and many talk of being mysteriously drawn back, over and over again. Even in our own apparently secular age visitors, when asked why they return, will mention St Columba, the imperious and energetic Irish monk who settled there in the sixth century and whose reputation is somehow intermingled with the spiritual atmosphere of the island itself.

He came, it is said, in May 563, on the evening of Pentecost (Whitsun), a man in his early forties, tall, fair and muscular, with curly hair and piercing grey eyes.[1] With him he had twelve other monks who were very obviously not his equals but were taking their orders from him. Among them were his uncle, Ernán, his cousins the brothers Baithéne and Cobthach, and his devoted personal attendant, Diarmait.[2] They dragged their wood and leather boat up on to the pebbled shore and prepared to spend the first of many nights on Iona, for that was to be their home. It seems probable that Columba had gone first to the hill fort of Dunadd on the mainland, to see his kinsman, Conall, King of Dalriada, and that the King had made him a gift of the entire island.[3]

1

There Columba would build a monastery, and he would be its first abbot.

How do we know any of this? It is, of course, difficult to reconstruct the life of someone who lived so long ago, but there are, for this particular man, unusually informative sources: a poignant Irish elegy, composed shortly after his death; a Latin *Life* written more than a century later by St Adomnán, one of his successors as abbot; and an Irish *Life*, probably composed four hundred years after that. There are fleeting references in the Irish annals, relevant passages by the Venerable Bede, who wrote his famous ecclesiastical history of England in 731 and, of course, there are later legends and poems. However, none of these is contemporary with him, they are of varying reliability and they were not intended to be biographical.[4] This can be frustrating for modern historians who are looking for verifiable facts. Amidst the legends, the prophecies and miracles, however, there is valuable circumstantial detail. Instead of criticising, it is therefore better to accept such sources on their own terms, albeit with caution, bearing in mind that we are not dealing with objective historical data – if there is such a thing. However we regard them, these tales contain truths and they are the means by which Columba's story has been preserved, resounding down the centuries to our own time.[5]

So who was this Irishman who has been of remarkable significance in Scottish life, perhaps the country's most popular saint, venerated by Roman Catholics and Protestants alike and respected by many of no faith? Columba was born in about 521. We do not know the exact date, but the year has been calculated from his accepted age at his death. His birthplace is traditionally said to have been Gortán, a village in Donegal, and although there is no mention of this before the twelfth century, it does seem probable that he came from that part of the country.[6] His father, Fedelmid was of royal descent, great grandson of the semi-legendary Niall of the Nine Hostages, High King of Ireland in the fifth century.[7] Ireland was divided into a surprising number of kingdoms at that time, Niall's many descendants were known as the Uí Néill, and influential Uí Néill relatives of Fedelmid ruled over important areas, including Donegal. In short, it is no exaggeration to say that Columba was very well connected indeed. Moreover, since the succession did not pass from father to son, he could have expected to be offered a position as a king himself, had he not followed a career in the Church instead.[8]

Little is known about Columba's mother, Eithne, other than that she came from a noble family and was the daughter of a man named MacNaue, who possibly lived in Donegal. A tenth-century list claims that, as well as Columba, she had a younger son and at least three daughters.[9] We catch a glimpse of her for a moment when Adomnán tells a charming but probably apocryphal story of her having a vivid dream when she was pregnant with Columba. In this dream, an angel appeared to her and gave her a wonderfully beautiful robe, embroidered with all manner of colourful flowers. A few moments later, the angel asked her to give it back, lifted it up, shook it out and let it float away on the breeze. Disappointed, Eithne watched it grow magically larger and larger until it measured more than all the plains and the mountains and the woods around her. A voice then spoke to her, telling her that she would bear a son who would be of such grace that he would be counted as one of the prophets of God. With that, she woke up, but she always remembered that prophetic, night-time vision.[10]

This brings us to the question of Columba's name. Adomnán was writing in Latin and so he used that version of the Irish name Colum. He added that the infant was baptised shortly after his birth but, according to a later account, the baby was at first called Crimthann, which somewhat disturbingly means 'Fox'.[11] With its connotations of cunning and deceit, that hardly seems an appropriate epithet for a future saint. However, it has been described as one of the most popular names in early Ireland, and indeed it was borne by various kings of Munster.[12]

Craftiness could have been seen as a desirable attribute for a successful ruler and might indeed have been chosen for Fedelmid's son. The thought that Columba may have begun life as Crimthann has led some experts to suggest that his family were pagans and that his name was changed to the one that we know him by when he was baptised.[13] Others have refuted this indignantly, preferring to think of him from the very beginning as Columba, which means a dove, is synonymous with gentleness and was also used frequently as a symbol of the Holy Spirit.[14] From the mid-seventh century onwards, 'Colum' was often extended to become Colum Cille, 'dove of the Church', distinguishing Columba from the many other Colums.[15]

It was common practice in Irish society for a child to be given to foster parents at an early age. In secular circles this was done to strengthen an alliance between the two families concerned, but it was also customary for a priest to accept as a foster child a young boy intended for a career in the Church. Various later Irish and Welsh saints are said to have been fostered from infancy[16] and, according to Adomnán, this is what happened with Columba, who was sent to be brought up by a priest called Cruithnechán, 'a man of admirable life'.[17] Later, as a young deacon, he was taught by Gemmán in Leinster, and then by a bishop identified by Adomnán as 'St Uinniau'. There is some doubt about this master's identity, for there was more than one bishop of that name. Possibly he was the distinguished Bishop Finnian of Moville, more probably he was Bishop Finnian of Clonard, teacher of various saints and perhaps Columba may even have been taught by both of these scholars.[18]

There then ensues a long gap in the story of his life. Until he was forty-one years old, Columba lived in Ireland, and yet almost nothing is known about that part of his career. His own abilities as well as his family connections must have made him a prominent figure, for he could not suddenly have developed his characteristic qualities of formidable energy and enterprise the moment that he set foot on Iona. It is tantalising that the monasteries at one time said to have been founded by him in Ireland during this period have proved to have been of a later date, but he was certainly an able and experienced administrator by the time that he left his native land.[19] Intriguingly, the Irish *Life* claims that during those years Columba contemplated going on a pilgrimage to Rome and Jerusalem, and later did actually travel to the French city of Tours, to visit the shrine of St Martin, who had introduced monasticism into Gaul and had died in about 400 A.D.[20]

St Martin was the son of a pagan Roman army officer. He too had taken up a military career and had been sent with his regiment to Gaul. Not long afterwards, on a freezing cold winter's day, he cut his cloak in half and shared it with a shivering beggar. That night he had a vision of Christ. Converting to Christianity, he chose to live as a hermit, but he was joined by a group of followers and he founded what became the first monastery in Gaul. Even when he was appointed Bishop of Tours ten years later, he insisted on living in a small cell near his cathedral. He destroyed pagan temples and went on to set up other monasteries in the area. He was in his eighties when he died, and his reputation was such that pilgrims flocked to see his tomb in a simple little chapel built over it.

Sixty years after his death, the numbers were so great that his body was moved to an impressive basilica specially constructed for the purpose and his stone sarcophagus was placed behind the high altar with a large block of marble above it, to make it more visible to the crowds who came to venerate his remains.[21] Whether Columba was among those pilgrims we shall never know. According to one account, he returned home with a somewhat macabre gift which had been presented to him in Tours: a precious copy of the gospels, which had allegedly been buried with the saint, on his breast. That Columba was given this special object sounds highly unlikely, but although the entire story of his visit may have been imaginary, it does indicate the importance of St Martin to the monastic movement in the Irish Church as well as elsewhere. Indeed, when Adomnán wrote his *Life* of St Columba he based its structure partly on the famous *Life* of St Martin by Sulpicius Severus.[22]

Even more intriguing than the apocryphal stories which swirl around Columba's earlier years is the question of why he left Ireland with such apparent finality in 563. No one ever suggests that he was seeking a quiet place to die, for that was not in his nature. Life expectancy might be short in those days, with all too many of his contemporaries dying in their thirties, but death was not what he was thinking about. No one knows for sure why he went, but a variety of explanations has been offered, the most dramatic of them concerning the Battle of Cúl Drebene. Possibly the reason for it being linked with his decision to go is that it took place in 561, just two years before his departure.

The details of the conflict are obscure, but what seems to have happened is that Diarmait mac Cerbaill, High King of Ireland, was defeated by an alliance of rulers from the north of Ireland. Included among them were an uncle and a cousin of Columba. It has been suggested that Columba himself was involved in the fighting, and that a livid scar on his side till the day he died was the result of a wound received at that time.[23] For a churchman to have engaged in combat would have been scandalous indeed, and most historians dismiss this theory, preferring the rather more innocuous explanation that Columba had successfully prayed for his relatives' victory. There were, however, dark thoughts that, perhaps with fox-like cunning, he had somehow instigated the battle at Cúl Drebene in the first place, in revenge for an attack on a young man who was under his protection.[24]

The following year a church synod was held at Teltown (Tailtiu) in County Meath, and at this synod Columba was excommunicated. Again because of the relatively short time between these events, historians have been tempted to link the two. Was Columba being punished for his involvement in Cúl

Drebene and for his part in causing the hundreds of lives lost on that occasion? This seems unlikely, for the sentence was revoked not long afterwards, and Adomnán would later insist that the excommunication had been improper, because the alleged offences were 'trivial and very pardonable.'[25] A later explanation for the excommunication would certainly fit that description. It says that Columba was in trouble for borrowing and copying without permission a particularly beautiful illuminated manuscript of the Book of Psalms which belonged to St Finnian. Everyone knew that Columba spent long hours copying manuscripts, and that he was particularly devoted to the psalms. Perhaps the High King of Tara had persuaded his friends among the clergy to concoct the accusation simply to get Columba into trouble.[26]

All we can say is that there is nothing definite linking Columba's departure from Ireland with either the battle or the brief excommunication and commentators nearer his own time preferred to see his journey in an entirely spiritual light. The Venerable Bede said that Columba went to convert Britain to Christianity by his missionary work among the Picts,[27] while Adomnán claimed that his sole reason for leaving Ireland was to be a pilgrim of Christ. 'White martyrdom', a term first used by St Jerome, was much valued in the early Irish Church. Red martyrdom implied death for one's religious beliefs, but white martyrdom meant deliberate separation from a person's home, family and friends, to go and live a life of asceticism elsewhere.[28] That is what Columba is believed to have been doing, and the *Amra Choluimb Chille*, the elegy written shortly after his death, also supports this view of his intentions.[29]

Whatever his motivation, he and his companions set sail in the spring of 563, presumably confident in the knowledge that they were not going to a hostile place. Most of what we now know as Scotland was the territory of the Picts, with Britons living in Strathclyde and Anglo-Saxons in Lothian. According to long-held belief, Irishmen from Dál Riata settled in the present day Argyllshire several decades before Columba's arrival, giving it the same name, subsequently altered to Dalriada. This view has since been challenged but, even if the inhabitants were not of recent Irish descent, they did appear to belong to the Uí Néill, and from the time of their arrival, Argyll and the Inner Hebrides were regarded as an extension of Ireland. What is more, a significant number of the people there are believed to have been Christian, as well as being allies of Columba's royal relatives.[30] He would have been well aware of these facts.[31]

It was the Annals of Ulster, written a century after the event, which say that before Columba landed on Iona he went first to Conall mac Comgaill the King of Dalriada, probably in his hill fort at Dunadd. Interestingly, a key source of the Annals is thought to have been a chronicle compiled on Iona from the early seventh to the mid eighth century. Adomnán too mentions Conall, saying that Columba stayed with him for a time not long after he arrived, explained his purpose in coming and was granted Iona.[32] Monasticism played a very important part in Irish Christianity, and monasteries were often established on islands, to be away from the distractions of more populated areas. There the monks would lead a life of prayer, meditation and study combined with work in the fields. Whether or not we believe another tradition that Columba the exile favoured Iona because, in keeping with the spirit of white martyrdom, he could not see his beloved Ireland from there, this particular island was a very suitable choice.

Iona is very small, only 5.5 km long by 2.5 km wide at its broadest point and the total area is about 800 hectares (2000 acres).[33] The Atlantic Ocean beats on its western shores with a ferocity and strong gales batter it in winter, while on the east side the Sound of Iona's deceptively sparkling blue and green waters in summertime give no hint of the dangerous currents beneath. The Sound is narrow, the shores of Mull are very close and so supplies of food and building materials could readily be brought over to the monastery. Indeed, for centuries a traveller wishing to cross to Iona would simply shout across the water for a ferry.

In Columba's day, Iona was known as Io, from the early Irish word meaning yew tree. Whether there were still yew trees when Columba came there is unknown, but studies of pollen found in the soil show that oak, ash, birch, willow and perhaps hazel grew there.[34] The north-eastern and central parts of the island are fertile, and archaeologists tell us that Iona has been inhabited from very early times, since the Bronze Age, in fact. There is one burial cairn dating from about the second millennium B.C., while the remains of a small fort survive from the subsequent Iron Age.[35] It has usually been assumed that Iona was uninhabited in 563, probably because Adomnán does not mention anyone living there. However, some historians have taken the view that it is very unlikely that there was no existing population at all, and an anecdote preserved in the later Irish *Life* may be a faint echo of an actual incident involving local hostility. According to this story, shortly after the Irish monks' arrival, they were suddenly confronted by two men claiming to be bishops, who tried to drive them away. Columba, always perspicacious, realised that they were imposters, lost no time in telling them so, no doubt in his characteristically forceful manner, and they immediately fled.[36]

Confronted or not by angry locals, Columba would have set his companions to work straight away on the construction of their monastery buildings. He had selected a site on the sheltered north-eastern side of the island. There have been long-running arguments as to the exact spot that he chose,[37] but the general consensus is that the church itself lay beneath the present day abbey.[38] The early buildings were all made of wood and probably thatched with reeds. The oak and ash trees would have been cut down for the purpose, for they vanish pretty quickly from the pollen records, and additional timber was probably brought over from Mull. The buildings were of timber, not because they had to be put up quickly, but because that was the way with Irish monasteries. These did not consist of one large, stone building with everything necessary for communal living. Instead, wattle and daub huts were dotted about with a few larger wooden structures all enclosed within a large earthen rampart with an outer ditch.

At Iona, a short stretch of earthworks is the only part of Columba's monastery to have survived. Largely rectangular in plan, such earthworks were there simply to delineate the area occupied by the monastic buildings and perhaps to indicate different divisions within it.[39] On Iona there was no east rampart, because the shoreline formed the boundary instead. The earthworks have been investigated in the past century by means of archaeological excavations, geophysical surveys and aerial photography, and the results show that they were modified and added to as time went on, with the result that they are now very complex.[40] It is a small, rather wavering ditch on the north side which probably belongs to Columba's era.[41]

The most important monastery building was, of course, the church, the focus of the community's daily life. It would have been the largest structure, with a window at the east end at least. During the hours of darkness it was not lit inside, apart from the candles on the altar, and when the monks came to services at night they brought their lamps with them.[42] We know that there was a side chapel, which was used for private prayer and may also have acted as a sacristy for storing relics. It did not have a separate entrance of its own, but was entered from the church itself.[43] The monks kept the Divine Office, the daily round of services customary in the Catholic Church. This involved a sequence of eight services during each twenty-four hour period, beginning with Matins at sunrise and continuing at three hourly intervals until Compline at the end of the day. Adomnán does not specifically list or describe them, for his readers would have been perfectly familiar with them, but he does mention four by name and three others are implied.[44] Sometimes Columba ordered Diarmait to strike a bell, even in the middle of the night, when he wanted to call the monks to pray for someone in particular difficulties.[45]

Differences between the early Irish Church and the Church of Rome have been greatly exaggerated, and most modern scholars have concluded that although the geographical distance between Rome and Ireland meant that variations of practice had come into being, they were usually of a relatively minor nature. Columba and his monks would have thought of themselves as members of the Church Universal just as much as their continental contemporaries did.[46] They all celebrated the same sacraments – the means of grace believed to be necessary for salvation. The seven sacraments of the later Roman Catholic Church (baptism, holy communion, penance, confirmation, marriage, holy orders and the anointing of the sick) were not defined until the twelfth century and were not officially recognised until 1439. In the sixth century there were only two.[47] The more important was holy communion, also known as the Eucharist, from the Greek word for thanksgiving. It was celebrated every Sunday in the church of the Iona monastery, with Columba standing in front of the altar to consecrate the bread and the wine, he and his monks wearing white linen robes. No work was allowed on that day, and the food eaten was better than at other times, whether in quality or amount is not specified.

Communion was also celebrated on saints' days and on the two great festivals of the Christian Church, Easter and Christmas. On one occasion at least, it was part of a service to commemorate a bishop who had recently died, and we learn that a prayer customarily chanted on such occasions on Iona, 'with melody', made reference to St Martin.[48] Gregorian chant was not introduced into Britain until 678, according to Bede, and it has been suggested that Gallican chanting might have been used at the Iona monastery instead.[49] Prayers were said, and hymns were sung too, in addition to the psalms. Indeed, various Latin hymns have been attributed to Columba in the past, and many modern scholars are inclined to agree that he really was the author of one of them, *The High Creator* (*Altus Prosator*).[50] During the mass it was customary to have a reading from the Acts of the Apostles, followed by a reading from the Gospels, which was in turn followed by a sermon or homily. The readings would have been chosen by Columba himself.[51]

Baptism was the other important sacrament. Many baptisms would be of recent converts who came as pilgrims to Iona. An Order of Baptism forms part of the Stowe Missal, a small early Irish mass book dating to the very late eighth or early ninth century, and its text is noticeably similar to that of sixth-century Roman Catholic baptismal services. The newly baptised person put on a fresh white linen robe and went forward to the altar to receive communion in both kinds, that is to say, both the bread and the wine, which was mixed with water. It was only later that the wine was reserved for the clergy and not shared with lay people.[52] From time to time Columba would baptise babies in the open air during his travels, on one occasion christening an entire Pictish household, parents, children and servants, after preaching to them through an interpreter. He also baptised people who were dying.[53]

Columba, as abbot, had his own lodging where he is said to have slept on the bare rock, with a stone for his pillow. (Plate 12b) He also had a writing hut for himself, supported on planks and at a higher level than the rest of the monastery. The most likely position for it was on Tòrr an Aba, a rocky ridge close to the other buildings. There he spent a good deal of time copying manuscripts.[54] This was not seen merely as a practical task with the purpose of providing additions to the monastery's library, or as an artistic exercise. Columba was a highly regarded scriptural scholar, 'learning's pillar' said the Irish elegy, and anyone who was engaged in copying the Psalms or the Gospels or any other biblical manuscript was expected to do so as a means of deep contemplation, meditating on the words they so carefully transcribed in elegant calligraphy.[55]

Columba read widely, knew Latin, of course, and the elegy says that he had not only studied the Bible, especially the Psalms and the Song of Solomon, but read Greek and was conversant with the movement of the stars and the tides of the sea.[56] If 'scriptorium' seems too elaborate a name for the simple room where he wrote, 'hut' hardly does justice to level of intellectual activity that took place there, making Iona an admired and advanced centre of learning.

The hut had a view out over the Sound of Iona and on one occasion, as Columba sat busily writing, he heard someone shouting for a ferry from the shore of Mull, which suggests that the door of the hut, which was usually open, must have faced east. With his customary prophetic powers, Columba warned his attendant that the man was clumsy and would upset his inkhorn when he arrived. Diarmait stood protectively in front of the door for a while, but he was called away at the vital moment and, sure enough, as the visitor eagerly advanced to greet Columba with a kiss, the edge of his garment caught the inkhorn and knocked it over, spilling the ink.[57] Interruptions such as these were all too frequent. One day Columba's cousin Baithéne, who was also his foster son, came and asked for some-one to read through a psalter which he had been copying, in case there were any mistakes. Columba impatiently demanded to know why he was being troubled with this, adding that if Baithéne looked at it himself he would find that only one letter of the alphabet had been left out.[58] This is another instance of Adomnán demonstrating Columba's prophetic powers, of course, but the story has a ring of truth about it and it probably did take place, even if his remark did not have the particular slant attributed to it.

On another occasion, one of the monks came to Columba as he was busy writing and asked him to bless the object that he was carrying. Absorbed in his task, Columba did so absent-mindedly, holding out his hand with the pen in it and giving the blessing, never raising his eyes from the book he was copying. When the monk had gone, Columba suddenly asked Diarmait, who as usual was with him, what implement he had just blessed. He was told that it was a dagger for the killing of bulls or cows. Columba exclaimed in dismay and hoped that the dagger would harm neither man nor beast. Of course it did not, nor did any of the other monastery tools. Even if we are sceptical about the supernatural element in these little stories, the vivid glimpse of the saint's life which they give us explains to an extent why such anecdotes have kept his memory alive for a remarkable length of time.[59]

So what was the rest of the monastery like? The monks had their own quarters. Their sleeping huts were probably shared and there would have been a much larger communal building too, where meals would have been cooked and eaten. The customary bake house and brew house could have been part of that building or, because of the danger of fire, they may have been separate huts. Generus the Englishman was the name of the monastery's baker.[60] In addition, a guest house provided short-term accommodation for the increasing number of pilgrims and visitors to the island.[61] Some arrived by sea from Ireland, others by way of Mull and when Columba expected an important visitor, he gave orders for the guest house to be prepared and told the monks to draw water to wash the feet of the guest.[62]

The dishes used at mealtimes were made of wood, metal and leather and the food available for visitors would have been quite varied. In the fields outside the abbey, barley was grown, and there were fertile pastures for cattle and sheep. Cattle were doubly necessary, for it has been calculated that the hides of more than a hundred calves were needed to make enough vellum for one manuscript Gospel book, and five times that number were required for a newly copied Bible.[63] Pigs were kept too and, apart from the bread and meat served, fish, shellfish and pieces of seals' flesh were readily available. There would also have been a herb and vegetable garden. The monks themselves fasted every Wednesday and Friday, and Lent was very strictly observed, with the only meal of the day being eaten in the evening and consisting of bread, milk and eggs. Columba kept three fasts each year: twelve days after Christmas; the first Wednesday in Lent and the first Wednesday after Pentecost. However, because most of the monks were involved in heavy manual labour, they would have needed nourishing food for the rest of the year. Columba also allowed them a celebration known as the Feast of the Ploughmen, when the crops had reached their full growth.[64]

To the north-east of the main buildings were several workshops, a customary feature of Irish monasteries. Excavations in that area in 1990 found evidence of metal-working in the shape of fragments of two triangular crucibles and the lug of another, all of a kind also found at Irish early Christian sites. There were traces of other materials on them, and when these were analysed they showed that the crucibles had been used for melting bronze and copper. They are believed to have dated from the Columban period.[65] Adomnán had mentioned ironworking at the monastery,[66] and the tools used by the monks and perhaps the vessels for church services were made there.[67] Outside the immediate monastery area there was at least one barn and a shed where the grain was stored.[68]

Grouped around the site were a number of tall, free-standing crosses. The Church in Ireland used such crosses on ecclesiastical sites, not only to commemorate individuals but to mark the places where significant spiritual events had taken place, and this custom was continued on Iona. Indeed, it has even been suggested that the idea originated on Iona.[69] Adomnán describes the reason for one such high cross. Columba's elderly uncle, Ernán, was prior of the monastery that Columba had set up on the small island which Adomnán calls Hinba.[70] When Ernán became seriously ill, he had himself taken back to Iona and was trying to walk up from the shore when he saw his nephew coming towards him. The effort was too much for him, and he collapsed and died there. A commemorative cross was set up on the place where he fell, just in front of the door of the monastery shed, and another was placed where Columba had been standing when it happened. Adomnán gives no description of these crosses and we do not even know if they were made of wood, which seems likely, or of stone, but he does record in a marvelling way that three of the crosses were still standing in his day, a century later. They would have been used as places where the monks and pilgrims could stop to meditate and pray.[71]

There is no record of how many monks were in Columba's monastery, beyond the original twelve who had accompanied him to Iona, and that figure probably reflects the traditional number of Christ's apostles rather being an exact calculation. Most of them would have been Irish, although the first to die was a Briton and as well as Generus there was another Englishman, Pilu and an unnamed Pict.[72] Irish monasteries usually had a prior, who acted as the abbot's deputy, but although Columba had sent Ernán to be prior of Hinba, there is no mention of a prior of Iona at this period, although of course that does not mean that the position did not exist.[73]

Very often a monastery would also have a bishop living in its community. This seems surprising to us, but at that time in the Irish Church a bishop was subordinate to an abbot, although his presence was necessary for the ordination of monks and he was always treated with respect. On one occasion Bishop Crónan from Munster paid an incognito visit to Iona, humbly behaving like an ordinary pilgrim. However, Columba quickly realised his true status and invited him to celebrate holy communion in his place, asking him why he had concealed his true identity instead of allowing the community to pay him the reverence due to his position. The Bishop's reply is not recorded, but no doubt it had something to do with Columba's reputation.[74] There appears to have been no actual Bishop of Iona until Cóeti, who died in 712.[75]

Not all the monks were priests who had taken vows of poverty, chastity and obedience, and in fact it has been suggested that most of them were not.[76] The skilled craftsmen who worked in the iron workshop, for example, would most likely have been lay brothers, as would some of those who toiled on the land, although manual labour was regarded as being a vital part of a monk's life. At every monastery a senior monk was the controller of work, and on Iona Baithéne occupied this position. He apportioned each man's daily task, whether it be threshing the grain, building fences, gathering fruit, milking, cutting down trees or hunting seals, all of which are mentioned by Adomnán. When the corn was cut it was carried on the monks' backs to the barn, but the milk each day was brought back in wooden vessels in a wagon drawn by a white horse that served the community for many years.[77]

Columba emphasised his authority by occupying his own quarters and by travelling separately from his monks when he went on journeys. Autocratic he might be, but they loved, admired and respected him and relied on his leadership. He alone decided who should and should not be allowed to land on Iona. He knew everything that was going on, not only in the monastery but on the island and beyond. Diarmait would have made sure that he was well-informed, and he would also have learned the latest news from visitors and from merchants who came by sea, mainly from Ireland and Gaul, to trade in Dalriada. Soon there was a constant stream of pilgrims arriving on Iona: churchmen and messengers, hopeful penitents, ill people looking to be healed and laymen seeking assistance.

Chapter 2

St Columba's Legacy

There is no doubt that his royal descent gave Columba a power and a status far beyond anything he might otherwise have achieved and he seems to have been recognised as the leading spiritual adviser to the Kings of Dalriada. It is significant that when his original patron King Conall died in 574, Conall's cousin and successor, Áedán mac Gabráin, is said to have asked Columba to ordain him as King of Dalriada.[1] It is hard to know what to make of this for, if it was really so, then not only does it indicate Columba's prominence in Dalriada but it would have been the first time in Western European history that the secular inauguration of a king was combined with the ritual of an ecclesiastical ordination.[2] Later, Áedán went to Ireland to confer with Áed, King of Cenél Conaill near Derry and Columba apparently went with him, facilitating an alliance between the two men. His close family connections with both kings, combined with his forceful personality, apparently gave him the opportunity of speaking to them on equal terms, and allowed him to advise on political as well as spiritual matters.[3]

A man of strong opinions, Columba was quick-tempered and fierce in his condemnation of wrongdoers, on one occasion pursuing a defiant thief into the sea as the man made his escape in a ship. Standing knee deep in the water, Columba raised both hands to heaven, prayed and then forecast the malefactor's sudden death. Not long afterwards the ship sank, and all on board were drowned.[4] However, he met requests for assistance with kindness and practical help. Tales were told of him increasing the number of cows owned by Nesán the Crooked, who had obligingly put him up for the night and Colmán, another poor man who had also provided a night's accommodation. There were instances of healing too, including the time when he saved Diarmait by praying at his bedside when the servant was gravely ill,[5] and he was even ready with marriage counselling when this was required.

The wife of a man named Luigne decided that she could not bear to stay with her husband for one more day because he was so ugly, and announced that she was going to enter a nunnery instead. Alarmed, Luigne persuaded her to go with him to see Columba, who listened to her complaints and then told her firmly that no one could divide those whom God had joined together in marriage. He himself and the couple should fast and pray together, he said, and this they did. The wife's feelings instantly underwent a transformation and she decided that she now loved the husband she had loathed the very day before.[6] Most famously of all, perhaps, Columba ordered one of his monks to rescue a crane which had flown in, exhausted, from the north of Ireland and fallen on to the beach. The monk was told to bring the bird into the monastery and tend it until it had recovered. Some commentators have seen in this a strikingly early example of concern for the environment, while others have remarked that Columba was only interested in the crane because it had come from Ireland. Read without prejudice, the anecdote simply shows that he had a kind heart.[7]

A favourite tale about St Columba, which has been handed down throughout the centuries, tells how he bravely decided to undertake a long and dangerous journey northwards to Pictland, with the purpose of converting the pagan King Brude and his people. Arriving at the royal fortress, he preached an impassioned sermon, instantly convincing the ferocious King that Christianity was the true faith and putting to flight Brude's wicked magicians. This anecdote made a thrilling bedtime story for Scottish children, its local associations giving it as much appeal as the Bible's accounts of David and Goliath or Daniel in the Lions' den, and it caught the imagination of artists too. At the end of the nineteenth century William Hole was painting a set of historical murals inside the Scottish National Portrait Gallery and one shows a tall and slender Columba clad in a white robe and a black cloak, holding aloft a cross and addressing a sullen King Brude, while a disgruntled, white-bearded magician recoils at the King's side, and several well-dressed but bored looking Picts are grouped around.

Victorians and indeed later generations shared the conviction that Columba's whole purpose in coming to Iona was to bring Christianity to what is now Scotland or indeed to Britain for the first time, but how true is this? Certainly St Augustine of Canterbury did not arrive in Kent to convert the Angles until 597, the very year of Columba's death, but it was the Romans who had brought Christianity to Britain and there were already Christians of Irish descent in Dalriada when Columba arrived in 563. There were also others in Galloway, said to have been converted from paganism more than a century earlier by that elusive figure, St Ninian. Recent historical research has thrown severe doubts on the very existence of Ninian, to the point where it has even been argued that there was no such person. His name is now believed to be a corruption of that of a ubiquitous Christian leader known in the sixth century as 'Vennianus', mainly active in Ireland but vaguely associated with other places too.[8]

Equally obscure are the facts about the conversion of the Picts. The Venerable Bede thought that Ninian had converted the southern Picts of Fife and Perthshire long before Columba's time but he also believed that Columba's purpose in coming from Ireland had been to convert the northern Picts.[9] So what do we actually know about his missionary activities? Did Columba really confront Brude, miraculously forcing him and all his people to become Christians? As usual, we must rely upon Adomnán as the most detailed source. According to his account, Columba did indeed make the difficult and potentially dangerous journey to Pictland, possibly more than once. However, he was not embarking on a missionary expedition. The first or only journey was undertaken, at least in part, because one of his monks, Cormac, had sailed north towards the Orkney Islands to look for a suitably isolated place to spend time as a hermit. The King of Orkney was subject to King Brude and so Columba, concerned for Cormac's safety, decided to visit Brude and urge him to see that no harm came to the monk.[10]

Travelling through the Great Glen by boat and on foot, Columba and his companions made their way to Brude's fortress, which was possibly at Craig Phadraig, near Inverness. Adomnán's details are vague, but he is the source of the picturesque stories of what happened next. Finding the fortress closed against him and although exhausted by his long journey, Columba went up to the gates, made the sign of the cross and then hammered on them for admittance. After an ominous silence, there was suddenly the sound of bars being drawn back and then the gates flew open and Columba and his companions marched in. Contrary to expectation, Brude was taken aback but welcomed the unexpected visitors politely, and from that day onwards he held Columba in great esteem. [11]

The other incidents said to have happened in Pictland do not form a consecutive narrative in Adomnán's account, but are scattered throughout the *Life*. They include the startling story of Columba's encounter with the Loch Ness Monster. Having heard from the local people that it had killed a man, he ordered one of his monks to enter the water in order to lure it out from its lair. The monk obediently dived in and, sure enough, the creature reared up from the depths and made for this new victim. Columba immediately ordered it to turn back and, to everyone's relief, it obeyed.[12] There were also several triumphant confrontations with King Brude's magicians. For instance, when Columba and his companions were singing psalms at the time of Vespers, just outside the royal fortress, the magicians came and tried to stop them, fearing that the local pagan population would be contaminated by the sound. Undeterred, Columba broke into Psalm 44 in such a loud voice that it struck terror into his opponents, who likened it to a deafening peal of thunder.[13]

That psalm, however, was far from being a threat, for it includes the lines, 'I speak my works to the king ... Thou art beautiful above the sons of men: grace is poured abroad in thy lips; therefore hath God blessed thee forever'. Flattery was not in Columba's nature, so could this have been a genuine tribute to a king who had already converted to Christianity? Archaeologists have found Christian burials on the southern edge of Pictland, dating from as early as the fifth century and so this idea is not as far-fetched as it might seem. Moreover, nowhere is there any mention of Columba either converting Brude or preaching publicly in his territories. What we do know is that by the following century there appears to have been a significant presence of Columban monasteries in northern Pictland, and as to Bede's claim that Columba converted the entire Pictish nation, both north and south,[14] it remains possible that he visited the lands of the southern Picts in Atholl and could have founded monasteries there. However, the sources are so sparse and so unclear that any definitive conclusion would seem to be out of reach.[15]

The same difficulty affects the other monasteries which Columba may personally have founded. Monasticism was very clearly his vocation and he appears to have been engaged in setting up a prestigious federation of daughter houses not only in Scotland but in Ireland too, with Iona at its centre. Even in the twenty-first century with its many different means of communication, Iona can seem a remote place, but in the seventh century sea travel was the principal way of getting about in that area and Iona was readily accessible from both east and west. Historians now believe that his laying the foundations of this highly influential monastic network is where Columba's true significance lies, although once again the lack of written sources presents real problems. We assume that Columba had established the monastery on Hinba, where his uncle Ernán was prior, and likewise Tiree had a monastery which he had presumably set up, administered by a prior whom he had appointed. These two communities were very closely connected with Iona, where ordinary visitors were allowed to stay for only three days and three nights while waiting to speak to Columba. Those seeking absolution were always sent on to Tiree or Hinba, for their penances would have lasted far too long for them to be accommodated on Iona itself. For instance, a man named Librán, who sailed over from Ireland and confessed to Columba that he had committed murder, was told that he must undergo a penance of seven years on Tiree, finally returning to Iona during Lent, to take communion at Easter.[16]

A daughter house was seemingly established near Loch Awe, while another was on the so far unidentified island of Elen. We know that Columba travelled assiduously, sailing to the Hebridean island of Skye, which was under Pictish control, probably visiting the island of Eigg as well and carrying out an open air baptism on the Ardnamurchan Peninsula.[17] Even so, it is impossible to tell which Columban monasteries were actually founded in his time and which belonged to subsequent years. Perhaps renewed archaeological investigations and radiocarbon dating may supply vital evidence. Despite the tales of Columba vowing never to return to his beloved homeland, he did in fact visit Ireland on several occasions, and he does seem to have founded monasteries there too.[18] Only one of his foundations may be dated with reasonable certainty, however, and that came much later, probably towards the end of the 580s, when Columba spent several months in central Ireland overseeing the establishment of a monastery at Durrow.

This project was no doubt accomplished with the support of his Uí Néill relatives, and his cousin's son, Laisrén, who had been one of his monks in Iona, was put in charge of Durrow, probably as prior.[19] So enthusiastic about the project did Lais-rén become that he drove his community far too hard, in the worst possible weather. Back on Iona, Columba was greatly distressed when he heard about this. Adomnán's version of the story tells how Columba's concern was miraculously conveyed to Laisrén, who instantly relented, ordering his monks to stop work, saying that they must eat and rest until conditions improved. However he may have received the message, super-naturally or by a traveller from Iona, Laisrén could not have ignored it, for Columba had supreme authority not simply over the Iona monastery but over Durrow and the other daughter houses he had founded.[20]

During his stay at Durrow, Columba also visited other places, including the monastery at Clonmacnoise, where it was noted that he was now 'a fairly old man'. His strength was beginning to fail and, in 593, thirty years after his arrival on Iona, he was praying to God to release him from his worldly life. He was in his early seventies but his prayer was not yet to be granted. By the spring of 597, now aged seventy-six, he was no longer able to stride around Iona to inspect the monks at their various tasks, but instead was taken in a wagon to watch them at their agricultural labours on the western side of the island. During his final days, he went to inspect the grain in one of the mon-astery barns. Diarmait was with him, and Columba remarked to him with satisfaction that there would be enough bread for the monks that year. On the way back to the monastery, weary with age, he sat down to rest, and the white horse which drew the wagon with the milk vessels came up to him, laid its head on his breast and wept, its tears falling on to his lap. Diarmait would have driven the beast away, but Columba refused to let him do that, explaining that it somehow had foreknowledge of his death. He blessed it, and then he slowly climbed the little hill where he had so often gone before to meditate and pray by himself. He sat there for a while, looking down at his monastery and then he blessed it too, declaring that native and foreign kings and their subjects, even barbarians, would hold it in great honour.[21]

Making his way to his writing hut, Columba took a piece of vellum and began to copy the thirty-third psalm from the Vulgate version of the Bible.[22] Reaching the foot of the page at the end of verse 10, which reads: '... but they that seek the Lord shall not want for anything that is good', he suddenly stopped, laid down his pen, and remarked that Baithéne would have to finish the task. He managed to attend the evening Office of Vespers in the church and, resting afterwards in his lodging, he urged his monks to live together in charity and in peace. When the bell rang for the midnight office, he hastened back to the church as quickly as he could and knelt to pray before the altar. Diarmait, taken by surprise, hastily followed, and as he hurried along the path he saw to his amazement that the entire building was suffused with light. Distraught, he ran inside, calling out in agitation, 'Where are you father, where are you?' He found Columba lying on the floor beside the altar. He sat down beside him, and lifted the dying man's head on to his lap. Seeing his eyes open, Diarmait helped him to raise his right hand, and with that final blessing, Columba passed away. It was 5 June 597.

After Matins, the monks carried his body back to his lodging, singing psalms as they went. The funeral ceremonies lasted for the next three days, during which time there were such fierce storms of wind and rain that no one could cross from Mull to take part. The monks noted sadly that this was in keeping with Columba's prophecy that only his own family of monks would be there. His body was wrapped in clean, fine cloths and buried, almost certainly on the site of the little chapel now known as Columba's Shrine.[23] (Plate 3) Archaeologists have variously dated the building to the ninth or tenth centuries or to the late Middle Ages, but the latest research suggests an even earlier date for it.[24]

Later, possibly about 750 or perhaps even as early as the

630s, his remains were moved from their grave to a special, highly decorated shrine made of precious metals including gold.[25] The translation of a saint's bones from their burial place was not done from some sort of vague sentimental attachment to his memory but because they were thought to serve a distinct practical purpose. When Christians had been martyred in the late Roman period, their graves had been venerated, but before long it had become the custom for their bones to be disinterred and displayed in a shrine high up behind an altar, as St Martin's were. The belief underlying this practice was that the soul in heaven could still communicate with the earthly body which, awaiting the Resurrection, could receive from it a heavenly power. With the remains so prominently placed, the celestial light reflected from them would be clearly visible.[26]

Whatever the date of the translation of Columba's bones, his shrine must have been fairly large and imposing, for it was described as being supported on pediments.[27] There would also have been a much smaller portable shrine, kept in the principal shrine but taken out to be carried from time to time to the other Columban monasteries in Ireland as well as in Dalriada during visitations made by the Abbot of Iona.[28] Similarly, a small, early eighth-century shrine shaped like a house and designed to be worn round the neck is now known as the Monymusk Reliquary from its later provenance. (Plate 5) In the nineteenth century it was identified as the Breccbennach, which was known to have contained a relic or relics of St Columba and was carried before the victorious Scottish army at the Battle of Bannockburn in 1314. This identification has recently been questioned, but whatever opinion one holds, the reliquary, preserved in the National Museum of Scotland, provides an interesting example of this type of portable shrine.[29]

The Irish elegy, the *Amra*, expressed the desolation experienced by all who had known Columba or experienced the supportive power of his protection. He had been a truly dominating figure and people felt lost without him. In accordance with his instructions, he was succeeded as Abbot of Iona and head of its monastic federation by his cousin, Baithéne. Apart from the glimpse we have had of Baithéne as an expert copyist of manuscripts, we know nothing about his activities or his personality. A short *Life* survives in a fourteenth-century manuscript, but it is concerned only with recounting his miracles rather than giving any biographical detail. His time as abbot was to be brief, for he died just three years after his famous predecessor, apparently on the same date in June. The next abbot of Iona was none other than Laisrén, the Prior of Durrow, whose father had been the first cousin of both Columba and Baithéne. This was not seen as a nasty case of nepotism, since it was customary in the Irish Church for the successors to abbots of a particular monastery to be selected from the same kinship group. An exception to this rule was Fergna, who followed Laisrén in 605. He had been one of Columba's monks, and Adomnán considered him to be a young man of good ability. He was probably not Irish but a Briton.[30]

Meanwhile, Columba's reputation continued to grow. Although he might no longer be with them on earth, people looked to him to intercede on their behalf in heaven and by the seventh century he was gaining recognition as a major saint. Until the tenth century, the Church had no official procedure for canonisation. Martyrs and people who had lived outstandingly holy lives were recognised by their own communities as saints if they could be shown to have prophesied events, performed miracles and possessed the ability to see into the minds of others.[31] Columba was regarded as having all these necessary qualities, and Fergna's successor, Ségéne, a nephew of Laisrén, appears to have engaged in a campaign to promote his kinsman Columba's reputation as a saint.

Probably in the 620s, Ségéne set about deliberately gathering recollections of Columba, summoning for interview the surviving monks who had been there in his time as abbot. Most of them had probably been young when Columba was in his seventies, but it is just possible that Diarmait was still alive and was able to act as an informant. The episodes in which he features in Adomnán's *Life of Columba* are particularly vivid, and must surely have been passed on at least at second hand if he was not there to impart them himself. Ségéne also appears to have questioned distinguished outsiders who had encountered Columba, and he then seems to have given his own nephew, Cumméne, also a monk in the Iona monastery, the task of putting together those treasured memories in a text entitled *Book of the Miracles of St Columba (Liber de virtutibus Sancti Columbae)*. This may well have been Adomnán's main source for his *Life of St Columba*.[32]

During Ségéne's long and effective abbacy of almost thirty years, from 623 until 652, the federation of Iona monasteries continued to expand on both sides of the Irish Sea, and an important connection was made with Northumbria too. When its King Aethelfrith was killed in battle in about 616, his seven sons had fled, finding refuge for the next seventeen years in Pictland, Dalriada and in Ireland. Oswald, the second son, was thirteen or so when he went into exile, and he is said to have converted to Christianity and been baptised in the Iona monastery. In 634 he was at last able to return home to Northumbria, soon afterwards succeeding his elder brother, who had reclaimed their father's throne. Anxious to continue the conversion of his people, Oswald asked Ségéne to send him a bishop to help and in this way Áedán, a monk from Iona, was given Lindisfarne, the little tidal island in the North Sea now more often known as Holy Island. He lived in the monastery there, and under his supervision, other monks trained in Iona went preaching throughout Northumbria, spreading the Columban influence.[33]

Ségéne also became involved in a much more controversial matter, the long-running and bitter debate over the date of Easter. This may sound like a trivial quarrel over the Church calendar, but it became far more than that. Easter was and is the most important festival of the Christian Church, and because two different systems were being used to calculate its date, confusion resulted. Easter is celebrated on a Sunday in the first lunar month of the year to have a full moon on or after the spring equinox. Traditionally, the Irish Church – and Iona – used a formula which regarded 21 March as being the spring equinox, whereas by the seventh century the Roman Church held that the equinox fell on 25 March. To make matters worse, the two systems reckoned a lunar month differently. Rome was anxious for uniformity, and in about 630 the southern Irish churches accepted the new formula, but the northern Irish churches and those of Dalriada, including Iona, refused to alter their position, with Ségéne acting as one of the leading opponents of change. They likewise refused to adopt the Roman style of tonsure. The Iona monks, in keeping with the Irish Church, shaved the front of their heads, whereas Rome had adopted the practice of shaving the crown.[34]

The matter did not end there, of course, and by the time Ségéne's nephew Cumméne became abbot of Iona in 657, the controversy had become increasingly acrimonious. The competing views were particularly obvious in Northumbria, where even the royal family was divided. Bede describes how Queen Eanflaed, who had been brought up in Kent, followed the Roman practice, while her husband King Oswiu kept to the Iona calculations, with the result that the Queen and her household were sometimes celebrating Easter while the rest of the Court were fasting in Lent. In an attempt to solve the dilemma, representatives of the opposing factions were called together at the Synod of Whitby in 664. Those who favoured the Irish way of doing things were led by Bishop Colmán of Lindisfarne, while the Roman faction had as their spokesman Wilfrid of Ripon, a very learned young priest who had actually studied in Rome and may have had connections with the Queen's family.

Colmán was defeated when he argued that the Irish calculation must be correct because Columba had used it and Wilfrid responded by citing the superior authority of St Peter who had, after all, been Christ's leading apostle. King Oswiu, no doubt for reasons relating to his own political manoeuvrings, declared himself convinced by Wilfrid's argument and Colmán retired in disarray to Iona. A few years later he moved on to found a monastery on Inishbofin, an island off the coast of Galway. Meanwhile, the Iona monks were all the more determined to keep to the traditions given to them by St Columba, and this they did for the rest of the seventh century, despite the efforts of their ninth abbot, Adomnán.[35]

Although he was himself a notable scholar with a cosmopolitan outlook, Adomnán's reputation has been overshadowed by that of Columba and despite the fact that he, too, would be recognised as a saint, his name is hardly remembered now, other than as the author of the *Life*. He was Irish, like Columba himself, and there were other similarities. Adomnán also was a mature man when he became Abbot of Iona in 679. About fifty-two years old, he too had important royal connections, for his ancestor Sétna, one of Columba's uncles, left descendants who had included no fewer than seven of the high kings of the northern Uí Néill.[36] Significantly, Adomnán enjoyed the friendship of Aldfrith, King of Northumbria. Not only had Aldfrith's mother been a daughter of a Northern Uí Néill king, but Aldfrith himself had been educated in the Iona monastery and was a distinguished scholar.[37]

We know relatively little about Adomnán's Irish years. He may have been recruited in Ireland when his predecessor at Iona, Abbot Faílbe, spent three years there from 673 to 676. To have been chosen as abbot of such a prestigious monastery as Iona, with its powerful federation of daughter houses, is an indication of Adomnán's standing as well as his scholarship, and there can be little doubt that his royal relationships facilitated his later career, just as Columba's had done. In 687 for example, Adomnán was chosen, presumably by the Uí Néill, to undertake an important diplomatic mission, escorting home from Northumbria sixty Irish captives who had been taken in a raid on the Southern Uí Néill kingdom of Brega three years earlier by Aldfrith's predecessor and held prisoner ever since.[38]

In 689, while on another visit to Northumbria, Adomnán became involved in the Easter controversy when his friends there persuaded him to adopt the Roman dating of Easter. On his return to Iona he completely failed to persuade his monks to agree to change – this in spite of their vow of obedience, which should have meant that they would meekly follow his instructions. Their loyalty to the memory of Columba was too strong.[39] Some historians have declared that Adomnán spent much of his time after that in Ireland, in exile from Iona,[40] but others point out that there is no supporting evidence for this having been so, and argue convincingly that although he did travel to Ireland in 692, he would merely have been undertaking the customary visitation made by the Iona abbots to the daughter houses there.[41]

Whatever the reality of his comings and goings, Adomnán made a considerable contribution to the scholarly reputation of his monastery. As usual, it is difficult to construct a chronology, but sometime after 689 he wrote his important work, *Of Holy Places* (*De Locis Sanctis*), still to this day considered to be of great value as a source of information. The inspiration for this book came from the unexpected arrival on Iona of a bishop named Arculf, who had been travelling in the Holy Land and was blown off course during his voyage home to Gaul. He told Adomnán all about his travels, Adomnán took notes on wax tablets and then transformed these into a book, vastly augmenting the information transmitted to him with details from manuscripts in the Iona library.[42] He presented a copy to King Aldfrith, who made it widely known in Anglo-Saxon circles, Bede thought very highly of it, and during the Middle Ages it was apparently far more famous than the *Life of St Columba*.[43]

Adomnán was also the author of another very different work of a highly influential nature,[44] the *Law of the Innocents* (*Lex innocentium*) which was promulgated at a great Irish synod

31

held at Birr, in Offaly, in 697, on the centenary of Columba's death. His text said that, in future, three sections of the population were to enjoy the special protection of the abbots of Iona. Women, children and clergy were already excused from military duty in wartime but, if any of them were to be killed or injured in time of conflict, in addition to other punishments, the perpetrator would have to pay a fine to the Iona monastery. Moreover, this was to apply not merely to the areas in Pictland and Dalriada where Iona had influence, but to the whole of Ireland. The chief rulers there had agreed in advance to the terms of this law, and attached to it is a long list of ninety-one prominent rulers and ecclesiastics who had promised to support it. The list begins with the name of Fland Febla, Bishop of Armagh and ends with Brude, son of Derile, King of the Picts. Significantly, the first non-ecclesiastical name on the list is that of Loingsech, the powerful High King of Ireland who was Adomnán's fourth cousin. Not only was this legislation seen as demonstrating Iona's importance and proper concern for the vulnerable, but it usefully increased the monastery's revenues and would be re-enacted time and again over the years.[45]

By now, however, the churches in Armagh and Kildare were beginning to challenge Iona's pre-eminent position. In spite of that, more new Columban daughter houses continued to be founded in Ireland, presumably with the support of the Uí Néill rulers, and Adomnán further enhanced Iona's prestige when he wrote his *Life of Columba*. We do not know when he started to compose it, but it would seem to have been written after his visit to Northumbria and his conversion to the Roman date for Easter in 692 and it has been suggested that it may in part have been inspired by a desire to help the Iona monks to set aside their differences over that controversy. Looked at in this context, the words Adomnán attributes to Columba on his last evening, urging his community to live in peace and harmony together, may well have been composed for Adomnán's own readers rather than being a direct quotation from the dying saint.[46]

32

If we know nothing of the appearance and little about the personality of Columba's successors, we are similarly ignorant about the physical circumstances of the monastery during those years. However, Adomnán's *Life* does give us the occasional, fleeting glimpse, as when he recounts the story of two miracles during his own abbacy which were accomplished thanks to the intervention of Columba. In one, he mentions that dressed timbers of oak and pine were being brought by water to Iona. It was customary for not only the bones of saints but objects they had used to become revered as relics and so, anxious about the weather for the voyage, Adomnán and his monks decided to lay some of Columba's carefully preserved garments and books on the altar of the church, singing psalms, fasting and praying to him for a fair passage. Just as they had hoped, the winds on the appointed day suddenly veered round and the cargo arrived safely. Some of the timbers were for the construction of a long ship, we are told, but others were brought 'for the great house'. We can only guess at what this would have been, for we do not even know if it was a new building or an existing one.

The second anecdote follows immediately upon the first and again concerns oak being brought to the island. The timbers were being towed from the mouth of the River Sale (probably the Shiel) on a calm day when a contrary wind suddenly sprang up and the sailors were forced to seek shelter in the harbour of a nearby island. Frustrated, they began to complain loudly, saying that they had expected better of Columba, who should have helped them. With that, the wind dropped and instead a gentle breeze carried them safely home. Tantalisingly, Adomnán says only that this wood was 'for the restoration of our monastery'.[47] The original wattle huts would have been long gone and the wooden buildings too must have been replaced by then. Archaeological information has so far been disappointing, but several structural timbers from that era have been excavated from the ditch of the rampart surrounding the monastery, post holes which would have been for timber buildings

33

have been found in the ground[48] and the surviving portions of the rampart itself may date from this period. Its walls are substantial, with a drop of at least 4 metres from the top of the inner bank to the foot of the ditch.[49]

Adomnán died in 704, reputedly at the age of seventy-six, although this figure may have been chosen to coincide with Columba's age at the time of his death. Despite his notable success in raising and strengthening Iona's position in the world, Adomnán had not succeeded in reconciling the warring factions who were arguing still about Easter and the tonsure. There is considerable confusion about the identity of his immediate successors, but the eventual reconciliation seems to have come about during the abbacy of his cousin, Dúnchad, who withdrew to Ireland and spent most of his time there. It may well have been he who sent Ecgberht, a learned English monk also living in Ireland, to persuade the Iona community to accept the Roman Easter. That can have been no easy task, but after some months Ecgberht was successful and the monks' stubborn adherence to the date favoured by Columba was finally set aside in 715–16. Two years after that, the Iona monks adopted the Roman form of tonsure.[50]

By that time Nechtan, King of the Picts, had already accepted the Roman dating of Easter, possibly having been convinced by some of Adomnán's followers in the Columban Pictish monasteries and then by corresponding with Ceolfrith, the Abbot of Jarrow and Wearmouth. Despite the fact that he and the Iona monks were now in agreement on this divisive issue, Nechtan is said suddenly to have expelled them from his territories in 717. Recent historians have queried the motives behind this crisis and indeed questioned its significance. The events are completely obscure and opinions differ, but speculation suggests that if a large-scale expulsion really happened, it would have had nothing to do with religious issues but could well have been caused by the Iona monks supporting one of the rivals for Nechtan's throne.[51]

Despite the alleged expulsion and the fact that its allies in northern Ireland were being temporarily eclipsed in a series of power struggles, Iona's monastery continued to flourish. Subsequent abbots vigorously upheld its reputation as an internationally famous centre of intellectual activity and one such was Cilléne Droichtech, formerly a hermit, who was abbot from 726–52. During his abbacy one of his monks, Cú Chuimne, worked with the Irish scholar Ruben of Dairinis on the *Irish Collection of Canon Law* (*Collectio Canonum Hibernensis*), sixty-seven books of law arranged for the first time by subject. This collection would be influential throughout Europe for centuries to come.[52]

Chapter 3

Visual Arts and Vikings

It was not long before Iona also became a great centre of creativity in the visual arts, with masons at work on imposing and intricately decorated high crosses which were then grouped around the monastery precincts. The successors to the plain wooden crosses of Columba's time, they were much more permanent, for most were made from a dark green crystalline rock imported from the Argyllshire mainland. The local rocks were much too hard and brittle to be worked easily.[1] The carvings, of course, were the great feature of the crosses, which displayed such elaborate designs that they were emerging as a highly important art form in their own right and are now recognised as being among the most significant works of sculpture produced in medieval Europe. Four of the few which are still in existence have been dated to around the second half of the eighth century or the early ninth century, the only one to survive intact being St Martin's Cross. (Plate 2) Made from a single slab which would have been brought by boat from the mainland, it has very short arms, but they have slots in the ends, which would have allowed the addition of ornamental mounts made of either wood or metal.

The east face of St Martin's Cross is covered with the designs of bosses and intertwined serpents familiar from other examples of early Christian art, while the west side has a fascinating series of carvings illustrating biblical texts. A primitive representation of the Virgin and Child features in a circle between the cross's two arms, while four Old Testament stories are depicted on the shaft. Daniel, who narrowly escaped martyrdom in a den of lions, thanks to God's intervention, is seen looking alarmed, as well he might, since two of the lions flank him so closely that their front paws are on his lap. Beneath him, Abraham raises his sword, ready to sacrifice his son Isaac, as God had required. (The boy survived, for this was actually a test of Abraham's faith.) A more relaxed scene below shows David plucking his harp in company with another musician who holds to his lips a set of triple pipes. The fourth carving on the shaft has a row of figures representing young David and the giant Goliath, both about the same size, because of the restrictions of space, and David with Saul. Twelve serpents and six bosses ornament the lowest part of the shaft and on the base are the much weathered remains of an inscription, too worn to decipher.

St Oran's Cross, unlike the others, is probably made from local stone and is believed to be the earliest of the surviving group. Who was St Oran? He does not feature in any of the usual dictionaries of saints, and Adomnán does not mention him, probably for a very good reason. An embarrassing legend, originating in the 12th century in a rather different form, was current by the 19th century, alleging that when St Columba wished to build a small chapel in the monastery graveyard, he found that the walls were mysteriously demolished every night. A strange, mermaid-like messenger emerged from the sea to warn him that he would never be able to put up the chapel unless someone was sacrificed and buried alive on the site. One of the monks named Oran, possibly a relative of Columba, bravely stepped forward and volunteered to be the victim. This sort of living sacrifice is not unknown in legends in the Highlands and elsewhere.

Three days after the burial, Columba ordered Oran to be disinterred, to see what had happened to him. There he was, still alive. Opening his eyes, he declared that neither hell nor heaven existed. Alarmed in case he might reveal some other unwelcome secrets, Columba quickly ordered the earth to be piled on top of him again, even more securely.[2] Whatever one cares to make of this strange tale, the present St Oran's Chapel at the corner of Reilig Odrháin (Oran's graveyard) is actually from several centuries after Columba's time. Whoever St Oran was, if he really existed, his cross was originally a fine one. Now only fragments remain, but they have designs of serpents and bosses, with the Virgin and Child flanked by angels and a man accompanied by a lion. Judging by the attitude of the lion, one paw on the man's lap and its jaws near his face, it was either about to lick him affectionately on the cheek or bite off his head. The man is most likely to be Daniel again, although it has been suggested that he could be David, who once killed a lion to save a lamb, or even St Jerome, but he is usually pictured with his tame lion lying at his feet.

St John's Cross, decorated with the customary bosses and intricate designs, is also in fragments. Its unusually wide and heavy arms, with a span of almost 2.2 metres, led to it being blown over time and again, and it has now been taken inside for safety and replaced outside by a replica. With its liability to be damaged by gales in mind, it is sometimes said that the ring at the upper part the high crosses was added for purely practical reasons, to strengthen the two arms. However, even crosses with short arms have the rings, which are usually believed to feature because they symbolise eternity or the Resurrection of Christ. The fragments of St Matthew's Cross, thought to date from about 850 to 950, are also on display under cover, while its granite base remains in place, not far from St Martin's Cross.[3]

Many are the theories about the origin and the design elements of these famous crosses. Were they made by Pictish or Irish carvers? Were they imitations of crosses found in Ireland or Northumbria or at Carolingian monasteries on the continent or did they pre-date the Irish crosses and were actually invented on Iona, as is now being suggested? There seems to be a distinct relationship between their designs and those on Pictish and perhaps Scandinavian carved stones. Did the decoration on jewelled brooches or on wooden objects inspire the intertwining serpents and the domes and the hollows of the bosses carved in stone? Continuing investigations may well provide the answers.[4]

Carving was not the only activity to earn Iona its artistic fame at this period. As we have seen, the study of scriptural manuscripts had always been a preoccupation there and beautiful illuminations were now being created to adorn the new copies of the Gospels and other biblical works produced in the scriptorium. It has been suggested, for instance, that the Book of Durrow with its highly decorated pages and its innovative illustrations may have been made in Iona in the late seventh century, although this is somewhat controversial speculation.[5] It is preserved in Trinity College Library, Dublin, as is the famous Book of Kells. Although its provenance remains unknown, many experts are willing to accept that it was created on Iona. Containing the text of the four Gospels (the Books of Matthew, Mark, Luke and John) and based mainly on the fourth-century Latin translation of the Bible by St Jerome (the Vulgate), the Book of Kells runs to 680 vellum pages. It is probably the work of at least three or four principal scribes, with three artist-monks providing the illuminations which feature the most amazingly complex, vividly coloured decorative borders, elaborate capital letters and full-page representations of figures such as the Virgin and Child (Plate 4), the four evangelists and scenes from the life of Christ.[6]

The range of colours used in the Book of Kells was for long the subject of speculation, but investigations in 2004, 2006 and 2007 involving micro-Raman spectroscopy have indicated the sophisticated use of largely local pigments. Orange-red came from red lead, and orpiment (arsenic sulphide) produced a deep yellow ochre and could have been brought to Iona from Ireland, for there were deposits in Galway. Gypsum, a naturally occurring mineral, supplied the white pigment used for the faces and hands of the various figures. Contrary to previous belief, there was no evidence of very expensive Afghanistan lapis lazuli. Instead, the blues came from indigo plants or from the large leaves of woad, widely grown as a dyestuff for cloth. Purple, as in the Virgin's robe, was derived from various species of lichen. A mixture of orpiment and indigo could give a shade of green, while a brighter green came from verdigris, apparently produced at that time by hanging copper plates over hot vinegar in a sealed pot and then scraping off the deposit. The brown and black inks, also used in the calligraphy, came respectively from crushed oak galls and from the soot of charred bones or wood.[7]

Experts are agreed that the Book of Kells must have been written in about 800 A.D. Its attribution to the Iona scriptorium is in part on the basis of later tradition which tells us that it was venerated as a relic of Columba, but also because of striking similarities to Pictish art in the decorative detail. Again, the spiral ornamentation closely resembles that on the Iona St John's Cross, while the Virgin and Child carving is clearly related to the portrayal of mother and child on St Oran's Cross. Because of its size and the richness of the illumination, the text of the Book of Kells was probably not used at holy communion in the abbey church but was more likely to have been displayed open, perhaps on the altar, on ceremonial occasions. However, it appears to have been unfinished.[8]

Why was this so, and why is it known as the Book of Kells if it was created on Iona? The answer may lie in a dramatic series of events which took place in the late eighth and early ninth centuries. In 795 the monastery at Iona was sacked by the Vikings.[9] Churches were one of their favourite targets, because of the expensive chalices, reliquaries and vestments to be found there, and of course these buildings were particularly vulnerable because they had no defences. Fragments of such treasures from Ireland and the west of Scotland have been discovered in graves in Norway.[10] Another attack on Iona followed in 802 and Abbot Cellach decided that it was simply too dangerous for the community to remain there. In 804 he therefore decided to build in Ireland a new monastery as a place of refuge for the Iona monks. He obtained a grant of land at Kells, County Meath, for that purpose.[11] It took ten years to construct the new monastery, by which time Iona had suffered an even more savage attack. In 806, the Vikings had returned, this time killing sixty-eight people whom they found at the monastery: monks, lay brothers and, presumably, penitents and other pilgrims.[12] After that, most of the monks would have moved to Kells even though the monastery was not yet complete, presumably taking the unfinished Book with them.

Even so, the entire community did not abandon Iona, for we know that in 825 there were still monks living there, with their prior, Blathmac, a high-born Irishman. In that year a marauding party of Danes invaded Iona and burst into the monastery church, expecting no doubt to find Columba's precious metal shrine in its customary place behind the altar. Instead, the space where it had stood upon its pediments was empty, for the monks had hidden it outside somewhere, in a hollow in the ground, beneath a thick layer of turf. Failing to find the shrine, the Danes demanded to know where it had been hidden. Blathmac was determined to protect the sacred relics of the beloved founder. He confronted the invaders on the steps of the altar, and refused to tell them where the shrine was hidden. They brutally hacked him to death where he stood.[13]

It has often been said that because of this particularly savage raid, Columba's relics were in 849 removed from Iona, some of them going to Kells, while others were taken to Dunkeld, in Perthshire. The Church had originally forbidden the division of relics, but this prohibition had faded away and when, for instance, Colmán had retired to Iona after his defeat at the Synod of Whitby, he had taken with him some of the bones of Áedán, founder of the Lindisfarne monastery, leaving the rest where they were.[14] It would have been understandable if Columba's relics had been divided for safety's sake between Kells and Dunkeld. However, Kells had been available since 814, so why were

41

they not carried there immediately after Blathmac's death? Why wait another 24 years and then choose to send some of them to Dunkeld? It seems that the explanation lies with political developments rather than with considerations of security.[15]

The rulers of Dalriada had, over a lengthy period of years, harboured ambitions to take over Pictland and this desire increased as the Dalriadans were pushed eastwards by Viking invasions. At one time it was believed that Kenneth MacAlpin (Cináed mac Alpin), King of Dalriada, simply conquered the Picts in battle and made himself their king too, in about 843. Historians have now challenged this version of events, highlighting among other things the fact that Kenneth was not the first king to rule over both Dalriada and Pictland. What exactly happened is obscure. Whether he took advantage of the defeat inflicted on the Picts by the Vikings in 839 to reverse recent Pictish dominance in northern Britain or whether he consolidated an existing trend for Scottish kings of Picts, Kenneth founded a line of kings who would continue to rule over a united kingdom of both Pictland and Dalriada, leading to the eventual creation of what we now known as Scotland.

The Church had played an important part in supporting Dalriada's kings ever since Columba's day, and Kenneth I apparently wished to maintain this close connection. It had originally made good sense geographically for Iona to be the centre of the Columban monastic network, with Ireland to the west and Dalriada to the east, but now all that had changed, with Kenneth's territories spreading so much further east, across the former Pictland. In this interpretation of events, it would seem that Kenneth rather than the Abbot of Iona instigated the division of the relics, perhaps completing a move originally planned by his predecessor Constantin, who was said to have 'built Dunkeld'. What of the Columban monasteries in Ireland, however? They could not be administered from far away Dunkeld, particularly when the Vikings were still virtually controlling the sea route between Dalriada and Ireland. A new Irish centre for the monasteries would have to be found, and Kells was the obvious place for it. In order to assume this new authority, however, Kells had to have significant relics in its possession, hence the division.[16] It is noticeable, though, that the most important, the portable shrine of St Columba, went to Dunkeld, and along with it seem to have been the Breccbennach, and the Cathbuaid, Columba's crozier which, like the Breccbennach, would also be carried in battle by Scottish armies. Despite these changes, Iona itself remained a place of significant sanctity even though it was left with a single major relic, one of the saint's hands.[17]

It seems likely that from then onwards the abbot of Iona was also abbot of Kells. After he had taken the Irish share of Columba's relics to Kells, Indrechtach, the then abbot, remained in Ireland, as his successors probably did too.[18] In spite of that, pilgrims continued to flock to Iona and when Kenneth I died at Forteviot in 858 he was interred in Reilig Odhráin, as were many of his successors.[19] Its fame as royal burial place was already well-known. In the late 770s the Irish Niall Frossach, who had abdicated from his kingship of Tara, had been buried on Iona, and four years after that Artgal, King of Connacht in the west of Ireland, had died on Iona and his grave was there too.[20] What had drawn these kings to spend their last years or months there? Quite simply, it had been the reputation of Columba. Indeed, he even came to be regarded as the patron saint of the Vikings who had settled in the Hebrides.

After the killing of Blathmac in 825 no further Viking raids were recorded until 986. The sources for what happened on Iona during the three centuries after the transfer to Kells of many of the monks and some of the relics are so vestigial that it is impossible to construct any chronological narrative, but we do know that the Vikings did not continue to swoop down on monasteries, pillage all their valuables and then return to Scandinavia. The ninth century in fact saw significant numbers of them settling in the Northern Isles and the Hebrides, marrying local women and converting to Christianity. Indeed, they appear to have supported Kenneth I in his bid to rule Pictland as well as Dalriada.[21] It is said that some of the Hebridean Vikings went to Iceland and built churches dedicated to Columba,[22] while in 980 Olaf Sihtricsson the Viking King of Dublin retired to Iona 'in penitence and pilgrimage'. One of the grave slabs, dating from slightly later, has a runic inscription naming Ful and Kali, the sons of Olvir, obviously another Viking.[23] By the following century, Norse respect for Columba was such that when Magnus Barelegs, King of Norway, raided both the Outer and Inner Hebrides in 1098, he spared Iona, apparently halting on the threshold of what was probably the little chapel known as Columba's Shrine, locking the door and ordering his men not to touch it.[24]

We still have no knowledge of the monastic buildings during this period, although a persistent tradition has it that the Iona monastery was rebuilt and endowed by St Margaret of Scotland. Margaret, a Saxon princess, had been born in Hungary, where her father was living in exile. She was brought up at its pious court and then at the court of King Edward the Confessor, after the family were recalled to England. Her intention was to become a nun, but following the murder of her father and the subsequent rebellion of her brother, she, her mother, sister and brother fled north and sought the protection of King Malcolm III of Scotland. He married her and as his consort she played an active part in public life, particularly concerning herself with the affairs of the Church. She engaged in public debates with representatives of the Scottish Church, Malcolm acting as her interpreter, for she was uneasy about several irregularities in its rites. She felt that Lent was not being properly observed and that there were errors in the way that mass was celebrated. She arranged for Benedictine monks from Canterbury Cathedral to found a priory at the Church of the Holy Trinity in Dunfermline and presented costly gifts to other churches. She also made a point of visiting Gaelic hermits, so could she ever have gone to Iona?

It seems highly unlikely that Margaret would have made that long and complicated journey, not least because she had eight pregnancies and her asceticism and constant fasting seriously undermined her health. However, it does not do to underestimate a female saint, for many were not meek and acquiescent but strong-willed and full of determination. Of course Margaret could have made gifts of money to an abbot of Iona if he had happened to be visiting the royal court or attending the great ecclesiastical council at which she allegedly reformed the Scottish Church. However, the only evidence for her supposed connection comes in one brief mention by the chronicler Orderic Vitalis, who was himself a Benedictine monk. It was he who said that she rebuilt the monastery of Iona which had fallen into ruins, 'furnished it with monks' and gave them revenues for its maintenance.[25] The available sources of information for that period are so scanty that there would appear to be no means of confirming what Orderic Vitalis wrote, but because of that very fact we cannot dismiss it out of hand.[26] We know that Margaret was particularly interested in Céli Dé (clients of God), an ascetic group founded within the Irish Church in the ninth century,[27] and the Annals of Ulster record that in 1164 there was at Iona a monk named Mac Forchellaig described as being 'head of the Céli Dé'. If the Céli Dé were associated with that monastic community a century earlier, in Margaret's time, she might have been in touch with them. Intriguingly, her son, Alexander I, commissioned a copy of Adomnán's *Life* from Simeon, an Iona monk, although of course that in itself does not prove her relationship with the monastery.[28]

We may never find out any more about St Margaret's supposed connection with Iona, but by the late twelfth century another powerful figure was taking a close interest in the monastery. This was Somerled, ancestor of the MacDonald Lords of the Isles. Apparently of mixed Norse and Gaelic descent, he boldly styled himself 'King of the Hebrides' and eventually ruled over what is now Argyll, and the Isle of Man as well.

Scottish and Norse kings vied with each other for possession of the Western Isles and although the Norse were successful, they were really too far away to exercise their power there. When not engaging in territorial expansion, Somerled was an active patron of the Church, and in 1164 he decided that it was time that Iona had a resident abbot again. He therefore dispatched a deputation to Derry, which had by now superseded Kells as the Columban monastic centre, to see if Flaithbertach Ua Brolcháin, who was its head in Ireland, would move to Iona.

The deputation included not only Mac Forchellaig of the Céli Dé but Augustine 'the great priest', Dubsíde the lector, who would have read the scriptural passages at services, and Mac Gilla Duib, a leading hermit.[29] This suggests that there was still, or again, a sizeable monastic community at Iona, but in the end Flaithbertach was not allowed to move there, because Muirchertach mac Lochlainn, High King of Ireland, relied upon his support at home. We do not know why Somerled had wanted to have a new Irish abbot for Iona. It has been suggested that he may have had it in mind to try to make it the centre of the Columban monasteries once more. Perhaps he was attempting to enhance his own prestige by doing this or there may have been some reason which made him suppose that the community was in need of reform. He might simply have been eager for the monks there to pray more effectively for his soul when he was gone, and this came sooner than he had expected. That very same year, he rose in rebellion against Malcolm IV, King of Scots, not for the first time, only to be killed in battle. According to a seventeenth-century account based on much earlier sources, Malcolm sent a boat with the body of Somerled to Iona for burial, at his own expense, in a gesture of reconciliation.[30] It was then left to Somerled's son, Ranald, to introduce a dramatic new development at Iona's monastery.

Somerled's wife was Ragnhild, daughter of Olaf the Red, King of Man, and they had four sons. The second eldest was Ranald, whose name is sometimes given in its Latin form, Reginald. He had taken part in his father's military campaigns, and the seal he used on his documents is described as having on one side a ship full of warriors while the other side showed an armed man on horseback, brandishing his sword. Ranald was not only a fighter, however. He seems to have been genuinely devout. The seal in question was attached to a charter by which he made a generous endowment to Paisley Abbey some time before 1192, possibly because it was the church nearest the place where his father had been killed. According to tradition, he also built the Cistercian abbey of Saddell, in Kintyre, which may originally have been planned by Somerled.[31] Possibly Ranald and his father had discussed Iona and its future, but it was not until almost forty years after his father's death that Ranald made a far bolder move. He transformed the Iona monastery into a Benedictine foundation.[32]

The Benedictine Order had become very popular by this time. The monasteries took their name from St Benedict of Nursia (now Norcia), a small town near Spoleto in Italy. The saint was born there in about 480 A.D. but, like St Martin, he was brought up in Rome. His family were wealthy and he could have expected a comfortable future, but as a young man he recoiled from what he saw as the corruption of that city and went to live the life of a hermit in Enfide, a village about thirty miles away, with only his old nurse for company. She was to act as his servant. However, as was sometimes the way with holy men living as hermits, his reputation as a miracle worker soon spread and he was besieged by visitors seeking his advice. To get away from them, he left the old nurse behind and retreated by himself to the even more isolated Subiaco Mountains, where he lived in a cave. Romanus, a monk from a nearby monastery, brought him food and gave him a monk's habit.

When Benedict had been there for three years, the head of a nearby monastery in the area died and its monks came and begged Benedict to become their next abbot. He reluctantly agreed, but the community found his very austere way of life so burdensome that some of them allegedly tried to poison him. Unsurprisingly, he immediately moved out and went back to Subiaco. He was not to be left in peace, however, for visitors flocked to see him. Always practical, he organised them into a dozen small monasteries. For some reason he left there abruptly in about 525 and moved to Monte Cassino, where he demolished a pagan temple and founded the great abbey where he would live for the rest of his life.[33]

It was soon after his arrival there that he composed his famous Rule which would earn him the title of the founder of Western monasticism and which was now adopted on Iona. This set of instructions for monastic life runs to seventy-three chapters, with a prologue, and it not only places great emphasis on spirituality and the need for poverty, chastity and cheerful obedience, but it gives minute detail for daily living, regulating the services of the Divine Office and giving instructions for the clothing to be worn by the monks, where they were to sleep and when they were to wash. With a keen understanding of human nature and an abundance of practical good sense (he had learned much from his unfortunate stay in the monastery near Subiaco), he wrote his Rule for all who wished to become monks, taking into account their differing ages, personalities and intelligence.

The monks would engage in three principal activities. They would spend four hours a day in prayer, with another four hours or so in reading suitable material: the scriptures and the writings of the early Fathers of the Church. For about six hours they would be occupied with manual work, because St Benedict knew that no one can spend their entire time reading and praying. He did not envisage lay brothers being part of the community, but non-monastic farm labourers would help in the fields and in the gardens, and those monks unsuited to strenuous outdoor activities would be occupied in other ways, cooking, baking, copying out Books of Psalms and scriptural passages for new novices and tending the old or sick members of the community. The abbot would be elected by the monks, and he was to strive to lead a perfect life, looking after them carefully and spending time teaching the more intelligent members of the house. The whole aim of the Rule was to help the monks to serve God in simplicity, in a self-sufficient place, and without contact with the outside world.[34]

The earliest Benedictine house in England appears to have been introduced by St Wilfrid, who may have brought back the Rule after his visit to Rome in the 650s. A number of other Benedictine monasteries seem to have been founded after that, until the Viking raids destroyed them. However, there was a revival in the tenth and eleventh centuries, which saw Benedictine houses rapidly established in the southern half of England. Until the 1070s, however, there was none north of the River Humber. St Margaret's foundation at Dunfermline, established before 1089, was the first in Scotland, to be followed by a small priory at Urquhart in Moray in about 1136, another at Coldingham in 1139, which was linked with Durham, and then in 1153 yet another on the Isle of May. Various reforming Benedictine Orders had come into being by this time, and in the twelfth century there were richly endowed Tironensian and Cistercian abbeys in Scotland, along with two Cluniac houses, while Augustinian abbeys, which followed a milder version of the Benedictine Rule, proliferated too.[35]

St Margaret had established her Benedictine priory by writing to Lanfranc, the Archbishop of Canterbury, for some monks. When Ranald introduced the new Order at Iona, he must have brought Abbot Celestine and other senior monks from elsewhere, to demonstrate the Benedictine way of life. One possibility is that Ranald may have imported monks from Durham. Iona and Durham already had a longstanding connection through their relationship with Lindisfarne, but there was also the fact that Ranald's elder brother Dugall had visited Durham Cathedral, where there were Benedictine monks. He had become a member of some kind of confraternity there, a confraternity being a group of lay men and, very occasionally, lay women, associated with a religious community. Those who joined the confraternity would all be remembered in the prayers of the church concerned, and might be buried in a monk's habit when they died.[36] So Dugall's contacts with Durham could have played a part in the choice. Moreover, Somerled's lands had been divided between his four sons, and Iona lay within Dugall's territories, so he would have had reason to influence the decision. However, the Annals of Ulster give Abbot Celestine's original name as having been the Gaelic 'Cellach' and it is more likely that Ranald continued the Iona tradition by recruiting his Benedictine monks in Ireland.[37]

It is also quite possible that some of the original Columban monks, if there were still any, stayed on in Iona, accepting the new Rule. After all, they too had been obliged to take vows of poverty, celibacy and obedience and they had always followed the pattern of the Divine Office in their daily services. They had studied, they had laboured in the fields and they had had their fine scriptorium. Of course it could be that they had drifted away from their original requirements and had no desire to accept a stricter regime and there would have been minor irritations too. The change to wearing black habits was possibly irksome, there would probably have been clashes with the new personalities in charge and of course fundamental to all was their loyalty to St Columba and his way of doing things. Six hundred years might have passed since his death, but his reputation lived on as strongly as ever. Perhaps it was hoped that any discontented members of the original community would be mollified by the fact that in future papal bulls and other official documents the new Benedictine abbey on Iona continued to be known as 'the monastery of St Columba'. The indomitable founder was not going to be forgotten. However, if there were those who were unable to subdue their resentment of the changes, they may well have moved to Kells or Derry or to one of the other Columban monasteries in Ireland.

Chapter 4

Black Monks and Black Nuns

However he effected the transformation on Iona from Columban monastery to Benedictine abbey, Ranald must have accomplished it by 1203 for, on 9 December that year, Pope Innocent III issued a papal bull addressed to the new Abbot Celestine and his monks. By this time, bishops had been given their own dioceses, but confusion had arisen because the Norse claimed that the Hebrides lay in their province of Nidaros (Trondheim) while rival bishops of the Isles were consecrated in York. However, Ranald had managed to obtain a special privilege for Iona. The Pope announced that in future Columba's monastery and its extensive properties in Argyll and the Inner Hebrides would be under his direct protection. In return, the monks would pay to the Holy See a token 2 bezants a year, a bezant being a Byzantine gold coin which was in wide circulation throughout Europe during the Middle Ages.[1] According to the Annals of Ulster, Abbot Celestine then busied himself erecting the new abbey, apparently in the enclosure where the monastic sheep were formerly kept. In the meantime, the monks would have continued to occupy the existing buildings.

The clergy of the Church in Ireland were furious when they heard what was going on, and in 1204 a large deputation, led by the Bishops of Tyrone and Tirconnell, along with the Abbots of Armagh and Derry and many of the monks of Derry, set out for Iona. They reputedly 'destroyed' the new monastery and elected Amalgaid ua-Fergail as Abbot of Iona. Their efforts were in vain, however. Ranald was a powerful figure. He had inherited the greater part of his father's lands and used the impressive title of 'King of the Isles and Lord of Argyll and Kintyre'. He continued determinedly with his plans, and the building of the abbey went on, apparently uninterrupted by his death in 1207.[2]

Ranald was reputedly buried in St Oran's Chapel, in the corner of Reilig Odhráin.[3] (Plate 8) There has been a great deal of speculation about the age of that Chapel. At one time it was supposed that it might have been built on the orders of St Margaret in the eleventh century, but this theory has been dismissed.[4] In recent years, a later date has been assigned to it and it is thought that it was possibly erected as a burial aisle by Somerled or more probably by Ranald himself, even before he started building the abbey. Whatever the circumstances, St Oran's is undoubtedly the oldest surviving stone structure on Iona.[5] As we have seen in relation to the high crosses, most of the rocks on the island were difficult to work, because they are very hard gneisses, formed more than 2500 million years ago, so St Oran's rubble walls were instead composed of the local flagstone and granite boulders. The east end of the island, however, has a band of softer sandstone resembling the Torridonian sandstone of the Western Isles and there were by now masons capable of using it for carvings.[6] They may well have come from Ireland, for the chapel's architecture is Irish in style, the main doorway decorated with chevrons and animal heads reminiscent of those seen in Irish churches of the late twelfth century. The rectangular doorway in the west wall also seems to be characteristically Irish.[7] Whoever constructed it, we do know definitely that St Oran's became the burial aisle of Ranald's son, grandson and their descendants, the Lords of the Isles.[8]

We have no details of the alarming late Viking attack on Iona which took place in 1210, just three years after Ranald's death, nor is there any description of the damage done. This might have had something to do with the continuing Norse reverence for Columba, which was again demonstrated in a story relating to the death of the Scottish king Alexander II. According to one of the Norse sagas, Alexander had a vivid dream prominently featuring the saint in a somewhat surprising role as protector of the Norse against the Scots. In 1249, Alexander had set out on an expedition designed to wrest the Hebrides from the Norsemen once and for all. One night he dreamed that three men appeared before him. The first was dressed as a king (Olaf of Norway), the second was a youthful figure (St Magnus, Earl of Orkney) and the third was the most imposing: huge, frowning and with an Irish tonsure. This was St Columba. He grimly warned the King of Scots to turn back and when Alexander told his men about his dream the next morning they pleaded with him to abandon the voyage. Alexander refused, and died soon afterwards.[9]

By that time, the church had almost certainly been completed and this is, in essence, the structure that we see today, albeit altered in the fifteenth century and heavily restored in the early twentieth century. The church would have been the first of the new buildings to be put up and it is now generally agreed that it must have been built on the site of its predecessor. As with St Oran's Chapel, the local grey or black flagstone and red granite were used, and the architecture was Romanesque in style. The church faces east, of course, and the ground plan is laid out in the traditional shape of a cross. It is thought that the long, narrow nave was built first. Beyond it lay a square chancel, about 5.2 metres square and the north and south transepts which form the arms of the cross were each of around the same size. Above the crossing, where the transepts join the main part of the building, was a sturdy bell tower. Not long after it was built it must have been decided that the chancel was inadequate, for between the years 1220 and 1250 it was extended a further 14 metres to the east and narrow aisles were built at either side of it. Later developments have altered the interior, but part of the masonry of the original chancel can still be seen at the west end of the north wall, and the floor level of the north transept dates to the early thirteenth century.

The church was dedicated to the Virgin Mary and the high altar may possibly have been placed at some distance from the east wall, to allow space for an ambulatory passage behind it. There would have been side altars in the transepts. There is no record of the dedications, but one of them would almost certainly have been to St Columba. A central niche in the east wall of the north transept contains what is left of a statue – its feet – and it has been suggested that these may have belonged to an image of Columba. The pilgrims who flocked to Iona may initially have been received in the north transept. By the late thirteenth century this had become inadequate and there was a plan to extend the south transept into a huge area, possibly intended for their reception. For some unknown reason, this was never completed. The project may well have been abandoned because the country's economy was badly affected by the financial burden of preserving Scotland's independence by fighting wars against the English.

The identity of the no doubt itinerant masons who built the church is unknown, but it has been said that the stonework of some of the windows resembles that of various Irish churches, and an investigation of a small group of masons' marks on the thirteenth-century stonework may yet yield some information.[10] There must have been quite a number of men employed there, for while the abbey church was being built, work also seems to have started on the cloister. Normally a Benedictine abbey would have its cloister to the south of its church, so that it would not be in the shadow of the taller building. On Iona, however, there was a stream usefully close to the north of the site, from which water could be led to the community's domestic buildings. This practical concern was more important than any considerations of light and shade. As a result the cloister was, unusually, on the north side of the church.[11]

A typical Benedictine cloister consisted of four ranges of monastic buildings, separated by a pathway and arcade from a large, central, open quadrangle. This was the pattern at

Iona, where the arcade had a lean-to wooden roof supported by octagonal stone pillars, the capitals of which were carved with scalloped and water-leaf ornaments. The monks could stroll there in quiet contemplation, even on wet days. Because the cloister buildings adjoined the abbey church, there was no south range at Iona, the north wall of the nave forming the south side of the cloister. The east range always contained the most important monastic buildings and the Iona chapter house is thought to have been the first of them to have been erected.

This was where the monks would gather together each morning after the Divine Office of Terce, which took place at 8.15 a.m. in winter and 8 a.m. in summer.[12] They would sit on stone benches along the walls of the inner chamber of the chapter house. Their meeting began with prayers and a reading from St Benedict's Rule, after which the abbot would ask any wrongdoers to confess their faults. Business matters followed. Property transactions were discussed, charters were read out, approved and sealed and the abbot might ask for the advice of his monks on new appointments or on any current difficulties. Having listened, he would then take the final decision. When all was done, the monks would leave in procession, walking up the steps back to the cloister and, if the Iona monks were following Benedictine practice exactly, chanting Psalm 5, 'Give ear, O Lord, to my words' ('Verba mea').[13]

Another small chamber in the chapter house building may have been where novice monks were taught and upstairs was a room which could have been the monks' library of manuscripts.[14] The main space on the first floor, however, was occupied by their dormitory, reached by the day stair at the north-east corner of the cloister. St Benedict had been careful to say that monks should sleep in dormitories and not in separate cells, with the beds of the young monks interspersed with those of the older ones, presumably to prevent them from chattering when they should have been asleep. A passage led through a narrow, two-storey building that linked the dormitory to the reredorter, in other words the latrine building, with its water supply coming from the nearby stream. A candle would be kept lit in the dormitory all night and the monks were to wear their habits in bed, so that they would be ready to rise in time for Nocturns at two o'clock in the morning. They would then make their way down into the church by means of the night stair, which took them into the north transept.

St Benedict had insisted in his Rule that the abbot of a monastery should share the same quarters as his monks but, as time went by, abbots became increasingly involved in public affairs and felt the need for greater privacy. This might account for an unexplained partition which seems to have divided the dormitory during the thirteenth century. Perhaps it created a private bedchamber for the abbot. At some later date a substantial abbot's house was built behind the north range, linked to both the reredorter and the monks' dormitory.[15] The north range itself was given over to the monks' other domestic arrangements. An elaborate doorway in the north-west corner of the cloisters opened into a downstairs chamber of unknown purpose, and a stair leading up to the refectory. This large room occupied the entire length of the north range. Its four windows looked out to the north and there was a bay in the north wall with a small pulpit which incorporated a cupboard where books could be kept.

During mealtimes, the monks listened to one of their number reading from the Bible or from the Rule as they ate. The abbot's table was probably directly opposite the pulpit. According to the Rule, for most of the year, the main meal of the day was to be taken at 2.30 in the afternoon, although in the spring, from Easter to Whitsun, it was at midday. The monks were not supposed to eat meat unless they were recovering from an illness and needed to regain their strength, and they fasted every Wednesday and Friday for much of the year. During Lent, on every day but Sunday, their only meal was in the evening and was restricted to bread, milk and eggs, as indeed it had been in

Columba's time. On other occasions, the abbot could vary the fare his community was allowed. He himself was permitted to eat meat, except on fast days, and he could have it served, along with wine, to guests or to any of the monks whom he cared to invite to his table. Otherwise, barley bread, eggs, vegetables, fish, shellfish and cereals would have been what the monks usually ate, accompanied by water or ale.[16]

Because of the danger of fire, baking and brewing were carried out in a separate, two-storey building on the west side of the cloister. It was entered by a doorway in its east wall. Inside were four hearths and it too used water from the nearby stream.[17] It seems that the west range was never completely built, perhaps because St Columba's Shrine occupied part of where it would have been or more probably because the money had run out by the end of the thirteenth century, when the rest of the cloisters were completed. However, it may have been, in part at least, where the abbey guest house was to be found, perhaps as an entirely separate building.

There were various free-standing buildings very close to the abbey and forming part of it. There was, for instance the St Michael Chapel. Its site is unknown but it may well have been the structure which in the twentieth century was restored and given the slightly abbreviated name of the Michael Chapel, for some unexplained reason. It stands close to the east range and might have been put up as the place where the monks could worship while the main abbey church was being constructed. It may later have served as the infirmary chapel. The infirmary itself was probably the larger, single-storey building nearby, also at right angles to the main abbey. Sick and elderly monks would have been looked after there.[18] Many of their illnesses would have been treated with extracts of the herbs and other plants which grew in the large and intensively cultivated abbey garden close by.[19] Finally, in a field south of the abbey there was another small chapel, St Mary's, perhaps used for prayer by the monastic community or by pilgrims on their way to the abbey.[20]

As pilgrims arriving from Mull walked from the shore up the long path leading to the abbey, they might have been surprised to see to their left, on the slope of the raised beach, another smaller but very similar building with a church and a cloister. This was the nunnery established by Somerled's son Ranald and built in the early thirteenth century at the very same time as the abbey itself (Plate 6). He founded it for his sister Bethoc, who became its first prioress. It was an Augustinian house, and only the second in Scotland. The earlier Scottish Augustinian house for women, at Scone, had been set up in about 1120.[21]

St Augustine of Hippo had drawn up the first general rule for a community of women attached to the Church. A native of Roman North Africa, he had lived from 354 until 430. After some years in Italy, where he wrote his famous *Confessions*, he had returned to Africa and founded a semi-monastic community, later becoming Bishop of Hippo. His Augustinian houses flourished and in 423 he wrote, in a letter to a community of women attached to the monastery in Hippo, what amounted to a Rule for them. After that, the number of such communities spread rapidly. The Rule was less rigorous for women than for men. The nuns took vows of chastity and obedience, but not of poverty, and they usually attracted as members the daughters of the nobility and even of royalty. A career as an abbess was a fine one for an intelligent, energetic woman and nunneries also provided a safe home for high-born daughters who were unsuited either physically or mentally for marriage. Augustinian nuns were known as canonesses and their days were spent attending the services of the Divine Office, taking care of church vestments and teaching the daughters of the aristocracy. That brought in some useful income to add to the offerings of pilgrims.[22]

Large Augustinian nunneries had the title of abbey, while the smaller ones were called priories, as was the case on Iona. Women's priories such as these were usually linked to existing Augustinian monasteries, but although the Iona nuns belonged to a different Order, their house obviously had a close relationship with the Benedictine abbey. There is no record of where the first nuns came from, but the general impression is that Ranald would have brought some of them, at least, from Ireland, where there were already various Augustinian houses. Others could well have been his own relatives, like Bethoc. We know practically nothing about his sister Bethoc or why he founded the nunnery for her. Was she particularly devout or was she an ambitious organiser, eager to have a career of her own? Had their father failed to find her a husband? Could she have been a widow, unwilling to marry again or did Ranald feel that her active role in the Church would enhance his own status? Nobody knows. Even her name is recorded in a series of different forms: Bethoc, Behag or in Latin Beatrice or Beatrix. Indeed her very existence might have been doubted were it not for a gravestone which survived until the early nineteenth century and described her as 'Behag, daughter of Somerled son of Gilbride, prioress'.

There is also another intriguing object which is almost certainly connected with her. In the National Library of Scotland there is preserved an illuminated manuscript known as The Iona Psalter (Plate 7). Close study of its text by experts suggests that it had been commissioned by an Augustinian canoness who took a special interest in the saints connected with Iona. Although it has been suggested, on very slight evidence, that it was produced in Oxford sometime between 1180 and 1220, it is generally believed to have belonged to Bethoc. Certainly that is perfectly possible. Oxford was well known for the production of high-quality manuscripts of this kind, with commissions coming in from quite distant places. Wherever it was written, the page with the first word of the first psalm is particularly elaborate. The psalm begins with the line 'Blessed is the man who walks not in the counsel of the wicked' and the first word in Latin is 'Beatus'. The very large letter B occupies two thirds of the entire page. In the centre is a sorrowful green face, while unpleasant, pinkish, four-legged creatures with tails coil round complicated, interlaced ribbons. It is perhaps no coincidence that the extravagantly illuminated B was also the first letter of the first prioress's first name.[23]

The Iona nunnery, like the abbey church, was dedicated to St Mary the Virgin and it appears to have been erected during the first two decades of the thirteenth century. Both the nunnery church and its cloisters were of high quality, architecturally, in the Romanesque style and with sophisticated detail. Constructed of the usual local materials, it may have been built by some of the Irish masons who were working on the abbey church. The chancel of the nunnery church was square and the nave was of the same width, but with the customary slightly lower floor level. The nave would have been occupied mainly by stalls for the nuns, although lay women too seem to have attended services. Probably pilgrims or relatives and pupils of the nuns, they would have entered by the main door, which was towards the west end of the north aisle, while the nuns themselves probably used the only other entrance, which led from the cloister into the nave. Their choir would have sat in the chancel. The north aisle had a small chapel at the east end and a stair in the wall leading to a little room above which may have been used as a sacristy. Both the chancel and the north aisle chapel had rib vaulted roofs, an advanced feature which was not found elsewhere in the Hebrides at that time.[24]

The nuns' church and cloister appear to have been put up simultaneously, with the cloister in the conventional position on the south side of the church, but otherwise the nunnery closely resembled in layout that of the abbey. The nuns' chapter house was on the ground floor of their east range, with stone benches around its walls, and their dormitory was on the floor above. Two other chambers were to be found on the ground floor, a very large one with stone benches along two of the walls. This may have been used as a parlour, and it could be that a wooden staircase led from there up to the dormitory. The purpose of the other room is unknown. The nuns' cloister had no north range, because of its position south of their church, and so its refectory was a long, sunny room in the south range, one storey high and lit by three windows in its south wall. Their guest house was probably situated in the west range.[25] The spacious quadrangle within their cloister would have been about 9.7 metres square.

As well as their buildings, the nuns owned a large area of hill pasture in the south of Iona, along with a certain amount of arable land there. They also had a small group of land holdings which they had been given in central Mull, and one or two other properties in the nearby little islands of Inch Kenneth, where a follower of Columba is said to have founded a monastery, and Eorsa, which was probably uninhabited. They likewise had the right to present the vicar to the parish church of Findoc on the island of Coll.[26] Apart from the very occasional mention of such properties, we know nothing of the life of the Iona nuns, not even the names of Bethoc's successors as prioresses until very late on. The only fleeting glimpses of them come in the form of four small silver spoons and an ornamental gold headband excavated at the nunnery and dated to the twelfth or thirteenth century.

A child's grave slab made of sandstone from the same period was found close to the nunnery, but it probably had nothing to do with the nuns and was instead related to another twelfth-century building. It appears that by this time there was a local population of lay people on Iona, and immediately north of the nuns' church was St Ronan's, built at about the same time as the nunnery and believed to have been the parish church for the island. This is not absolutely certain, for there is no written record of it until 1372, when a priest named Mactyr, son of John the Judge, was appointed to be its rector, replacing Dominic, son of Kenneth, who had died several years earlier.[27] Made of the usual materials and standing on the site of an earlier Christian chapel, it was lit by a little east window and by two other windows at the east end of the chancel, facing each other. Women islanders and children were often buried nearby.

The nuns and the local men and women were not the only people whose identities have been lost, for until the middle of the fourteenth century we know the names of only two of the Iona abbots: Celestine himself, the first Benedictine abbot and an elusive Finlay, who was consecrated about 1320.[28] This is all the more tantalising because, among the various gravestones of armed men formerly in Reilig Odhráin and now preserved under cover at the abbey, there are several belonging to unnamed ecclesiastics dating from the fourteenth to the fifteenth century. These were probably carved by various masons working in a similar style under the patronage of Somerled's descendants the MacDonalds and their allies.[29]

The earliest representation of a possible abbot may be on the slab bearing the figure of a tall, very thin ecclesiastic. He is wearing his alb, the long, linen robe beneath his sleeveless outer garment, the chasuble. On his head is a small, fairly low mitre, its style suggesting that he died in the late thirteenth or early fourteenth century. His right hand is raised in blessing and with his left hand he holds his crozier. Beneath his image, two unidentified monk-like figures embrace each other. Another such gravestone consists of a tapered slab with a Latin inscription and a panel carved with the figure of a priest in Eucharistic vestments. He stands with his hands together in prayer, in front of an altar raised up on a plinth. On the altar are the communion chalice and a cross, while another man wearing an alb stands behind the priest.

For all the accidental anonymity of the early abbots, documentary sources do begin to throw some light on their activities. Western European abbots in general found themselves increasingly involved in public affairs, summoned to the royal Court to give advice, serving on important committees and attending Church conventions in other countries. This was so even on remote Iona. Successive abbots did not remain at home in their own comfortable house. Instead, they were to be found travelling surprising distances, leaving the prior in charge of the abbey during their lengthy absences. At this time Iona was still in the Norse province of Nidaros and a Norse saga mentions that in 1226 the Abbot of Iona was in attendance at the Court of King Haakon IV of Norway. It seems that he had accompanied Simon, the new Bishop of the Isles, who had gone there to be consecrated.[30]

Just over twenty years after that, the then abbot of Iona was in Lyons, where Pope Innocent IV was staying to escape anti-papal disturbances in Rome. The abbot had gone there to petition the Pope to allow him to have an episcopal ring and mitre, although of course he was not a bishop. In the letters which Pope Innocent issued agreeing to the request, he rather quaintly described the abbot as coming from 'a distant part of Norway'. At the same time he forbade the Benedictine abbots in Scotland to try to force Iona's abbot to attend their general chapter. They had been demanding that he be present, pointing out that although Iona was in the Nidaros diocese, its abbey held lands in Scottish territory too.[31] Norway finally ceded the Western Isles to Alexander III, King of Scots, with the Treaty of Perth in 1266, after their defeat at the earlier Battle of Largs, but Iona Abbey would remain technically in the province of Nidaros until 1472.[32]

At the end of the fourteenth century, we suddenly have for the first time a dramatic insight into the career of one of St Columba's successors. He was Fingon Mackinnon, known in later Gaelic tradition as 'the Green Abbot'. He first enters the records in March 1359 when the Pope instructed the Bishop of Dunkeld to investigate the unlawful occupation of the abbacy of Iona by a monk called Fingon, and remove him if he were unfit for the position.[33] Nothing is heard of him for the next thirty years and more, until 1393 when Duncan Patricii, priest of the parish church of St John the Evangelist on the Isle of Mull, somewhat insecurely sought from Pope Clement VII confirmation of his own appointment. He had been presented to the living by Abbot Fingon, Duncan said, and the Abbot certainly had the right of presentation, but Duncan appeared to be in some doubt as to the legality of Fingon's position.[34] Four years later, Fingon himself was seeking papal confirmation that he really had been elected Abbot of Iona about forty years earlier, on the 'free resignation' of the late Abbot Peter.[35]

Pope Benedict XIII obligingly issued the necessary letter of confirmation, but that was not the end of the story. There were those who remembered perfectly well that after the death of Abbot Peter, Fingon Mackinnon the Iona monk had unlawfully claimed to be the next abbot. He was the son of Gilbride, chief of the Clan Mackinnon and, according to the seventeenth-century manuscript which called him 'the Green Abbot', he was devious, wicked and manipulative.[36] So what was the significance of this nickname? Fingon might have chosen to wear secular clothing, favouring the colour green, but it is much more likely that the epithet referred to his unfortunate character rather than to his attire. William Dunbar, the late fifteenth-century poet wrote of Pluto, King of the Underworld, wearing a cloak of green and, during the seventeenth-century Scottish witch trials, various witnesses testified that they had seen the devil, dressed in green. In a similar vein fairies, sometimes considered to be evil spirits, were also often described as wearing green, which was regarded as an unlucky colour, associated with death.[37]

Whatever the connotations, on the surface at least Abbot Fingon appeared for a time to be on reasonably good terms with John MacDonald, 1st Lord of the Isles, who took a close interest in the affairs of Iona Abbey. As we have seen, St Oran's Chapel had become his family burial place. Fingon may have sat on his council and when John died in 1387 Fingon and his monks met the mourners bringing his body to Iona at Martyrs' Bay, the customary landing place for such arrivals, leading them in procession along the cobbled Street of the Dead to the abbey, where there would be eight days and nights of funeral ritual. At some other point, Fingon even managed to place in St Oran's Chapel a gravestone commemorating his own family.

The gravestone has an effigy of Gilbride, his father, shown in a pointed helmet, grasping a spear and wearing a large sword at his belt. A shield which conceals his left arm has on it a design of a galley, a salmon chased by an otter and a somewhat indeterminate animal which is probably a lion. Two inscriptions on the slab commemorate Gilbride himself, his sons, Ewan and Cornebellus, Cormac's son Fingon, Fingon's son Finlay, and another Ewan, of unspecified parentage. Family feeling and indeed family feuds were never far from the Abbot's mind.[38]

Just three years after the peaceable burial of John, 1st Lord of the Isles, Fingon was stirring up a rebellion against Donald, the new Lord, by encouraging Donald's younger brother John Mor to rise up against him.[39] The revolt was unsuccessful, Donald forgave his brother and Fingon escaped any punishment for his part in this episode because he was a churchman. Matters were smoothed over, and in 1395 John Goffredi, rector of the parish church of St Congan in the diocese of the Isles and a relative of the Lord of the Isles, left his parish to become a monk in 'the Monastery of St Columba' at Iona.[40] Meanwhile, Fingon went on living all too comfortably in his Abbot's House, letting the abbey go to rack and ruin.

No new building work had been undertaken during the fourteenth century, perhaps because the existing accommodation was regarded as being satisfactory, or perhaps because there was no money available to pay for it. That said, neglect must certainly have played a part in the disaster which followed. On 27 May 1403, Pope Benedict XIII approved a dispensation for the wedding of Anna Macleod to Lachlan Macgilleon, who were distantly related and therefore required special permission to marry. There was nothing extraordinary about that, but one of the conditions for the dispensation being granted reveals a startling state of affairs. The couple could become husband and wife, it said, provided that, as soon as the marriage had taken place, they paid a sum of money to the building fund of the monastery of Iona, 'which has collapsed.'[41]

Chapter 5

Disaster and Renewal

This startling piece of news, so laconically conveyed, is borne out by another papal document, five years later, which supplies a little more information. On 22 December 1408 Pope Benedict XIII permitted Dominic Dominici, the illegitimate son of one of the Iona monks and an unmarried woman, to become a monk there himself. It was noted that he was allowed to do so in spite of the fact that a large part of the chancel, the chapter house and other abbey buildings were in ruins. Apparently the timberwork had collapsed. Winter gales and heavy rainstorms would always be a problem, with the perpetual damp taking its toll, and of course neglect would have made matters much worse. Moreover, 'wicked men' were said to be occupying a great part of the abbey lands.[1]

John Goffredi, by now the prior, had no doubts about where the blame lay. He sent a list of allegations to the Pope and, on 26 August 1405, Benedict XIII ordered the Bishops of Glasgow and Dunkeld to summon Abbot Fingon to hear the charges against him. Goffredi was claiming that Fingon had lived with concubines and had wasted the abbey's resources, not least by using some of the income to provide dowries for three of his daughters by one of the concubines. He had deprived the abbey of goods worth 400 merks sterling, and the Pope declared that if these allegations were proved, then Fingon must be removed.[2] Unfortunately no record of the judgment against him has ever been found, but it would seem that he was indeed deposed, with John Goffredi taking over as abbot instead.

1 Iona Abbey from the west (© Peter Backhouse).

2 St Martin's Cross and the Sound of Iona (© Peter Backhouse).

3 St Columba's Shrine, in the shadow of the replica St John's Cross
(© Peter Backhouse).

5 The Monymusk Reliquary, traditionally said to have held relics of
St Columba (© National Museums of Scotland).

FACING PAGE: 4 The Virgin and Child enthroned, from the illuminated
Book of Kells (© The Board of Trinity College, Dublin).

6 The ruined Nunnery, an Augustinian priory (© Peter Backhouse).

FACING PAGE: 7 Page from the Iona Psalter, with the decorated initial B
(© National Library of Scotland).

8 St Oran's Chapel and Reilig Odhráin (© Peter Backhouse).

A high cross at Kirkapoll, on the island of Tiree, and later removed to Inveraray Castle, declared itself to be 'the cross of Abbot Fingonius and of his sons Fingonius and Eague'. By the time that the Green Abbot eventually died, at some point before 1421, the younger Fingon was prior of Iona Abbey.[3] It has been argued in mitigation of Abbot Fingon's irregular private life that the marriage of Gaelic churchmen was officially accepted. This view has been challenged,[4] and Fingon's domestic arrangements could equally well be seen in the context of the many non-Gaelic Scottish clergy who shared their lives with the women always described in the documents of the time as 'concubines'. Indeed, by 1425 James I, King of Scots was drafting a letter to the abbots and priors of the Benedictine and Augustinian houses in Scotland, declaring that he was filled with apprehension by the 'downhill condition and most threatening ruin of holy religion'. Everywhere in the country, he said, monasteries were defamed and regarded with contempt. If they did not mend their shameless ways, he might come to regret past royal generosity to them.[5]

There are no documentary sources to prove that this was the situation at Iona, but Fingon's reputation is certainly highly suspicious and there can be no doubt that the abbey buildings suffered during his term of office. It was left to his successor, Dominic, son of Gille-Coinich, to retrieve the situation. In very difficult conditions, Abbot Dominic made valiant efforts to raise the money necessary to fund the reconstruction work. There were no doubt gifts from local supporters – Donald, Lord of the Isles gave the abbey two parishes in Mull and one in Tiree in 1421[6] – but no repairs could begin. A petition of 1426 explained that this was because of local warfare, the financial burden of entertaining the pilgrims who were still coming in large numbers and because 'wicked and perverse noblemen' had encroached on the abbey lands.[7]

Visitors to Iona in our own time, impressed by the tranquillity of the island, might find it difficult to accept that local warfare was ever a problem, but the row of fourteenth- and fifteenth-century grave slabs of armed men with weapons who had been buried in Reilig Odhráin tells a different story. (Plate 9) In fact, the Scottish monarchs of the period, having given up the seemingly impossible task of imposing their rule on the Western Isles, had turned instead to a policy of encouraging rivalries between powerful local families, in the hope that they would be too busy fighting each other to rise up against the crown. As a result, the petition said, such was the monastic community's poverty that the monks had hardly enough barley bread and ale for their meals. To make matters worse, it was emphasised that not only the supporting timberwork but the masonry itself of the abbey church, chancel, bell tower and other buildings had completely collapsed. In 1428 Dominic was petitioning the Pope, asking him to allow the sale of special indulgences to pilgrims coming to Iona for St Columba's annual feast day. These would allow the soul of whoever bought one to spend three years fewer in purgatory. The proceeds would go towards the abbey reconstruction work.[8]

To add to Dominic's problems, one of Abbot Fingon's grandsons was causing endless trouble. The son of the illegitimate Prior Fingon, he was also called Fingon MacKinnon and he was agitating to become a monk at Iona. When he was a young man, Dominic had probably known the Green Abbot personally, but even if he did not, he obviously remembered all too vividly his reputation and as a result he was utterly opposed to allowing this would-be novice to join the monastic community. Indeed, he managed to make the younger Fingon swear an oath to the effect that he would never become a monk on Iona without the Abbot's consent. Having sworn the oath, Fingon apparently dismissed it from his mind and continued his efforts to be accepted.

Still highly suspicious of his motives, Dominic sent another petition to the Pope in 1426, declaring that this persistent applicant wanted to enter the monastery 'by reason of succession rather than devotion'. He went on to explain that he was completely unwilling to receive him, on the grounds that Fingon's grandfather had been 'the greatest tyrant' and because of the demerits of others in the MacKinnon family. 'A bad tree cannot bear good fruit', he added tersely. His reaction may be imagined when he received a swift reply in the form of a papal letter ordering him to accept Fingon as a monk.[9] Obviously a man of influence and determination, Dominic did not meekly comply however, but declared that, if Fingon were appointed, the Lord of the Isles would remove the precious relics his ancestors had given to the abbey and would also take away the bones of his forebears who were buried there. No doubt the gifts would have included the magnificent gold and silver reliquary which Donald, 2nd Lord of the Isles had presented to enclose the hand of St Columba.[10]

The struggle between the two men went on for years, and in December 1443 Dominic sent to the Pope another lengthy complaint about Fingon, declaring him to be 'hateful' to both the abbey and the Lord of the Isles, because of his dishonest 'life and conversation'. He not only kept a concubine 'of noble birth', whom he had furnished with a settlement consisting of 40 cows, but he had led a group who carried off some of the abbey's goods.[11] Unfortunately for Dominic, this document had the reverse of the desired effect. Fingon must have had influential friends, for when the Pope held an inquiry to look into the matter, he promptly excommunicated the Abbot and monks of Iona for refusing to accept Fingon. Undeterred by this latest and most serious rebuff, Dominic fought on, enlisting the support of King James II himself, and in the end he must have triumphed. Fingon disappears from the records, whereas Dominic remained abbot until his death more than twenty years later.[12]

Despite all these distractions and setbacks, Dominic must have had the satisfaction of seeing the actual work of rebuilding start, probably about the middle of the fifteenth century.[13]

In view of the scale of the damage, the entire south side of the abbey church and part of its east wall had to be demolished and rebuilt, and the opportunity was taken to widen the chancel and to add to it a new south aisle, rather shorter than the chancel itself. This made room for at least two additional altars and the north chancel aisle was changed too. Half of it was demolished, its upper storey was done away with, the arches between it and the chancel were blocked up and it became a sacristy with an elaborate doorway leading from the main church interior. The massive walls built at this period were from 1.1 metres to 1.3 metres thick and, most unusually, the floor level of the nave was, and is, noticeably higher than that of the chancel. The walls would have been plastered, and traces of paint have been found there too. In keeping with other churches of the period, there can be little doubt that Iona Abbey would have had a vivid interior, perhaps even with wall paintings as well as brightly coloured and gilded statues of saints.

Three shallow steps led up to the high altar, which stood about 1.3 metres inside the east wall, under a handsome, traceried east window. It has been suggested that during Lent the customary veil which was hung immediately in front of a high altar would have been suspended from a beam fixed on surviving sockets up above and reaching from the north to the south wall. A spiral stair at the south-west corner of the crossing led up into the sturdy central tower, which now had elaborate windows too in its upper part, and a gabled roof. Above its bell chamber was a dovecot with two tiers of nesting boxes Some commentators have sentimentally supposed that the doves were kept in memory of St Columba, 'Dove of the Church', but the reality was rather more brutal than that. Great houses and abbeys often had a dovecot, simply to augment the food supply. In other words, pigeon was frequently served up at mealtimes. Back on the ground floor the nave, like the chancel, was also expanded, becoming 6.7 metres wide, but no side aisles to it were built, although a small tower was put in to join its north-west corner to St Columba's Shrine. The main door was created in the west wall and above it a large window with five sections.[14] After dark, of course, the interior of the church would be lit by candles.

Because the chapter house had also collapsed, substantial work had to be done there too and it was virtually rebuilt, somewhat hastily, judging by inaccuracies in its design, and using inferior materials which included fragments from the previous structure. A barrel-vaulted roof was constructed over its inner chamber, and stone benches were installed in recesses in the side walls. The dormitory upstairs may have been divided into cubicles by timber partitions at this period. Alterations were also made to the cloister arcade. Some of the pillars were replaced and some of the arches were blocked up with masonry, either for structural reasons or to make it more sheltered from the wind and rain for the monks who liked to stroll there. The windows in what is now the Michael Chapel were also altered at this time.[15]

Interestingly, the nuns seem to have taken advantage of the presence of the masons to have work done on their priory. There is no suggestion that it was in danger of collapse, but perhaps the prioress wanted to make sure that no such disaster would happen to her house. At any rate, some fairly substantial alterations were made. In the church itself, the nave arcade was blocked up and two large windows were put into the south wall, several clerestory windows were inserted and a new chapel was formed in the north aisle, with a vaulted ceiling and a doorway leading to a staircase in the wall. This gave access to what was probably the sacristy up above. It may have been at this same time that a wooden screen, presumably a rood screen, was inserted between the nave and the chancel, and a gallery was constructed at the west end. Its purpose is not known, but it could well have been for important pilgrims or, it has been suggested, for the nuns' choir, although this seems less likely.

As with the abbey church, the interior would have been

71

plastered and possibly had painted decoration too. Extensive work was also done on the nunnery cloisters. The cloister garth was increased from almost 10 metres square to 14 metres, with the walks about 2.1 metres wide. For some reason the spacious refectory in the south range was rebuilt, using blocks of granite brought over from the Ross of Mull.[16] The only brief glimpse of any of the nuns of this period comes in a mention of one of them in a petition of 1422. This was Christina, who is described as being the daughter of one of the monks at the abbey.[17]

The most striking feature of both the reconstructed abbey and the nunnery was the wealth of fifteenth-century decorative carving still to be found there. The capitals of the pillars inside the abbey, for instance, have not only leaf designs as formerly, but biblical scenes. There is a crucifixion in the chancel, with Christ on the Cross, the Virgin Mary and St John standing in attitudes of mourning at either side. Along from this, two angels with large wings flank a representation of the Virgin and Child, while Adam and Eve stand guiltily beneath their fruit tree on an arch between the south transept and the chancel, she semi-naked and hastily wrapping a garment round her legs while a stern angel with an upraised sword watches them. On the north arch of the crossing they are portrayed again, more boldly catching at the branches of their tree, perhaps about to pluck a fig, for some versions of the Bible story say that Eve tempted Adam with a fig rather than an apple.

There is a demon, possibly even the devil himself, vying with the Archangel Michael for the souls of the departed, who are being weighed in a pair of scales. Lions, dogs and fabulous animals like the wyvern, an intimidating dragon-like creature with wings, two legs and a barbed tail, prowl round the capitals, occasionally accompanied by or threatening a medieval man. Several lively scenes depict more realistic aspects of fifteenth-century life, with men in hoods, doublets and hose engaging in combat and elsewhere carrying out the slaughter of a cow, while a mounted warrior followed by a foot soldier rides round the capital of one of the pillars in the chancel arcade. The carvings in the nunnery church are very badly weathered, but on some of the corbels in the wall of the nave there can still be seen a human head, an animal's head and an Annunciation scene, with the Archangel Gabriel telling Mary that she would give birth to Jesus Christ, while another angel looks on and holds up a scroll. The capitals of the pillars are mainly scalloped or have animal carvings.

Architectural historians are inclined to agree, on stylistic grounds, that the carvings along with the fifteenth-century reconstruction were mainly undertaken by Iona masons, albeit of Irish descent, and on the east arch of the abbey church crossing are carved in Latin the words 'Donald Ó Brolchán made this work'. He is believed to have been the master mason.[18] His is the only name actually carved anywhere, but there are also a number of masons' marks from this period, many of them in the form of single capital Lombardic letters, from an alphabet which originated in Italy, as its name implies, and was frequently used in manuscripts, church carvings and medieval stained glass windows throughout Western Europe. There is also the rather comical carved head of a startled looking man on the crossing arch, and it is thought that he may well have been one of the masons, portrayed there by a mischievous colleague. (Plate 12a)

The masons' work was not confined to the architecture of the churches, of course, for the longstanding practice of putting up high crosses had not died away. The imposing MacLean's Cross was erected at this same period, between the nunnery and the abbey, at the junction of three medieval streets. (Plate 11) Still in what is believed to be its original position, it is carved from a single slab 3.15 metres high, and has noticeably short arms. Both sides of the cross are intricately decorated with interlacing and anyone standing in front of it, facing east, sees the carved figure of the crucified Christ in the circle near the top. Unusually, he is shown wearing a long robe and not simply the loincloth more familiar from crucifixes. However, this representation was not unique, for he is also portrayed wearing robes of this kind on a number of Irish Romanesque crosses. On the left arm of the MacLean cross there was a chalice, now destroyed, and on the back, the very top is carved with two animals, while there has been an angel on the right arm. A panel at the foot of the shaft shows an armed man with a lance, and an inscription in Lombardic capitals which is almost entirely worn away. Perhaps it recorded the name of the unknown chief of the MacLean family who commissioned it.[19]

Having overseen his important building programme, Abbot Dominic died in about 1465, and was buried near the high altar in the abbey church, as befitted such a remarkable man who had devoted so many years to his monks and their buildings. A tomb with a full-length effigy has been identified as his. Unfortunately the features have entirely worn away, for his is the only effigy made of Carsaig sandstone. It was no doubt chosen because it was easily carved, but that makes is far less durable. Dominic is dressed as he would have been when he celebrated mass, and his Eucharistic vestments are reasonably well-preserved. He carries a crozier, two angels support his pillow and there were two lions at his feet. It has been suggested that Donald Ó Brolchán himself would have carried out the carving, for he must have known the Abbot well.[20]

Abbot Dominic was succeeded by Angus, an illegitimate grandson of Donald, Lord of the Isles, but he seems to have held the position for only two years before, somewhat ironically, yet another member of the MacKinnon family took over.[21] The Green Abbot's brother Niall, chief of the MacKinnons, had a grandson named Lachlan, also the MacKinnon chief, and it was his son John who was now elected to the abbacy, although he had not been one of the Iona monks.[22] He too was obviously proud of his family connections, for he commissioned a large, free-standing MacKinnon cross. The shaft still survives. On one side are intertwined scrolls above a galley. On the opposite side is a griffin, the legendary animal which has the head and wings of an eagle combined with the body of a lion. The shaft's edges are decorated too, and feature a cat's head, while the inscription in the usual Lombardic capitals records that this was the cross of Lachlan MacKinnon and his son John, Abbot of Iona, and was made in 1489.[23]

Some of the tombstones of the period occasionally identify one or two of the other abbey personnel for us. A grave slab, probably dating from the mid-fifteenth century, has the small figure of a cleric in Eucharistic vestments and records his name. The Latin inscription translates as: 'Here lies Brother Cristinus MacGillescoil, sometime Prior of Iona, on whose soul may God have mercy' and, interestingly, another fourteenth or fifteenth-century grave slab which used to be in Reilig Odhráin, must have been that of a smith, for along with a cross, plant scrolls and a sadly illegible inscription, there are two or perhaps three anvils.[24]

John MacKinnon continued the rebuilding of the Abbey during his long term of office. After thirty-one years as abbot, he died in 1498 and was buried in the church, beneath a tomb bearing his effigy (Plate 10). Its design was based on Abbot Dominic's and it would appear to be the work of several masons. The Archangel Gabriel and another winged figure, possibly St John, support the pillow of his carved figure, which rests on the backs of stone lions. His round, plump face has a wrinkled brow and a somewhat surprised expression. He wears Eucharistic vestments and held his crozier (now gone). The inscription gives his name and the incomplete date of his death, '15...'. He must have overseen the preparation of the monument, and optimistically overestimated the length of his life.[25]

By that time the political landscape of the Western Isles was changing as the Campbell family rose to prominence. Colin Campbell, 1st Earl of Argyll, was for a time high in royal favour and was the Chancellor of Scotland in the reigns of both James III and James IV. He determinedly built up his power in the west and when his son Archibald succeeded him as 2nd Earl, he too set out on a similar course, becoming Master of the Royal Household. He also used his influence to encourage the young James IV to move against his rivals, the MacDonald descendants of the Lords of the Isles.[26] James was already determined to exert effective royal control over the north-west territories of his kingdom which had so long defied any such previous attempts by the monarchy. Probably in his parliament of May of 1493, he forfeited the ineffectual John, Lord of the Isles, who had notably failed to control his own followers. His lands were annexed to the crown, and James made three subsequent expeditions, personally securing the submission of a number of clan chiefs, and taking the islands of Islay and Tiree. [27]

Iona Abbey could no longer look to the support of the Lord of the Isles, and Archibald 2nd Earl of Argyll had plans for the abbey and its extensive properties. On the death of Abbot John, he persuaded the King to send a petition asking the Pope to make Iona Abbey the seat of the Bishop of the Isles. As we have seen, the history of that bishopric had been a complicated one until the Treaty of Perth in 1266, when the Hebrides were surrendered by the Norse to the Scots. The Isle of Man formed part of the bishopric of the Isles, and that is where the bishop's seat was. In 1334, however, Man came under the control of the English and by the end of the century there were once more two competing bishops. During the Great Schism in the papacy, which began in 1387, there were rival popes in Rome and in Avignon, the English supporting the former and the Scots the latter. As a result, the bishopric of the Isles had to be divided in two, with an English bishop still based in Man and a Scottish bishop whose cathedral was apparently the church of Snizort on the Isle of Skye. The royal petition inspired by Argyll was therefore asking that Iona Abbey replace the Snizort church until the Isle of Man was recovered from the English.[28]

James IV's request was officially granted, but it is believed that it was never carried out, for there is no sign that the Iona monks formed a cathedral chapter, nor was Iona ever termed a

cathedral in official documents at this time.[29] The Earl of Argyll
continued to pursue his plans, however, and the following year
Iona Abbey was granted for life *in commendam* to none other
than his kinsman John Campbell, Bishop of the Isles.[30] This
meant that no new abbot would be appointed, and the Bishop
would draw the revenues from the abbacy, although he would
not be involved in its daily administration. The grant to him
was careful to say that the usual services in the abbey church
must be maintained and the customary number of monks must
be 'in no way diminished'. It did not say what that number
was. Originally an abbey had been held *in commendam* as a
temporary measure when the position of abbot was vacant, but
by this time abbeys were all too often granted *in commendam*
to illegitimate royal sons, ambitious noblemen or demanding
churchmen in order to augment their resources. Successive
bishops of the Isles continued to hold Iona Abbey *in commendam* and there never was another abbot.[31]

It suffered financially as well as losing some of its status,
for the bishops drew upon its revenues to support their own
dwindling finances. This probably explains why the chapter
house was finished so hastily, presumably in the early sixteenth
century, and with inferior materials. Whether or not the church
was now known to people as a cathedral, the bishops of the
Isles did apparently live on Iona, probably in the Abbot's
House, at least for part of the year and Bishop John Campbell
certainly died on Iona on 14 June 1510. He was interred in 'St
Michael's burial aisle' (which may or may not have meant the
present Michael Chapel) by his own choice.[32] The Bishop's successor, nominated by James IV, was George Hepburn, Abbot
of Arbroath and Treasurer of Scotland, but he was killed at the
Battle of Flodden in 1513, whereupon Bishop John Campbell's
nephew, another John, was nominated in his place, although
he was never consecrated. However, when he resigned in about
1529, that did not prevent him from demanding a pension from
the revenues of the Isles and Iona.[33]

The Campbells were definitely in the ascendancy at that point and a sixteenth-century grave slab formerly in Reilig Odhráin commemorates 'four priors of Iona from one clan': John, Hugo, Patrick, who was a Bachelor of Canon Law, and another Hugo. The second Hugo probably commissioned the slab, for the date is unfinished and simply reads '15...'. Tantalisingly, their surname is not given, but it is believed to have been Campbell.[34] After the younger Bishop John Campbell's resignation, however, a rival family came to the fore, in the shape of the Macleans of Kingairloch, which lies on the mainland, to the north-east of Mull. Farquhar Maclean, who was bishop from 1530–44, had been an Iona monk. Little is known about his career, but he does not seem to have been a particularly forceful character, for he sought permission to wear his bishop's rochet, a type of surplice which reached to below the knee, instead of his usual monk's habit. This, he hoped, would make the local people have greater respect for his authority. He resigned in favour of his brother Roderick, who had been a priest, not a monk.[35]

Intriguingly, Roderick is said to have studied at the German University of Wittenberg in 1534, the leading intellectual centre of the Reformation. Martin Luther and Philip Melancthon the famous Reformers both taught in that University. Roderick does not seem to have deviated from the old faith, however, and in 1549, describing himself as being 'of Iona', he published in Rome a translation into Latin verse of the first two books of Adomnán's *Life of Columba*.[36] In that same year Donald Monro, Dean or more probably Archdeacon of the Isles, visited Iona and was told that no fewer than four Irish, eight Scandinavian and forty-eight Scottish kings, including both St Margaret's father-in-law, Duncan and the famous Macbeth were buried in Reilig Odhráin. Certainly the early Scottish rulers had a devotion to St Columba for, from the tenth to the twelfth century, four of the kings were named Malcolm, which is the anglicised version of the Gaelic Máel Coluim, meaning 'servant of Columba' The graveyard was well-built, he noted, with stone and lime walls, and there were three little chapels, each with a broad grey marble or whinstone slab in the gable. On one was inscribed in Latin 'Grave of the Kings of Scotland', while the other two bore the inscriptions 'Kings of Ireland' and 'Kings of Norway'.[37] Historians have concluded that the number is a vast exaggeration but it has as yet been impossible to do any excavations in the area because the graveyard is to this day used for burials by the local community.[38]

One interesting development during Farquhar Maclean's episcopacy appears to have been the acquisition of a bell made in Mechelen, in the Low Countries. Dedicated to St Anna, it is inscribed in Flemish with the words: 'I am Anna, cast by Peter van den Ghein in the year of Our Lord 1540'. Beneath the words are five small shields. The first one has an image of the Virgin and Child with St Anna and the second has a coat of arms superimposed on a crozier. A cherub holding a napkin bearing the face of Christ is on the third shield and the heads of two more cherubs decorate the fourth and fifth shields. After a chequered history, the bell was found in a farm in Hertfordshire in the 1940s and brought back to Iona, where it hangs in the abbey cloister,[39] but did it really belong to the abbey? It might just have been commissioned by the long-term Augustinian prioress of the nunnery, for she was named Anna MacLean, she could have wished to honour her patron saint in this way and it was not only bishops who carried croziers. Prioresses did too.

Anna, daughter of Donald MacLean and granddaughter of Charles MacLean, may well have been a sister of the two bishops, Farquhar and Roderick. We know that she was prioress in 1509, when she obtained from James IV a letter of protection defending the nunnery against the depredations of the MacLean lairds of Duart and Lochbuie and Ranald, son of Alan MacDonald of Clan Ranald. Almost all her activities are entirely unknown, but she is believed to have commissioned a large cross at Soroby, one of the nunnery's churches on Tiree. On the shaft are inscribed in Latin the words, 'Here is the cross of Michael, Archangel of God. Anna, Prioress of Iona.' The upper part shows Michael with a dragon, while the lower section depicts a nun, probably Anna herself. St Michael was known for leading souls to heaven, and Anna possibly commissioned this cross in contemplation of her own death. The style of the black-letter inscription places it firmly in the early sixteenth century.[40]

When Anna died, she was buried in the nunnery church, before the high altar. Her grave slab, attributed to the same Oronsay carver who produced the Soroby cross, features the large carving of an imposing figure. Anna stands with hands clasped, wearing a narrowly pleated rochet over a more widely pleated cassock, and from her shoulders falls a long, heavy cloak which is fastened by a small brooch at her neck. Her hair is covered by another long, thick cloth and in general her appearance is remarkably similar to the image of Bricius Mac-Mhuirich on his grave slab. He was a prior of Oronsay, another Augustinian house, which was dedicated to St Columba. Both are the work of the same Oronsay sculptor, although some of the details are different. The prior's cloak is shorter and Anna has a little lapdog lying on each side of hers, while above the angels hovering at either side of her head are two popular symbols, a round mirror and a double-edged comb.[41]

Sometimes these have been interpreted as signs of worldly vanity, but it has been noted that they frequently occur on Pictish carved stones from the fifth to the ninth centuries, and are often associated with important secular men and women who had died. It has therefore been suggested that the mirror and the comb instead indicated a high status, and this could well have been carried over into commemorative Hebridean stone carvings.[42] Anna's grave slab has been broken and the lower half of it is almost entirely missing. However, an eighteenth-century drawing (Plate 25) shows it to have had a depiction of the Virgin and Child, the Virgin wearing a tall, mitre-like headdress, with a sun and a moon, symbols of the Creation, replacing Anna's comb and mirror.[43]

Looking at her carved figure, it is tempting to believe that Anna was a formidable personality, but unfortunately there are no surviving documents with her signature to allow us to assess her likely level of education, let alone her competence as the administrator of her nunnery. In 1532 no fewer than six of the seven Iona monks were able to sign their own names, but the situation in nunneries was usually rather different. By the early sixteenth-century there were only eleven convents in Scotland, some of them with fewer than half a dozen nuns, and time and again, their documents show that they did not know how to write, for they had to ask a notary to guide their hands when they were asked to sign their names as witnesses to land transactions. The sisters of the Dominican convent of St Catherine of Siena in Edinburgh were an exception but the lack of documentary sources makes it virtually impossible to say whether the Iona nuns shared their level of education.[44] They did, however, have in their possession in about 1550 a Sarum Hours of Our Lady which had been produced in Flanders in the early sixteenth century. [45]

We know that prioresses in English nunneries usually belonged to noble families, and that they tended to live in very comfortable circumstances befitting their social status rather than their profession. They travelled about quite extensively to conduct their community's business and they were often accused of wearing luxurious clothes, being excessively imperious and keeping a plethora of pets. True, the English nunneries generally had only half the revenues of male monasteries but a prioress often had her own house with a staff consisting of at least one or two gentlewomen to wait upon her, as well as a cook and a laundress. There is no evidence to tell us about the lifestyle of the Iona prioresses, but if they too had gentlewomen and pets keeping them company, that might explain the carvings of lay women on some of their grave slabs, not to mention the presence of the two little lapdogs beside Anna.[46]

When Prioress Anna died, she was succeeded by Mary MacLean, daughter of a Farquhar MacLean and very likely one of her own relatives. [47] It has been claimed that there is no evidence of a community of nuns on Iona by the late fifteenth century,[48] but the carved stones prove otherwise. One worn grave slab of the period, found at the nunnery, has the figures of two nuns wearing their habits, consisting of long veils and cloaks over long dresses. The mirror and comb symbols are present, and the panel below has a priest beside an altar with a chalice on it, while the panel above has two lay women in gowns, cloaks and rather smart caps or hats. If they were not gentlewomen attending the nuns, they must have been patrons or relatives of the main figures. Unfortunately, the inscription bearing the words 'Here lies ...' in Latin is otherwise illegible.[49]

A couple of other grave slabs which have been dated to the period 1500–60 are more informative. The first features two women standing together in separate niches, and although its top and lower right corners have been broken off and much of the inscription is now illegible, a drawing made in 1699 tells us that it commemorates Mariota, the daughter of John, son of Lachlan, Lord of Coll, who would have been a MacLean. Mariota is presumed to be the figure wearing lay clothes, but the name of her companion was too worn to be read even in the late seventeenth century. From her costume, the second woman was a nun and could have been Mariota's sister. The other grave slab is even more significant. Amongst its worn symbols are a mirror and comb, but it is the Latin inscription which is intriguing, for it translates as: 'Here lie Fuinnguala and Mariota MacInolly, sometime nuns of Iona.'[50] Can this be an indication that they had died after the Scottish Reformation?

Chapter 6

A Romantic Ruin

With the Reformation of 1560, Columba's monastery ceased to exist as the home of a living community. Ever since 563, almost 1000 years before, it had been the focus of life on Iona, surviving warfare, Viking attacks, neglect and physical decay, some monks living there even in the most dangerous times and significant numbers of pilgrims continuing to make the journey to the island. We do not know exactly what happened on Iona when the Scottish Church severed its ties with Rome, but what can be said is that there was no monarch-led Dissolution of the Monasteries in Scotland as there had been in Henry VIII's England, with monks and nuns forcibly turned out and their buildings attacked.[1] The actual damage done by angry mobs to Scottish abbeys and churches has been greatly exaggerated and highly-coloured tales of more than three hundred crosses on Iona being torn down, smashed and thrown into the sea by infuriated Reformers do not appear to be true. This story, still related today in some shape or form, seems to be a greatly inflated version of an event which, as we shall see, took place eighty years later.

The abbey buildings were certainly not demolished, but what happened to the personnel? There could be no more abbots of Iona Abbey, but there was still a Bishop of the Isles. This may seem surprising, in view of the centuries' long controversy over whether or not bishops could be permitted in the Calvinist Church of Scotland, which was supposed to be governed by a series of church courts and not by a hierarchy. However, unpopular though they might be in certain quarters, bishops with Protestant views, or at least Protestant sympathies, were allowed to survive the Reformation and continue their work, because a full system of Presbyterian church government was not yet in place.[2]

The Bishop of the Isles would presumably have continued to regard the abbey church as his cathedral, although both he and it were now officially Protestant. After a brief interlude of MacLeans and Campbells vying for the bishopric, 'Big John' Carswell was granted that position in 1565. A huge man, seven feet tall (his skeleton was found and measured at the end of the nineteenth century), he had a reputation for ruthless avarice but he was nevertheless a staunch supporter of the Reformed Church, like his patron, Archibald, 5th Earl of Argyll. He was very active in his diocese and his great work was a Gaelic translation of the Book of Common Order, the service book used by John Knox and his congregation of English exiles in Geneva. Certainly his translation was couched in the classical Gaelic of the bards, which would not have been understood by most Gaelic speakers, but it was the first book ever to be published in Gaelic.[3]

The fate of the Iona monks is not documented. Some of them may have moved to Ireland, but it has been estimated that more than fifty per cent of Scottish priests stayed on in their parishes as Reformed ministers, and monks often continued to live informally in the buildings they had previously occupied, still drawing revenues from the monastic lands.[4] By law, even those Scottish monks who now became Reformed ministers were entitled to retain their monastic income, despite the fact that they were drawing a stipend from their new profession. Whether any of the Iona monks did this is doubtful, but a legal document of 1573 was signed by the Bishop of the Isles and witnessed by two monks, James MacLean and a colleague named Murchardus. This suggests that they were still resident at the abbey.[5] As to the nuns, we know that in 1567 Mary

MacLean, former prioress of the nunnery, received a royal grant of its revenues, but in 1574, perhaps unable to maintain her hold on them, she granted the lands to Hector MacLean of Duart, very likely one of her relatives.[6] In 1587 an act of parliament deprived bishops of their properties, which were annexed to the crown, and James VI then granted Iona abbey and its buildings to Hector MacLean.[7] What he did with them is unknown, but in 1606 another act of parliament restored their properties to the bishops.[8]

Despite the leading Reformer Andrew Melville's determination that bishops should be abolished in the Church of Scotland, King James VI was equally determined to strengthen their position. He saw them as useful instruments of crown policy, hence his famous remark made during his English years: 'No bishop, no king'. It had been agreed that he could nominate Reformed ministers to vacant Scottish bishoprics so that they could sit and vote in parliament and in 1605 the minister of Paisley, Andrew Knox, was promoted by the King to be Bishop of the Isles. A native of Renfrewshire, he was a pugnacious individual with a ferocious temper, who was known to have struck one of the Paisley burgesses during a dispute. However, James had seen in him the qualities that he required and he was to prove an energetic proponent of royal policy in the Western Isles, working tirelessly to curb the power of the rival leading families and pacify their interminable quarrels.

The significance for us is that in 1609 he summoned a number of clan chiefs to Iona, and succeeded in persuading nine of them to agree to a code of regulations known as the Statutes of Icolumkill (Iona), which bound them to obey the King, support Protestantism and accept the Scottish laws.[9] Does this mean that Bishop Knox was regularly using Iona as the seat of his bishopric? There must have been a suitable building where the meeting could take place; probably the abbey church itself. Might he also have felt that the serene atmosphere of the island and the recollection of St Columba and his monastery would have a good effect on his warring visitors, despite the fact that they were no longer Roman Catholic and about to swear the next day that they would uphold 'the true religion', in other words, the Reformed Church? It is impossible to say. Perhaps he simply thought that its isolation would make it a secure place to meet, with no opportunity for the clan chiefs to bring huge retinues of supporters with them.

In 1617 parliament ratified the King's return of the Iona Abbey lands and buildings to the bishopric of the Isles and legislated for the re-establishment of a diocesan chapter. This certainly sounds as though the abbey church was actively being used as a cathedral. An Irish Franciscan missionary, Father Patrick Hegarty, visited the island in 1625 and reported that he had been able to celebrate mass there, presumably out of doors, the first time this had happened since the Reformation. Although he made only three converts to Catholicism, he observed that there were two buildings, the abbey church and the nunnery church, which were 'worthy of veneration' because of their antiquity. They were also to be admired for the splendour and magnificence of their structure, he said. He was similarly much impressed by Reilig Odhráin and was told the usual story about the royal burials. [10]

James VI died that same year, and was succeeded by his son Charles I. Anxious to enhance the prestige of the Scottish bishops, Charles gave orders for the repair of various cathedrals, including Dunkeld, Glasgow and Iona.[11] The Bishop of the Isles at this time was Neil Campbell and in the spring of 1635, the King issued a royal warrant to the Lords of the Exchequer, directing them to pay Bishop Campbell the sizeable sum of £400 sterling for the work needed at Iona Cathedral. It had already been arranged that this money would be taken from the feu duties which Sir Lachlan MacLean was supposed to pay each year to the cathedral, but it was claimed that he had failed to send in the sum and no building work had yet begun. In fact, Sir Lachlan had made part payment to the Lord High Treasurer of £277:2:2½, which accounted for two years' duties and, at some point after that, substantial alterations were effected to what had been the former abbey church, as well as a house being built for the Bishop.

It was decided to do away with nave and the south choir aisle of the church. The nave seems to have been in a semi-ruinous condition by this time, and the aisle had apparently lost its roof. Probably this was the result of natural causes. As we have seen, roof timbers had collapsed before, bringing down the masonry they supported. Had irate Reformers damaged the building, they would have been more likely to attack the chancel. At any rate, the upper parts of the nave walls were now demolished to provide building materials, and the arches of the arcade between the aisle and the chancel were blocked up, as was the arch between the aisle and the crossing. The west arch was also blocked up, seemingly to divide the cathedral into a chancel and an ante-chapel. It was probably thought that this would suffice, at least for the time being, because the members of the chapter would have their stalls in the chancel and it was not likely that a large congregation would be attending services.[12]

At the east end of the chancel stood the altar, on the site of the former high altar. An altar was a feature which Charles I was determined to have and which his Presbyterian subjects heartily disliked, considering it to be 'popish'. They did not even want a communion table at the east end, because early seventeenth-century Scottish Presbyterians normally took communion seated at trestle tables put up for the occasion, feeling that this arrangement resembled more closely the Last Supper. We have no contemporary description of the altar, but until the 1770s there existed in the chancel a large slab of white marble which may well have dated from the 1630s and had formed its top. William Sacheverell, a tourist visiting what remained of the abbey in 1688, described the marble as being very fine, about 6 feet long and 4 feet wide, curiously veined and polished.[13] Possibly it was quarried locally, although a later visitor described the veins as being grey rather than the characteristic green of Iona marble and it might have been imported by sea.

Any Protestant church, large or small, had to have a pulpit, not merely a small reading desk, for the Reformers placed much emphasis on the Word of God, and the sermon now formed the main part of a service, along with readings from the Bible. As a result, a pulpit, probably a wooden one, was put in, standing against the south arcade on a plinth made partly from the base of a late medieval cross.[14] A cathedral also needed bells. Some of the existing bells were sent to the Low Countries to be re-cast, while an entirely new one was commissioned in 1638 from the famous bell founder Michael Burgerhuys of Middelburg. His work was already known in Scotland, for he had supplied two new bells for Edinburgh, one for St Giles' in 1621 and another for the Magdalen Chapel in 1632.[15] The new Iona bell was engraved with the arms and initials of both Charles I and Bishop Neil Campbell. At some point in its later history, it was moved to the Old Lowland Church at Campbeltown, Kintyre.[16]

Bishop Campbell may never have had the satisfaction of hearing his new bell toll out from his cathedral tower for, in that very same year of 1638, he was deposed as Bishop of the Isles. This was not the result of any misdemeanour on his part, but because there had been such a strong reaction by Scots to Charles I's attempted ecclesiastical innovations, in particular to his efforts to introduce a prayer book along English lines into Scottish church services. His opponents drew up the document known as the National Covenant, promising to defend what they believed to be the true religion against any who sought to interfere with it, meaning the King, and at the end of the year, the General Assembly of the Church of Scotland met in Glasgow, condemned all his changes and deposed the archbishops and the bishops. This was the prelude to the Bishops' Wars, which themselves preceded the Civil War.[17]

With its bishop gone, Iona abbey church now needed a

minister, and in 1641 one of the Mull ministers, Martin MacGillivray, was appointed to that position. His stipend of 800 merks a year (a merk being worth thirteen shillings and four pence) was supplemented by a further 200 merks to pay for 'upholding of the fabric' of the building.[18] A synod of Argyll had been set up in accordance with one of the acts of the 1638 Glasgow General Assembly and two years later the Assembly ordered the destruction of what it termed the many surviving idolatrous monuments in the country.[19] The leading landowner in Argyll was now the famous Archibald Campbell, 1st Marquis of Argyll. Indeed, he was considered to be the most powerful nobleman in Scotland.[20] A committed opponent of King Charles I's ecclesiastical policies, he was a devout supporter of the National Covenant and, according to one contemporary account of 1644, he had by then carried out the synod's instructions by causing to be broken up and overturned all the crosses and memorials of the saints to be found in the Western Isles. His activities seem to have been the origin of the tales of mass destruction of Iona's high crosses at the Reformation. Sailing across from Mull with his men, he had ordered them to destroy monuments and altars in the former cathedral and he was allegedly only prevented from carrying away its great bell by the protestations and curses hurled at him by a nonagenarian former nun of the MacLean family.[21]

In 1645 Martin MacGillivray the minister was censured for his royalist sympathies by the synod of Argyll, and after that some of the local ministers from the mainland took services in the abbey church, but no new minister was appointed during the 1650s. The Marquis of Argyll was now drawing the bishopric rents, from which any stipend for a minister and funding for repairs were supposed to come, but when the synod approached him about these, no satisfaction was forthcoming. To complicate the situation, after Charles II's restoration to the British throne in 1660, the Church of Scotland had bishops once more. However, the title of Cathedral of the Isles was transferred from Iona to the more accessible Rothesay, on the Isle of Bute and until 1829 Iona would be without its own minister. Even so, the islanders continued to meet for Sunday prayers in what had reverted to being the abbey church or in one of the small chapels nearby. Indeed, as late as 1764 mourners at funerals would walk in procession with the corpse round the now ruined abbey before the burial of men in Reilig Odhráin or women in the cemetery beside the nunnery, despite the separation of the two genders being frowned upon by the Church of Scotland.[22]

The island of Iona itself came into the possession of the Argyll family in about 1690, finally wrested from the MacLeans of Duart during the latest phase in the continuing feud between the two families. Having acquired it, along with other territories, the 1st Duke (formerly 10th Earl) of Argyll was not likely to have had at the forefront of his mind a discarded cathedral on one of his smallest islands. He was in fact a strong supporter and close adviser of William III, whose legislation in 1690 finally did away with bishops in the Church of Scotland.[23] So what was the condition of the abbey and the nunnery buildings when he acquired Iona? A hundred and thirty years had passed since the Reformation. The alterations effected as part of Charles I's ecclesiastical policy appear to have been incomplete and short-lived. No further maintenance was undertaken and as always Iona was battered by gales and by rain. Just as the buildings had fallen into a state of disrepair due to neglect during the Green Abbot's time, so did the timber gradually rot and fall and the masonry crumble and collapse.

The islanders carried off stones and even grave slabs for their own building purposes, and used the nunnery church as a byre for their cattle. The floors of the churches and chapter houses were covered in rubble and filth, and tall weeds choked not only the graveyards but the church and cloister interiors. Yet still people came to Iona, some of them famous men who published reports of what they saw, allowing us an occasional sight of the situation during three centuries of desuetude. Their motives were varied, and so were their reactions, but somehow St Columba's reputation lived on, not least because of Adomnán's vivid *Life*. One of the first travellers to make his way there and write a description of what he saw was the William Sacheverell who noted the white marble altar slab in 1688. Apart from the fact that he would become Governor of the Isle of Man in the early 1690s, little is known about his career, but he had been returning from a tour of northern Ireland when, sailing near the Mull of Kintyre, he decided that he must visit the 'so much celebrated' Iona.

It was no easy journey. Setting off on 23 August, he and his companions travelled on horseback across Mull, marvelling at the dramatic scenery of this 'wild, desert country' and then, after some trouble, finding a boat in which they rowed across the Sound of Iona. Sacheverell was impressed with the abbey church, which he observed had once been large and noble – considering where it was, he added quickly – and by the remains of what he described as the convenient and neat monastic buildings. Several of those in the cloister were still standing, such as the chapter house and the library above it. Some good lodgings, he thought, must have belonged to the abbot. He took the trouble to measure the church, the chancel and ruined nave, both of which were just over six metres long and he was told that there had once been a fine peal of bells in the lofty steeple.

After gazing at the surviving tombs of Abbots Dominic and John, he went outside and scrutinised a pile of stones at the west end, said to have formed a monument to 'Columbus', as he and his contemporaries disconcertingly called the saint, with a little chapel beside it – presumably Columba's Shrine. He saw one complete high cross (probably St Martin's) and more than half of two others. The enclosing wall round the abbey was almost demolished, but he found that Reilig Odhráin was almost entirely covered with the monuments and the gravestones of various kings. Recounting a version of the story of St

Oran, which he thought 'comical', he admired the monuments inside the chapel and moved on to look at the Bishop's House. It consisted of a large hall, open to the roof, and a chamber which he thought the bishops must have entered by climbing up a ladder. Beneath the chamber was what he described as a buttery, but its roof had fallen in. All in all, he thought that the house was very mean.

Walking down to the nunnery, he found it to be a pretty square building with a neat chapel. He noticed many flat grave-stones there, including what must have been Prioress Anna MacLean's. Like the abbey church with its large dock leaves, the nunnery was overgrown with henbane and other tall weeds, one variety being four feet high, with large, purple stalks, thick fat leaves and big buds. Sacheverell did not know its name, but when he later described it to a knowledgeable friend, he was told that it would have been deadly nightshade. So what was his general impression of Iona Abbey? He seems to have been pleased with much of the architecture, but his perception of St Columba was depressing, to say the least, for he was prepared to blame him for what he imagined to be the worst excesses of destruction at the Reformation.

Having been told a story about Columba ordering the drowning of some pagans who had refused to convert to Christianity, Sacheverell decided that the saint's severity and austere nature had led directly to a sour form of religion which ultimately resulted in almost all the Iona crosses being destroyed at the Reformation. He had been told, correctly, that this had been done on the orders of the synod of Argyll, but he had placed this event in the sixteenth century instead of the seventeenth. To restore his spirits, he took a stroll, admired the fertile fields and the fine views, was shown the greenish pebbles to be found in the sea and learned that about eighty families lived on the island. His feelings of vexation subsided and he was able to enjoy a plate of mutton in a neat little house occupied by a member of the MacLean family.[24]

The next well-known description of Iona was not supplied by a stranger but by Martin Martin, a native of Skye. He had graduated from Edinburgh University in 1681 and then studied medicine at Leiden before settling in London. In 1703 he published *A Description of the Western Isles of Scotland*, which gained great popularity. Unfortunately, his historical knowledge was somewhat confused. Although he knew that, in the time of Columba, the monastery had been 'a seminary of learning', he thought it famous for its founder's severe discipline and believed that it was sixth-century Columba who had built both the early thirteenth-century Benedictine abbey and the Augustinian nunnery. He was also told a strange tale about Columba having cursed thirty of his own relatives who were living on Iona with him, declaring that most of them would die, the aim being that no more than five could be resident there at any one time.

He likewise repeated an old story alleging that Columba would allow no women on Iona, nor would he have cattle or sheep or goats there, because they would require women to look after them. This last was patently untrue, for we know that the Columban monks kept livestock, particularly cattle. Martin's details of the abbey church follow closely Sacheverell's description, but he was much more taken up with the various tombs and grave slabs. By the time he saw them, the three large royal tombs in Reilig Odhráin were still there, but the inscriptions which Donald Monro had seen in 1549 had by now worn off. Martin had little to say about the nunnery, but when he went down to the beach at Columba's Bay, he did admire the pretty, variegated pebbles.[25]

It would seem that both Sacheverell and Martin had originally been attracted to Iona by Columba's reputation, which they had admired until they listened to some of the tall stories of the islanders, but in the eighteenth century there were visitors who arrived out of scientific rather than spiritual or historical curiosity. Naturalists and geologists were eager to look for the unusual types of flora, fauna or rock formations to be found there. There was, for example, Joseph Banks, the famous English naturalist, who came to see Staffa in 1772 and spent a few hours on Iona on the way back. In a letter dated 12 January 1773 to Thomas Falconer, one of his contacts, Banks referred to that previous journey, dismissing Iona as being unremarkable, apart from the fact that it was the first seat of Christianity, although he did concede that the buildings were extensive and 'rather pretty' – when one considered the era in which they were put up.[26]

Falconer was a relative of the Welsh naturalist Thomas Pennant, who had helped and encouraged Banks during the early years of the latter's career, although they were later to fall out.[27] Pennant also visited the area in 1772 and wrote a detailed and immensely popular account which included the first published description of Staffa and earned both it and Iona enormous publicity. Arriving on Iona, he was not impressed by the hundred and fifty or so inhabitants, whom he described as being stupid and lazy, despite their much vaunted claims to have been descended from Columba's monks. After a brief and somewhat inaccurate biographical paragraph about the saint, he went on to describe the nunnery, reporting that the attractive ribbed roof of its church was intact, although the church itself was still being used as a byre. However, he bribed one of the local men to dig away a pile of cow dung on the floor, revealing Prioress Anna MacLean's grave slab, which was undamaged.

Remarking that the nunnery could not possibly have been there in Columba's day since the saint was a famous misogynist who would not allow women on Iona, Pennant continued to the abbey, scrutinising MacLean's Cross on the way. Eager, like everyone else, to see the early tombs of the various kings, he hurried to Reilig Odhráin, only to find to his disappointment that almost nothing remained, except for a few ridges in the soil. So the actual stone tombs resembling little chapels must have disappeared between 1703, when Martin saw them, and 1772. Repeating the grisly story of St Oran, Pennant noted in detail the various tombs in the chapel itself before continuing to the abbey church.

Inside, he remarked upon the carvings on the pillars, including the little scene of souls being weighed in a balance, and thought them 'quite peculiar', but he admired what was left of the ever diminishing white marble altar. In the ninety years since Sacheverell's visit, people had broken off and carried away pieces of it as amulets and good luck tokens. Indeed, Pennant could not resist doing so himself. The abbey church he thought magnificent, but the monastic buildings behind it were by now in a very ruinous state, with only a small portion of the cloister left. He does not mention the chapter house, so it may have gone completely by that time. He then traversed a large part of the island, he too visiting Columba's Bay. Next morning at 8 o'clock he sailed back across the Sound to Mull.[28]

A year after Pennant's visit, we have the evidence of two famous literary figures who made the journey for largely historical reasons and were deeply impressed by the spiritual atmosphere. Dr Samuel Johnson the celebrated lexicographer and his friend James Boswell were staying on the island of Coll with Sir Allan Maclean when they decided to have an excursion to Staffa and Iona. Travelling in a boat rowed by four men, they had to bypass Staffa, for the swell was too high for them to be able to land, but they sailed on along the coast of Mull, arriving at Iona on the evening of 19 October. They spent the night in a barn, sleeping on the hay, which was what visitors had to do, since there was no inn on the island. Next morning, they set off for the abbey, finding that both it and the nunnery church were roofless, but solid and 'not inelegant'. No doubt confused by the alterations of the 1630s, Dr Johnson's interpretation of the abbey, which he referred to as 'the Episcopal church', was rather odd, for he decided that it had originally consisted only of the chancel, with the tower at one end, and then when it proved too small, the nave was added, thereby placing the tower in the middle.

Despite the floor being covered in mud and rubbish Dr Johnson, like Sacheverell and Pennant before him, was interested in what remained of the marble altar, most of it gone now because of the islanders' belief that a fragment would provide protection against shipwreck, fire and miscarriage. Boswell was shocked to see the conditions in the nunnery church but, well used to visitors' requests by this time, one of the local people obligingly cleared away the dung so that they could see Anna MacLean's grave slab. Interestingly, Dr Johnson observed that the remains of a large room whose walls still stood and which had probably been the nuns' refectory would be capable of being repaired. When he saw the Bishop's House, two storeys were still standing, along with a chimney.

Reilig Odhráin was a great disappointment to Boswell because of the lack of identifiable graves of kings, but Dr Johnson pointed out to him that, nearby, the fishponds and the aqueduct of the monastery gardens were still discernible. Boswell, a Presbyterian by upbringing, who as a student had entertained thoughts of converting to Roman Catholicism and becoming a monk, slipped away next morning and knelt in front of St Martin's Cross to say a brief prayer before going into the abbey church to pray to St Columba. Finally, he went down to Columba's Bay to say another prayer and of course gather some of the famous pebbles. Despite the general state of the buildings, Dr Johnson, a somewhat unconventional High Church Anglican, was impressed with what he had seen, making his famous remark that a man was little to be envied if his piety did not grow warmer among the ruins of Iona.[29]

As befitted a famous historical novelist and poet, Sir Walter Scott when he looked round in 1814 was similarly preoccupied with the island's past. He spent a good deal of time examining the carved stones and the graves, and thinking about the monks who had once inhabited the abbey. (Plate 26) From the architectural point of view, he usefully noted in his diary that part of the church tower had fallen since his previous visit, which had taken place four years earlier.[30] Other poets who came to the island were generally less inclined to notice details of the architecture or the gravestones, but they were very sensitive to atmosphere. John Leyden, the Scottish poet, linguist and friend of Scott, composed a short verse entitled 'To the Setting Sun, written in the Isle of Iona in 1800', alluding to 'that green happy isle' with the spirits of the dead thronging round.[31] Ten years later, John Keats was simply astounded at the sight of the ruins, attributing the state of the buildings to violent attacks by fanatical Protestants at the time of the Reformation. [32]

William Wordsworth arrived fifteen years after that, armed with Martin's account and was inspired to write four sonnets. The first is in praise of Iona's past saints, and the second, 'On Landing', regrets the sad welcome the visitor receives from a ragged child trying to sell pebbles from the beach, but praises the spirituality which lives on despite the abbey church itself being surrounded by ruins. The somewhat desolate scene conjured up thoughts of perjurers and hell in his third sonnet while, in the fourth, he leaves for home, inspired by Columba's cell and Christian piety's 'soul-cheering spark', which shone out on Iona like the morning star.[33] Wordsworth had no need of a boat with four strong men to row him first to Staffa and then to Iona, for by the previous year a steamboat from Oban was calling twice weekly in summer. The service had been set up rather more erratically in the late 1820s and indeed one of the first to sail by that method from Oban was Felix Mendelssohn, composer of the famous Hebridean Overture (Fingal's Cave). Unfortunately his 1829 visit to both Staffa and Iona was marred by the rough seas which made him dreadfully sea sick.

These famous men give us some indication of the fame of Iona Abbey during its years as a ruin, and allow us to see the abbey through their eyes, but there were other visitors who were not content to sigh, shake their heads and express regret to their friends about the state of the ruins. These were the increasingly numerous antiquarians who came to the island, As early as 1757 an effort had been made by Archibald, 3ʳᵈ Duke of Argyll to protect the ruins to a certain extent by enclosing them with a wall. Two new leases of farms on the island were granted that year, one of the conditions stipulated by the Duke's factor being that within seven years the tenants were to build a stone wall six feet (1.8 metres) high, at a distance of forty feet (12.2 metres) from the ruins. Tenants were also told to keep the ruins of the abbey and the nunnery free from weeds and other 'nuisance', but they paid no attention to that and, to make matters worse, the new walls were soon crumbling.

When Grimur Thorkelin, the Icelandic antiquary, came to Iona in 1787 with a group from the Committee of the British Fisheries Society, they were all considerably frustrated at being unable to see the inscriptions on the grave slabs in the nunnery, and their complaints were passed on to John, 5ᵗʰ Duke of Argyll. Involved with his own distinguished military career, he sent Lord Mountstuart, later 4ᵗʰ Earl of Bute to view the situation and report back to him. What Lord Mountstuart told him is not known, but when the famous German mineralogist Rudolf Raspe added his voice to the pleas of other visitors in 1789, the Duke instructed John Maxwell, his factor, to obtain an estimate for rebuilding the enclosing wall, and this was done two years later. However, the wall did nothing to remedy the falling masonry of the abbey and its buildings, and during the late eighteenth century the east gable of the abbey chapter house, the north wall of the north transept and St Mary's Chapel to the south all collapsed.[34]

George William, 6ᵗʰ Duke of Argyll, succeeded his father in 1806 and when he visited Iona the following year, the islanders are said to have scrubbed the tombstones clean in advance, but of course the difficulties continued.[35] In 1814, Sir Walter Scott observed that the footsteps of the islanders and 'Sassenach visitants' were rapidly destroying the inscriptions on the grave slabs, and damage of this kind was becoming an increasing problem. Not only did the marble top of the altar

9 Grave slabs of West Highland warriors buried at the Abbey
(© Crown Copyright Historic Scotland reproduced courtesy of Historic
Scotland www.historicscotlandimages.gov.uk).

10 Effigy of Abbot John MacKInnon (© Peter Backhouse).

FACING PAGE: 11 MacLean's Cross, with the nineteenth-century
parish church in the background (© Peter Backhouse).

12a Carved medieval head on the west arch of the Abbey crossing, possibly of one of the masons (© Peter Backhouse).

13 George Douglas Campbell, 8th Duke of Argyll, about 1860,
by George Frederic Watts (© National Portrait Gallery, London).

FACING PAGE: 12b The stone traditionally said to have been Columba's
pillow. (© Crown Copyright Historic Scotland reproduced courtesy
of Historic Scotland www.historicscotlandimages.gov.uk).

14 Ina McNeill, Duchess of Argyll, about 1896, by William Clark
Wontner (© CSG CIC Glasgow Museums Collection).

15 Ruined Abbey chancel, looking east, before the 1874–5 repairs
(© RCAHMS Licensor www.rcahms.gov.uk).

17 Monument to the 8th Duke and Duchess of Argyll by Sir George Frampton (© Peter Backhouse).

FACING PAGE: 16 The Abbey chancel restored (© Peter Backhouse).

18 The communion table and silver cross (© Peter Backhouse).

19 The large font, just inside the west door of the Abbey
(© Peter Backhouse).

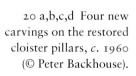

20 a,b,c,d Four new carvings on the restored cloister pillars, *c.* 1960 (© Peter Backhouse).

21 Christopher Hall at work on the cloister carvings, *c.* 1960
(© RCAHMS Licensor www.rcahms.gov.uk).

22 'The Descent of the Spirit' sculpture by Jacques Lipchitz, 1959, in the Abbey cloisters (© Peter Backhouse).

FACING PAGE: 23 St Columba, stained glass window by William Wilson, in the north transept, 1965 (© Peter Backhouse).

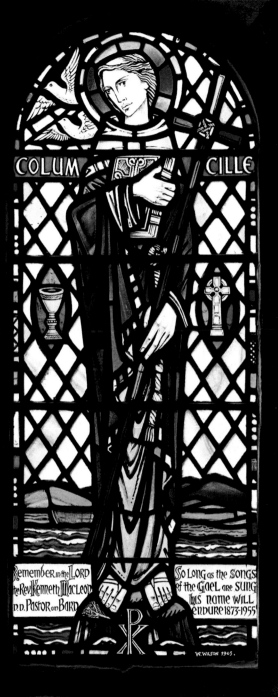

COLUM CILLE

Remember in the LORD
the Rev Kenneth Macleod
D.D. Pastor and Bard

So long as the songs
of the Gael are sung
this name will
endure 1873-1955

W. WILSON 1905.

24 The Abbey chancel, ready for a candle-lit evening service
(© Peter Backhouse).

virtually disappear altogether because of the attentions of the tourists, but in 1830 Mr Rae Wilson, an orientalist, insisted on digging in Reilig Odhráin and in the nunnery cemetery in search of more grave slabs, despite the remonstrations of Allan MacLean, the local schoolmaster who was acting as a guide to the ruins.[36] On 25 August 1847, F. W. Cox from Croydon was describing his annoyance at the damage being caused by tourists to the monuments[37] and two years after that David Laing, the distinguished Scottish antiquary, told the Society of Antiquaries of Scotland, of which he was treasurer, about the deplorable state of Iona Abbey, which he had just visited with the Norwegian scholar, P. A. Munch. Nothing happened and by 1854 the Society was urging George, 8th Duke of Argyll, to take action to preserve the abbey, the nunnery and the grave slabs.[38] The Duke, aged thirty-one, had inherited the family titles seven years earlier, and although he seemed to spend much of the year in London, where he was an active politician, perhaps he might have the time and the energy to do something.

Chapter 7

George, 8ᵗʰ Duke of Argyll

George, 8ᵗʰ Duke of Argyll was the younger son of a younger son and it had at first seemed very unlikely that he would ever inherit the family titles. He had been born on 30 April 1823 at Ardencaple Castle, Dunbartonshire, which his father, Lord John Campbell, inherited from a relative, and there he lived until he was thirteen. His elder brother, another John, was two years older than he was and he had a younger sister, Emma, who was two years younger. Their father liked a quiet life. He had a practical turn of mind, spent hours in his workshop, creating fine objects of rare woods and ivory, and for years studied the mechanics of the flight of birds. His wife, Joan Glassell, daughter of an East Lothian landowner, was very different; a plain young woman but highly intellectual and with 'a poetic temperament', according to George's description of her. He had no recollection of either her appearance or her voice, for she died when he was only four, just two weeks after giving birth to a second, short-lived daughter. He did, however, remember being taken to kiss her cold cheek as she lay in her coffin, and how panic-stricken he was when he and the other mourners were temporarily shut in the chancel of Kilmun Church, the burial place of the ducal family, whose coffins were kept there on shelves.[1]

A delicate, sensitive and highly intelligent child, George was already absorbed in his own thoughts and interests. Early on he developed a fascination with ornithology, and once he could write he was soon recording in a private notebook his detailed observations of the birds that perched in the trees around the

Castle. He kept the notebook locked in a drawer, so that no one else could read it, not even his brother, with whom he shared various other interests. He would later be told that, when his nurse once scolded him for whistling on a Sunday in that strictly sabbatarian household, he had replied in genuine bewilderment, 'Why not? The birds whistle on Sunday'. For the young trainee Church of Scotland ministers whom his father employed to be his tutors, he had nothing but contempt, describing himself later as having been idle and listless in the schoolroom but full of activity out of it.

When George was thirteen, his elder brother died and he became convinced that his own life would be equally short. As a result, his thoughts turned to religion, which was to become an abiding interest. He remarked in his memoirs, written in his old age, that ever since then he had pondered the difficulties of the Christian life. Two years later his uncle, the 6th Duke of Argyll, died leaving no legitimate children. With that, his father became 7th Duke and George found that he himself was now Marquis of Lorne and heir to all the titles and estates. After that, his life widened beyond the bounds of Ardencaple. His father found a new tutor for him, an Englishman named J. S. Howson, who would later become Dean of Chester. George quickly decided that the future Dean was not a man of much originality or ability, but he did introduce the boy to the poetry of Wordsworth, Coleridge and Southey. Until then, although George had always been an avid reader, he had no access to poetry, because his father's largely scientific library had not included works of literature.[2]

His uncle the 6th Duke had lived in England, entirely neglecting his estates and so George's father, determined to remedy that, spent a lot of time visiting his tenants, taking his son with him. They were received enthusiastically and George made his first public speech in Campbeltown in early August 1840, when he was seventeen. His hearers were very much impressed, for although he was so small and slight and seemed much younger than he really was, he possessed a very powerful speaking voice. Shortly afterwards, his long and prominent career in politics began when he went to London to see his father take his seat in the House of Lords. George became very interested in the controversy in the Church of Scotland about lay patronage (the practice of ministers being nominated by the local landowners rather than being elected by the congregation) and wrote the first of his many pamphlets on the subject.[3]

He soon had a wide and influential circle of friends, men and women of all ages. During his youthful travels on the continent he began his lasting friendship with the elderly Mary Somerville, the celebrated Scottish mathematician, whom he met in Rome and who greatly impressed him with the singular simplicity and modesty which completely concealed her brilliant intellectual powers. Elizabeth Fry the prison reformer left him in awe of her majestic figure and her 'ineffable expression of sweetness, dignity and power,' but she too became a friend, Most influential of all, however, was the beautiful Harriet Howard, Duchess of Sutherland, whom he judged to be one of the most charming women of her time. In 1842 he was invited by the Marquess of Breadalbane to stay at Taymouth Castle, which Queen Victoria and Prince Albert were about to visit, and it was there that he met the Duchess and her eldest daughter Lady Elizabeth Leveson-Gower.

Two years later, on 30 July 1844, just three months after his 21st birthday, he married Elizabeth, and found that she surpassed all the praise heaped on her by her friends. Indeed, 'On some subjects, excepting philosophy and the natural sciences, she was more widely read than I was at that time.' She not only brought him many new interests, but her family connections gave him much happiness and would be of considerable support to him in his public career. His mother-in-law was mistress of the robes to Queen Victoria and a leading political hostess and, through her, he soon became a close friend of both the Queen and Prince Albert.[4]

At first George settled down with his wife at Rosneath on the family estates but, with the death of his father in 1847, he became 8th Duke of Argyll and spent most of the year in London, for he was not only an active member of the House of Lords but he occupied a long series of important governmental posts. A Liberal, and later a Liberal Unionist, he was Lord Privy Seal at three different times, in the 1850s, the 1860s and again from 1880–1, Postmaster General from 1855–8 and Secretary of State for India from 1868–74.[5] He was a keen supporter of his friend Lord Shaftesbury 'in his great efforts for the redemption of women and children from exhausting labour in the mills', he got to know Harriet Beecher Stowe through his anti-slavery stance and energetically opposed Gladstone's Home Rule policies.[6] Idiosyncratic, independent and full of confidence in his own opinions, he was never quite trusted by Gladstone, however, who thought him erratic and unpredictable. (Plate 13)

Throughout all this, he remained keenly interested in theology and Scottish ecclesiastical affairs. Apart from the innumerable pamphlets and speeches he composed, the first book that he published was entitled *Presbytery Explained. An Essay, Critical and Historical, on the Ecclesiastical History of Scotland since the Reformation.* During the day he would plan what he wanted to say and then, such were his powers of concentration, in the evening he would sit and write in the same room as his wife and 'her children'. They had five sons and seven daughters.[7] The Duke was a profound thinker, and his geological studies later led him into the controversy about the creation of the world. All the scientific evidence, he thought, pointed to man having descended from one man and woman and, rather than evolving since then, human beings had degenerated. He expounded these views in published papers and books, clashing with both Charles Darwin and T.H. Huxley in the process.

Despite moving in the very highest social circles and working incessantly at his political responsibilities, the Duke did not forget his very extensive Scottish estates, which ran to about

175,000 acres. He estimated that between 1847 to 1897 he spent over £554,000 on agricultural improvement and tried to address the problems of overpopulation in the Hebrides and the results of the 1846 potato famine by becoming a sponsor of 'assisted emigration' to North America and Australia.[8] So did he have any interest in Iona in the midst of his busy life? 'It is very difficult to make others understand the immense enjoyment I have always had in the scenery of the Hebrides', he once wrote. He had first gone to Iona, as a teenager, in the company of his father, and it became a regular visiting place.[9] Every year, he and his Duchess spent August and September at Inveraray Castle, receiving guests and touring the Hebridean estates, 'a visit which was always to us the special holiday of the year'. There the Duke insisted on prayers and Bible readings at breakfast, as he presumably did in London, and wore full highland dress at dinner in the evenings.[10]

On 12 September 1868 he was writing to tell Gladstone that he was about to spend a week in Iona, where he had recently established a little inn. The hills and the colours of the sea were wonderfully beautiful there, he said, and he wanted to observe them in both the morning and the evening light. The following autumn he went back again, taking Arthur Stanley, Dean of Westminster and his wife Lady Augusta Bruce with him,[11] and in 1870 he published his latest book, which was simply entitled *Iona*. The short text runs to 141 pages, and the frontispiece is a reproduction of one of his own sketches of the ruined abbey. In his early days, he had taken lessons in oil painting from Montague Stanley, a young Scottish actor who had given up the stage for religious reasons and become a landscape artist.[12] Throughout his life, the 8th Duke found painting a great source of enjoyment and relaxation.[13]

The first chapter of his account of Iona is devoted to the life of St Columba, and it begins with an intriguing historical perspective. He points out that it was only a hundred years before Columba's birth that the Roman legions had finally been withdrawn from Britain. The tesselated pavements and the foundations of Roman towns and villas which were, in the Duke's own day, being accidentally uncovered by the plough were still, during Columba's childhood, 'the luxurious habitations of a Roman people'. He went on to observe that Columba was the contemporary of the Byzantine emperor Justinian and his famous general, Belisarius. Pope Gregory the Great was elected in 590, when Columba was seventy, and St Benedict was also alive during his lifetime, although Columba had probably never heard of the saint and his famous Rule.

Explaining that the Romans had never conquered Ireland, hence the comparative isolation of its early Church, and noting both the Irish monastic preoccupation with copying the Scriptures and the unusual status of their bishops, the Duke moved on to a critique of Adomnán's *Life of Columba*. Much of his analysis might have been written in the early twenty-first century rather than in 1870 for, like many present day readers, he recoils from what he describes as the 'childish and utterly incredible' miracle stories. He goes on to dismiss what he terms the inadequate explanation offered by philosophical historians who resort to saying, '"History to be true must condescend to speak the language of legend. The belief of the times is part of the record of the times."' He himself considered that much of Adomnán's text was deliberate invention, because his intended readers saw everything through the lens of Christianity, readily transforming the providential into the miraculous. He concluded that the imperishable interest of Adomnán's book lay not in the actual miracles but in the incidental but very vivid evidence which it provides of the saint's life and character. No other historical personage of the time in any way connected with British history was to a similar degree known to us as Columba is, and 'when we land upon Iona, we can feel that we are treading in the very footsteps of a man whom we have known in voice, in gesture, in habits and in many peculiarities of character.'[14]

An account of Columba's arrival and the subsequent history of both his career and his monastery occupy the second chapter, poetic descriptions of the scenery mingled with what we today would accept as a largely accurate account of the monastery buildings, while the third chapter carries on the story until Columba's death, with a carefully judged assessment of his character: fierce and passionate, but also affectionate, grateful, compassionate and easily moved to tears. The Duke finishes with the Viking raids and the establishment of the Benedictine Abbey, followed by a short geological account of the Iona landscape. His book was first published in London in 1870, and by 1913 it had gone into its 5th edition and was being printed by Mackay's, an Oban bookshop, for the benefit of the tourists. Apart from its readability and the inherent interest of the subject, it gives us a very useful insight into the thinking of the man who was now responsible for the survival of the abbey.[15]

Presumably in response to the Society of Antiquaries' 1854 complaint, on 30 June 1855 John Campbell, the Argyll factor for Mull and Iona, was passing on to the Duke a specification for repairs to St Oran's Chapel, with the most dilapidated areas marked with a cross as needing immediate repair.[16] Unfortunately the specification does not appear to have survived, but an estimate of proposed repairs to the abbey itself by William Forrest, mason, at around the same time is extant. The foundation of the south corner of the chancel needed to be supported and secured, and various windows required attention. (Plate 15) The pillars of the west arches of the chancel would have to be conserved and its north east arch would have to be built up. Breaches in the wall to the south needed to be repaired, as did the pillar between arched recesses of the chapter house. Forrest did not give the costs of the individual items, but he said that he could not do the work and provide the necessary scaffolding for less than £45 sterling. However, the most urgent repairs could be done for £40.[17]

There is no indication of whether the work was set in hand,

but on 30 August 1858 the monuments were still causing concern. In about 1830 the lower part of Prioress Anna MacLean's grave slab had been smashed by a fall of masonry in the nunnery.[18] There had also been deliberate vandalism, with a group of sailors in 1819 breaking off the hands and crozier from the effigy of Abbot John MacKinnon, someone then damaging his nose and later souvenir hunters making off with three of his lion pedestals.[19] The 8th Duke of Argyll would have liked the carved stones to be placed under cover. He was advised that the cost would be prohibitive, but the stones already inside the building were put along the walls, the complete ones upright. Those in Reilig Odhráin were left where they were, for many of them had been placed there by the islanders on the graves of their friends and relatives.[20]

Whatever was done or not done certainly did not satisfy John Stuart when he went to visit the island. On 5 October 1867, as the energetic and effective Secretary of the Society of Antiquaries of Scotland, he wrote an indignant letter to Charles, 3rd Earl Stanhope, whom he knew to be interested in historical antiquities and their preservation. He had just been on a journey to early ecclesiastical sites, he said, and it had been a matter of great regret to him to observe the condition of the ruins at Iona. The pointing of the masonry had been washed out by the weather, the walls looked very dilapidated and, because the site was open and easily accessible, the ruins were not being treated with the desirable care and reverence. Indeed, 'some of the rude visitors had forgotten that it was not a water closet.' The tombstones in the graveyard were trodden upon by 'the multitudes who in the summer season almost daily rush across them to visit the ruins', with the result that the carvings were rapidly being worn away.

He went on to give Stanhope some very interesting information. Some years before, he said, Sir James Simpson and he had a conference with the Duke of Argyll on the subject, suggesting to him that the whole ruins might be given to the crown. Simpson, as well as being the leading obstetrician who had developed the use of chloroform anaesthesia, was keenly interested in archaeological remains and served as President of the Society of Antiquaries of Scotland. It had seemed to them both that the Duke was 'not indisposed to accept our suggestion' and when Mr Stuart conferred with the 1st Commissioner of Works, William Cowper, later 1st Baron Mount Temple, he had the impression that the crown would be perfectly willing to go along with this. However, nothing further had happened, and so Mr Stuart was hoping that Lord Stanhope would raise the matter with the Duke. This he must have done, for the letter is among the ducal archives but, for whatever reason, nothing came of the idea.[21]

Six years later, however, a major programme of repair was set in hand, There was no question of restoring any of the buildings, but the ruins would have to be made safe and measures taken to reduce the risk of further deterioration. On 7 June 1873 James Ferguson sent the Duke a report on what required to be done. Part of the wall of the nunnery needed attention, and there was an arch which should be repaired. One of the pillars of the nunnery church had fallen down and one of its arches was faulty too. Two of the gables of St Oran's Chapel should be made up and levelled. As to the abbey itself, the arches in the side walls would have to be repaired, the north east side of the chancel was in a very bad state and two windows there should be built up. Water had gathered on top of the chapter house arch and would ultimately cause it to collapse if something was not done about it and the condition of the foundation of the east wall of the cloister was very poor. Two of the windows there should also be built up, and the north wall of 'the Dining Hall' (refectory) were positively dangerous.[22]

Robert Rowand Anderson, the Edinburgh architect, was chosen to undertake the work. At the age of forty, he was on the verge of his very distinguished career. He had been making his name as a designer of Scottish Episcopal churches and two years earlier had won a competition for the Catholic Apostolic church in Edinburgh. He was then elected to the Society of Antiquaries of Scotland,[23] and there he made the acquaintance of the lawyer and historian, William Forbes Skene. It seems to have been Skene who suggested to the 8th Duke of Argyll that Anderson would be a suitable person to see to the ruins on Iona.[24] Anderson arrived there on 11 August 1874, took up residence in the St Columba Hotel which was and is close to the abbey, and on 1 September was writing to tell Skene that he had been 'busy among the ruins' ever since.[25]

He went on to explain that his great problem was the lack of men and materials. He could not find a mason anywhere in the area and in the end had to send to Edinburgh for them, and to Glasgow for timber for scaffolding. He had managed to employ only four masons, but he was very pleased with the progress being made. He had decided to begin with the nunnery and not only had an immense amount of rubbish been cleared away, but gaps in the walls had been built up and the freestone corners restored. Because of the lack of manpower Anderson did not begin any serious work on the abbey that year, but he reported that enormous quantities of rubbish and fallen stonework had been removed from there too. The cloister courtyard was now clearly visible and the transept and nave were also ready for work to begin. Scaffolding would have to be put up on the whole exterior of the east gable in order to repair it, but unfortunately it was too late in the season to start that safely.

The weather had, in fact, been very broken during the second half of August and some days the steamer from Oban was not able to call at Iona at all. However, 'The bathing is splendid and I have not missed a day', Anderson told Skene. He was only sorry that he could not stay for much longer, but he had to get back to Edinburgh to begin work on the Edinburgh University Medical School. During his stay, there had been very few archaeological finds, but he made a list of them and sent them to the Duke before he left. There were twelve of them, and they consisted of small items such as a key and part of a small stone cross with the figure of Christ found at the abbey chapter house, a bronze ring and some medieval pottery dug up outside the abbey refectory, and a pair of scissors and a bone pin discovered at the nunnery.[26]

While he was on Iona, Anderson made the acquaintance of the eccentric archaeologist, Sir Henry Dryden, who had been making drawings of the ruins. Sir Henry was, he said, 'very energetic at his work and made himself very agreeable.'[27] A Northamptonshire squire, much loved by his neighbours and tenants, he was meticulous in his drawings, and his contemporaries liked to say that he once travelled two hundred miles across France to check a half-inch discrepancy in a measurement.[28] He does not appear to have gone to Iona at the invitation of the Duke of Argyll, but on his own initiative, as a result of the urgings of the London antiquarian, J. H. Plowes, who had visited Iona in August 1871 and had told him how interesting he would find the ruins. Plowes had recommended the St Columba Hotel, provided Sir Henry took his own wine and spirits, 'for not even whisky is to be got here – the Duke of Argyll will not allow it to be sold anywhere and he is the proprietor of the island.'[29]

As spring approached the following year, Anderson began to think again about the problem of getting masons for that summer's work, preferably from somewhere near Iona instead of having to bring them in from a distance. The previous year's foreman had been satisfactory, but the other men had been very badly behaved and it had been impossible to replace them because no others could be found on the west coast. It would therefore be advisable to engage masons before the work season began, and that would save expense.[30] The Duke told his factor to make enquiries, but ten days later was saying that he himself was in 'rather a fash [troubled state]' about Iona because of the difficulty of finding masons.[31] Fortunately the problem was solved, and that summer seven of them were at work, using freestone quarried at Carsaig and Gribun on the Isle of Mull, along with lime brought from Lismore. In all, the total amount paid by the Mull factor for the work from 1874–9, excluding the architect's fees, was almost £1,900.[32] One of the Duke's daughters, Lady Frances Balfour, later recalled that during Anderson's work her father frequently visited the site to supervise. He was always anxious that the character of the abbey should not be destroyed, she said later, and more than once considered its complete restoration, having models made to see how it would look.[33]

In spite of his keen personal interest, no further restoration work seems to have taken place for the next twenty years. The Duke appears to have been satisfied with Anderson's efforts, but of course financial considerations probably explained the lack of any more extensive conservation. Apart from the normal expenses of running his estates, the Duke's notes to his factor about building work had at times been greatly outnumbered by his instructions for setting up soup kitchens and trying to feed the starving.[34] There were personal distractions too. In 1870 Queen Victoria invited the Duke's eldest son, the Marquis of Lorne, and four other young British aristocrats to stay at Balmoral, one at a time, so that a suitable husband might be selected for her fourth daughter, Princess Louise. The handsome, fair-haired Lorne was chosen, and the wedding took place the following year.

The couple seemed happy enough at first, but both were unconventional characters. Louise was artistic, became a sculptor and was interested in politics, supporting the women's movement, although of course her position as a member of the royal family very much limited what she could do. In 1878 Lorne was appointed governor-general of Canada and soon discovered a deep affinity with that country, where he declared that he would like to stay forever.[35] Louise disliked it, and spent as little time there as she possibly could. Back in London, her

111

flirtatious behaviour attracted attention and there was gossip in the press about her relationships, while rumours swirled around to the effect that Lorne was homosexual. Whatever the truth of the matter, they had no children, and in the mid-1880s Louise seems to have asked for a formal separation, although that did not take place. All this was obviously a serious embarrassment to the Duke.[36]

He also had to deal with another urgent building project, for in 1877 a serious fire at Inveraray Castle destroyed the centre of the building, which then had to be restored. Worse still, in 1878 his Duchess, to whom he was devoted, collapsed and died while sitting next to Gladstone at a dinner at Carlton House Terrace in London.[37] By 1880 the Duke was much taken up with government affairs once more, having been made Lord Privy Seal again, but he resigned in 1881, and in that year he remarried. His second wife was Amelia Maria Anson, daughter of Thomas Claughton, Bishop of St Albans and widow of Colonel the Honourable Archibald Anson, the Earl of Lichfield's son.[38] With all these distractions, it was another ten years before the Duke's thoughts seem to have turned to Iona once more.

In 1891, however, he commissioned John Honeyman, the prominent Glasgow architect, to draw up plans for restoring the chancel of the abbey, but for some reason the work was not carried out.[39] However, with the approach of 1897, the General Assembly of the Church of Scotland decided to mark the thirteenth centenary of St Columba's death by holding on 9 June a thanksgiving service for the introduction of the Gospel into Scotland. It was felt that Iona Abbey would be the most appropriate place for this, and when the Church approached the Duke of Argyll for permission to hold the service there,[40] he replied, 'I shall be delighted to help the General Assembly in any way to celebrate the date on that spot'.[41] Of course the abbey was still a ruin and, given the chronic uncertainty of the weather conditions on Iona, it would hardly be practical to hold an important service in a building without a roof. However, the Duke was of the opinion that Robert Rowand Anderson's 1870s consolidation of the walls had been so successful that it should be possible to put on a temporary roof, and that was what happened.[42] The chancel and sacristy were re-roofed, the windows were glazed, a pulpit and a harmonium were installed and benches were put in for a congregation of about 250 people.[43]

On the morning of 9 June, a Gaelic service was duly held in the abbey, led by the Iona parish minister, the Reverend Archibald MacMillan, and large numbers of the islanders attended. At noon, there was a communion service in English. About three hundred people crowded into the church for that, including eminent clergymen such as the Very Reverend Dr James MacGregor of St Cuthbert's, Edinburgh and the Very Reverend Dr Herbert Story, principal of Glasgow University, while a special party of guests brought by Lord Balfour of Burleigh arrived on his steam yacht. A second service in Gaelic followed in the afternoon, and there was a third Gaelic service in the evening.

Other denominations were also eager to celebrate the occasion. A small group of Episcopal clergy met in their recently erected House of Retreat in the village, and on 15 June the Roman Catholic Church held a Great National Pilgrimage to Iona, with pontifical high mass in the abbey ruins at 10.30 a.m. Archbishop MacDonald of St Andrews and Edinburgh preached a eulogy on St Columba, and there was a papal blessing at the conclusion of the service.[44] The Duke's daughter, Lady Frances, noted afterwards that the temporary but effective preparations at the abbey had their effect on the whole of Scotland and many appeals were made to her father that it might be allowed to remain in its restored condition.[45]

The Duke gave much thought to this, and several of his family members were deeply interested too. Lord Archibald Campbell, his second son, made delightful watercolour sketches of scenes on the island and filled four volumes with stone rubbings which he took there in the 1890s,[46] while Lady Victoria, the Duke's third daughter, had a particularly intense fondness for the abbey. When she was about five, poliomyelitis had left her with both legs permanently paralysed. Throughout her childhood she used a wheelchair and was later fitted with steel callipers which made it possible for her to walk for short distances, supported by two sticks. Despite this severe disability, she was always determined to join in the family activities and Iona was one of her favourite places. When they were at Inveraray, she and 'a friend', probably her sister Frances, used to visit the islanders and then she would make her way slowly through the ruins where, with help, she would scramble up to the ledge of the south window of the church to gaze out. In that particular place, Victoria dedicated her life to God and to helping the people of the Western Isles.[47]

Closely resembling her father in nature, and deeply attached to him,[48] Victoria probably spoke to him about the abbey, and by this time there was another influential woman in his life who was keenly interested in it. His second wife, Duchess Amelia, had died in 1894 and was buried with her first husband in Cannes,[49] but the following year, on 26 July 1895, the Duke married Christina Erskine McNeill, always known as Ina. (Plate 14) The Duke was at this time seventy-two, while Ina had celebrated her forty-eighth birthday two days earlier.[50] Although *The New York Times* report of their wedding inaccurately referred to her as his cousin, the relationship was more distant. She was the daughter of Archibald McNeill of Colonsay W.S. and in 1870, when she was in her twenties, one of her uncles, Sir John McNeill, had married the Duke's sister.[51]

Born in Edinburgh, where her father was principal clerk of the Court of Session, Ina had been brought up with her parents and her elder sister, Susan, at 73 Great King Street, the house owned by another of her uncles, Duncan McNeill, Lord Colonsay.[52] Eventually, after her father's death and Susan's marriage, Ina and her mother moved to 58 Manor Place, which was not far away. By the time her mother died in 1886, leaving Ina all her household furniture and half of her silver plate, Ina was thirty-nine and all thoughts of marrying had long since faded away.[53] Instead, in 1888 she became an Extra Woman of the Bedchamber and private secretary to Queen Victoria, a position which she retained until her marriage to the Duke.[54]

Their wedding took place by special licence in the chapel at the Bishop's Palace, Ripon. It was strictly private, for one of the Duke's younger sons had recently died. The bride in a white, pearl-embroidered travelling dress and a bonnet trimmed with white roses wore not only a gift from Queen Victoria in the form of a miniature set in diamonds but a pearl necklace with a pearl and diamond heart-shaped pendant given to her by the Duke and a diamond bracelet from the people of Colonsay.[55] After a honeymoon at Castle Howard, the couple went to Inveraray, and in the months that followed it seems that the new Duchess eagerly shared in her husband's plans for Iona.[56] Like him, she took a keen interest in Church affairs and in 1898 she had the east end of the eighteenth-century Inveraray Parish Church remodelled and the side ceilings decorated with vivid Celtic patterns in red, blue and gold.[57]

Never physically strong, despite his apparently unflagging energy, the Duke was by this time in poor health, suffering increasingly frequent and painful bouts of the gout which had plagued him for years. In the face of continuing demands that he do something about making Iona Abbey permanently available for services, he was concerned not only about its immediate state but about its future. Like his contemporaries, he regarded the abbey as a cathedral and he was very conscious that, although the other Scottish cathedral buildings belonged to the Church, Iona, the most important of them all, was privately owned. Given its long history, he felt an enormous responsibility for it. Obviously, at his age, he might not be there for much longer to manage affairs, and who knew what his heirs might or might not do to maintain it.

He made it clear that he was casting no aspersions on the Marquis of Lorne but, although Lorne was now fifty and had shown many good qualities as Governor of Canada, one of his great failings in his father's eyes was that he obviously had no desire to spend his life at Inveraray. Instead, he retained his enthusiastic desire to live abroad. Unfortunately for him, Queen Victoria had ended his hopes in that direction by announcing that she must have Princess Louise close to her. Obviously the couple, who had held separate celebrations for their silver wedding anniversary,[58] were never going to have children and so the safest course to take would be to make some special arrangement securing the future of Iona Abbey. In the summer of 1899, the Duke therefore came to a decision and by 30 September, he was writing to his daughter Victoria: 'Dear V., I have made over by deed, signed and sealed, all the ruins of Iona to the Church of Scotland.'[59]

Chapter 8

The Trustees' Restoration

That same day, the Scottish press, at the request of the new Trustees of Iona Cathedral, published the Deed of Trust which the Duke had signed.[1] Recalling that it was fifty-three years since he had inherited the family estates, he explained that this meant that he had found himself to be proprietor of the architectural remains on Iona. Unlike the other ancient Scottish cathedrals this, the most important of them all, had long been wholly deserted. He had laid out a considerable sum, he said, in preserving it from further decay and had strengthened the walls to the extent that they were now almost ready to be re-roofed. Despite the fact that the ruins 'may be safe in my hands and in the hands of my immediate successors', he knew that not all those to whom the cathedral might descend would be appropriate owners of 'buildings of such great historic interest to the whole Christian world' and so he had decided to transfer them to a public trust in connection with the Church of Scotland.

The Iona Cathedral Trust would consist of various ex officio members: the Moderator of the General Assembly of the Church of Scotland, the Procurator of the Church of Scotland, the Principal Clerk of the General Assembly, the ministers of St Giles', and Glasgow Cathedrals, the principals of the Universities of Edinburgh and Glasgow, the principal of St Mary's College, St Andrews and the principal of the University of Aberdeen. To the Iona Cathedral Trust he gave the abbey ruins, St Oran's Chapel, the nunnery and the adjoining burial grounds,

117

with all the ancient tombstones and the enclosing walls. He bound himself and his successors to make all the writs relating to these properties available to the Trustees, but only for the purpose of defending their rights to the abbey and the other buildings.

The gift was made with four conditions. The first was that the Trustees would be acting on behalf of the Church of Scotland. The second was that the abbey would be reroofed and restored so that it could be used as a place of public worship, under the direction of the Trustees, and that the other ruins would be carefully preserved. It was his wish that the Trustees would occasionally allow members of other Christian churches to hold services in the cathedral, as he himself had permitted them to do. He added that, to prevent any doubts on the matter, the parish minister and kirk session of Iona for the time being 'shall have no part in the management of the said subjects or of the worship in the cathedral, although the Trustees could grant them permission to use it for worship'. This clause was presumably inserted because he and the minister, the Reverend Archibald MacMillan, had fallen out over services on Iona by other denominations, their quarrel dating back to January 1892 when the minister had organised a petition against the erection of an Episcopalian chapel and retreat house on Iona.[2] Thirdly, the Trustees must never sell, alienate or burden with debt the properties which he was giving them and fourthly, if the Church of Scotland were ever to be disestablished, then the Secretary of State for Scotland along with the Lord Advocate and the Sheriff of Argyll were to decide which body most nearly represented the previous Established Church of Scotland.

This clause is explained by the fact that the Church of Scotland's national status had been recognised in 1690, when an act of parliament restored its Presbyterian system of church government. Since the Reformation the Church had always maintained its freedom from state intervention, but in the nineteenth century it came to be regarded as something more, not simply a national but an Established Church, recognised and supported by the government. In the 1870s and 80s the breakaway Free Church of Scotland in particular was involved in a campaign to have the Church of Scotland disestablished. This was vehemently opposed by Queen Victoria, by Gladstone and indeed by the 8th Duke of Argyll. The matter was raised unsuccessfully in parliament in 1882 and, after that, the controversy largely died away. However, the Duke obviously feared that disestablishment might yet happen. In fact, Articles Declaratory of the Church of Scotland, recognised by parliament in 1921, have since made it clear that it never was an Established Church.[3]

The Duke had signed his Deed of Trust at Inveraray Castle on 22 September 1899 before two witnesses, Duchess Ina and Francis Robertson, one of his doctors. The press were quick to praise his generous initiative and the 'patriotic and pious feeling' that had inspired it,[4] describing Iona as 'the very fountainhead of the religious and ecclesiastical history of our kingdom, and of a large part of the Europe outside these islands', thanks to the actions of St Columba. However, as the Duke himself had anticipated, there was a good deal of criticism too. Tired of endless sectarian controversy and as devoted as ever to the Church of Scotland, he had said in his letter to Lady Victoria, 'My Deed will be grief to the Roman Catholics, to the Anglicans, and to the Scottish Anglicans. All pretty nearly equally disliked by me.' As her sister Lady Frances would remark, he could not but have known that 'those who desired to claim St Columba as belonging, not to the Church Universal but to some branch or sect, would be jealous that the Church of Scotland should have in trust this shrine and beacon of the Light of Christianity.'[5]

The Scotsman, while praising her father's ecumenical generosity in allowing other denominations to hold services, nonetheless asked indignantly, 'Are we to see "Popish" services conducted in an ecclesiastical building belonging to the Protestant and Presbyterian Church of Scotland?' The leader writer felt that any such awkwardness could have been avoided had the Duke made his gift to the Scottish nation rather than to the Church of Scotland.[6] One of the paper's readers, G. S. Aitken of Queen Street, Edinburgh, wrote on 3 October to demand, rather oddly, that architectural drawings of the church should be made, for they would prove that there had been Roman Catholic monks at Iona only since the foundation of the Benedictine Abbey. Others wanted it to remain a romantic ruin, an anonymous correspondent who called himself 'Critic' supported the view that the abbey should have been given to the nation and not any one ecclesiastical denomination, while Mr Cowley-Brown and 'A Member of the Church of Scotland as by Law Established' engaged in a tense debate as to whether St Columba had been a Roman Catholic or an Episcopalian.[7]

The Trustees had by then held their first meeting, on the very day that the Deed of Trust had been announced in the press. They assembled at 123 George Street, Edinburgh. The Moderator of the General Assembly for that year was the Right Reverend John Pagan, and Sir John Cheyne was the Church of Scotland's Procurator. The Very Reverend Robert Herbert Story, an imposing figure with a long white beard, was both Principal of Glasgow University and Principal Clerk of the General Assembly of the Church of Scotland. He had long been known to the Argyll family, for his father had been minister at Rosneath, on the Argyll estates.[8] The Very Reverend Dr James Cameron Lees, minister of St Giles' Cathedral, was a friend of Queen Victoria and a close associate of Lady Victoria Campbell;[9] the Reverend Dr Pearson McAdam Muir was minister of Glasgow Cathedral, and the principals of Edinburgh and Aberdeen Universities were Sir William Muir, the eminent Indian administrator and Islamicist and Sir William Geddes, a distinguished professor of Greek. William John Menzies W.S. was appointed to be the Trust's agent.[10]

The Trust Deed was laid before them, and they composed a letter thanking the Duke for the honour he had done them in appointing them as Trustees and assuring him that they would endeavour to make the cathedral fit for public worship as soon as was practicable. In his reply of 6 October, the Duke emphasised the fact that he wanted the restoration work to be done 'in the most conservative spirit', keeping as much of the old masonry as possible and, where any new work was required, adhering strictly to the old lines and proportions, especially with regard to the windows, so that their original tracery might be copied exactly. The gabled roof of the tower should be reinstated, as shown in an illustration to Pennant's published description, since it was 'peculiar'. He himself did not know of any suitable architect, but he hoped that the Trustees would take care to select one who was well skilled in Gothic architecture.[11] For some reason he did not suggest John Honeyman, whom he had previously employed to draw up plans.[12]

Some of the Trustees were particularly suited to the task of overseeing the restoration scheme. Principal Story had been deeply involved in the provision of new university buildings at Glasgow, Dr Lees had initiated a programme of restoration at Paisley Abbey and had collaborated in the major restoration scheme at St Giles' Cathedral in the early 1880s and one of the major achievements of Sir William Geddes at Aberdeen had been the restoration of the chapel and the extension of the Marischal College buildings. However, as one critic succinctly put it, they were 'excellent men, but burdened with many other cares and generally past their prime'.[13]

Of course the Trustees themselves realised from the start that they were confronted with what was to be a major problem. The Duke of Argyll had given them no endowment fund. Lady Frances was later to explain that 'at the time when the gift was made it was hoped that the Scottish people would hasten to endow the Trustees with funds adequate for the carrying out of the necessary restoration.'[14] Of course the Trustees may have been optimistic at the start that there would be an excellent response to the Duke's gift and, meeting again on 3 October, they decided to ask David MacGibbon and Robert Rowand Anderson to send in estimates for undertaking the work, stressing that no time should be lost. Despite this request, nothing happened at once and it was not until 10 January 1900 that William Menzies, their agent, was able to report that he had met both architects, but Anderson had been unwilling to prepare any plans until he knew who was to judge between his and MacGibbon's. The Trustees considered getting a neutral estimate based on Honeyman's 1891 plans, but in the end they decided to do nothing about an architect for the time being. There would have to be a public appeal for funds first, but the Second Boer War had broken out on 12 October 1899, British troops were being sent to South Africa and it hardly seemed an appropriate moment to start asking people to contribute money.[15]

When the news of the postponement reached the Duke's family, they were deeply distressed. No doubt led by Duchess Ina, they wrote at once to the Trustees saying that His Grace had not been told of their message because of the state of his health, and urging them to make an effort to proceed with the restoration right away. Admitting that they were unable to think what to do next, the Trustees could only decide to hold another meeting 'soon', but no date was fixed and weeks passed with nothing being done.[16] Meanwhile, the Duke's expressed hope that he would live to attend a service in the restored church was fast fading, and he died peacefully at 2.30 in the morning on 24 April 1900 at Inveraray Castle, with Duchess Ina, his son Archibald and his daughters Victoria and Frances at his side.

The Duke had left instructions that Duchess Ina was to make all the arrangements for his funeral. He wished to be cremated, his ashes put in an urn and placed as close as possible to his first wife's coffin in Kilmun Church. In due course, an urn with Duchess Ina's ashes should sit next to his. Unfortunately, the Duchess was so upset by his death that she was unable to see anybody about the funeral and during an uneasy interlude there were family arguments as to what should happen, some members (probably his heir) favouring Westminster Abbey, some (Duchess Ina herself) preferring Iona, while others (presumably his children) wished his body to be laid beside his first wife and his ancestors in the burial aisle at Kilmun. It was said that Queen Victoria had to intervene to settle matters, and in the end the Duke was not cremated but embalmed. Dressed in his uniform as Lord Lieutenant of Argyll and wearing his Garter robe, his body lay in state in a glass-topped coffin in the north drawing-room of the castle until being taken in procession to Kilmun for his funeral on 11 May.[17]

The many tributes to the Duke spoke of his generous gift of Iona, and on 28 June the Trustees finally held their long deferred meeting. It was explained that the delay had been caused by the fact that wealthy and influential members of the Church of Scotland were against raising money at present and so nothing could be done. However, the Duke's death seems to have shocked the Trustees into action for, at the end of July, 653 copies of an appeal leaflet were sent out. Unfortunately only 12 of the recipients responded but, by November, subscriptions amounting to £418:1/- had been promised. On 2 July 1901 another public appeal was launched[18] and three months later, Duchess Ina, now Dowager Duchess of Argyll, took a hand in the matter. She was dividing her time between a flat she rented in Chelsea and Macharioch House in the south-east of Kintyre, bequeathed to her by her husband in life rent. There she occupied herself with completing his unfinished autobiography, nor had she forgotten their cherished plans for Iona.

In September 1901 William Menzies received a visit from the Dowager Duchess's friend, Miss Helen Campbell of Blythswood, who told him that the Duchess had consulted the architectural firm of MacGibbon and Ross and obtained from them rough estimates of the cost of roofing various portions of the abbey church to see if she could fund part of the work herself. She would then seek the Trustees' permission to do so.

The Trustees replied cautiously that if the money could be got, then they might take the opportunity of roofing the chancel and transept, to protect them from the weather.[19] On 25 November the Duchess herself wrote to Menzies, emphasising her husband's desire that the ruins should be roofed over as soon as possible. If this could be done, she would like to place a monument in his memory in the south transept. 'Life is short', she wrote, 'and I should not like to delay longer the decision regarding a fitting memorial to one who I feel would be best commemorated in His own Cathedral of Iona, associated as it is with the earliest dawn in our country of that Christian Faith in which He lived and which His noble Life exemplified.'[20]

Even then nothing happened and, impatient with all the delays, the Dowager Duchess on 4 December 1901 again requested politely but firmly an immediate commencement of the work. No doubt at her instigation, two anonymous lenders, in fact Helen Campbell and her brother Walter, came forward to offer a loan of £1,500 each and the Trustees agreed to go ahead.[21] Nothing could ever be done on Iona in the depths of winter, of course, but in mid-February MacGibbon and Ross, on the basis of the estimates they had given the Duchess, employed J. Mitchell and Son to reroof the chancel with oak.[22] They estimated that this would cost £1,095, with a further £649 for the south aisle roof and £366 for the roof of the south transept. In addition, it would cost £100 to glaze the windows. The north transept would not be included in the restoration and instead the arch to it would be built up with brick at a cost of £10. With allowances to the contractor, the total cost would be £2,270.[23]

As the work progressed, there was increasing criticism of what was being done, Lady Frances Balfour leading the attack in a fiercely eloquent letter to *The Scotsman*. Writing on 15 July 1902, by which time the chancel, the tower and the south aisle had been reroofed, she was almost willing to accept what had been done to the first two, she said, but she was bitterly critical of the work on the south aisle, characterising it as a 'terrible external disfigurement' and 'cheap and nasty'. Two new doorways and a window had been inserted, with heavy stonework completely out of character with the rest of the building, and in her opinion the church now looked like nothing more than 'a United Presbyterian mission hall.' To make matters worse, nothing had been done about its beautiful east window, which was in a bad state of repair and partially blocked with rubble. She ended by saying that no one was going to subscribe to any appeal for the restoration if this was what was going to happen.[24]

MacGibbon and Ross replied, defending their work and making the unfortunate comment that Lady Frances had obviously not been familiar with the building before the restoration work. She retorted that she must 'fervently thank them for the work they have not done' and rallied her influential allies.[25] The following spring not only was the Reverend Dr Donald Macleod, retired minister of St Columba's Church in London, retained to take charge of the Trustees' fundraising process[26] but, on 28 May 1903, John Honeyman was called upon to prepare a complete restoration scheme, with the freedom to change any of the work that had already been undertaken. The Trustees, aware of the criticism in the press, said in their report to the General Assembly that year that they hoped that his appointment would set at rest any fears about the restoration.[27]

Honeyman's great advantage was that he knew exactly what the 8th Duke had wanted to be done: the reroofing of the chancel, its south aisle, both transepts, the tower and the sacristy but leaving the nave as a ruin because so little of it remained and no one knew what it had looked like. Honeyman recommended that all the outside walls ought to be pointed right away and that the paving of the interior and reroofing of the north transept and sacristy ought to be undertaken as soon as possible. Thomas Ross of MacGibbon and Ross was to work along with him in what not surprisingly proved to be an uncomfortable partnership.[28] Meanwhile, on 14 April 1903, the Trustees had granted the Duchess permission to decorate the south transept, also giving her the legal right to be buried in the elaborate sarcophagus that she wished to erect there, subject to their approval of its design.[29]

'Surely Iona should be preserved as a monument to keep alive the memory of the brave spirit, the pious labours and the noble sacrifices of St Columba', said the Trustees in their 1904 report to the General Assembly, expressing deep gratitude to Colonel Cooper who had nobly given £1,000 and to Mr Robert Gordon, the very first donor to respond, who had twice contributed £250. However, more money was needed.[30] The plan for the summer of 1904 was that the entire floor of the restored areas of the church would be paved, the north transept and the sacristy would be roofed and the south transept's interior would be completed, this last at the Dowager Duchess's expense.[31] On Honeyman's recommendation, the firm of E. C. Morgan and Sons undertook the masonry and joinery work, for Morgan had been for many years principal clerk of works to the famous ecclesiastical architect Sir Gilbert Scott.[32] That summer Ross's offending window in the south aisle was removed, and Honeyman promised to substitute another at a cost of less than £10. The wallhead junction put in by Ross was leaking badly, and so it too would have to be replaced. When Principal Story saw it during a visit in June 1904, he reported to his colleagues, 'I should strongly advise that Mr Ross should have nothing further to do with the Cathedral.'[33]

The previous year, thoughts had begun to turn to the other buildings. Should they not be restored too? Once the church was completed, would not its whole appearance be spoiled by the adjacent ruins? On 23 May 1903 James Cooper, the influential Professor of Church History at Glasgow University, was urging the Trustees to consider including them in their reconstruction plans so that a seminary for Highland divinity students could be established there, with the premises used as retreats for laymen during the summer vacation.[34] The following week, the General Assembly discussed the possibility of making Iona a centre of culture and education once more, where missionaries could be trained, or ministers could attend lectures. These seemed to be excellent ideas, but Principal Story was present and, in a speech which was as amusing as it was cogent, he pointed out that none of this could happen without the necessary funding.[35]

In spite of the doubts, by the autumn of 1904 Honeyman was drawing up plans to restore the nave, the chapter house and the adjoining buildings, something he himself had been urging for the sake of making available an interior space for the protection of all the carved stones. The south transept was now ready for the Duke's monument but, because it was made of marble, the Dowager Duchess knew that it would be very susceptible to damage by the chronic damp and so she was anxious to have hot air heating installed first.[36] Throughout that year Thomas Ross had failed to give John Honeyman any assistance, and the following spring Ross announced that he was withdrawing from the project. Honeyman was then allowed to appoint John Keppie, his own former business partner, to act as his assistant. Because of deteriorating eyesight he himself could no longer supervise the working drawings or the office work being undertaken by his previous staff.[37]

During the winter of 1904–5 Dr Donald MacLeod was busy fundraising in South Africa and managed to raise £402:15:6, his commission of 10% and his travelling expenses totalling £92:12:9.[38] The work was speeding ahead, and by March 1905 the church had been roofed from the east wall to the west arch of the crossing. The nave was still a ruin, but at long last the east end was ready for use. For almost three hundred and fifty years the church had stood empty, but now, just as the 8th Duke had wished, it would be used as a place of worship once more. The Trustees announced that Sunday services would be held there from 16 July until 10 September, beginning with a grand opening service on Friday 14 July 1905. Those who wished to attend could travel to Iona by Macbrayne's paddle steamer *Grenadier*, leaving Oban at 8.30 in the morning and returning in time for its passengers to catch the seven o'clock train for Glasgow and the south.[39]

The Scotsman gave a full report of the opening service, describing the congregation of about 300 people as being 'both large and of a very representative character – Protestant and Catholic Churchmen and dissenters were all gathered within the walls of the ancient edifice although the service was entirely conducted by the ministers of the Scottish Church.' Dowager Duchess Ina was there, with her friend Helen Campbell, there was a tutor and his reading party from Oxford and there were two Franciscan friars from Dublin. The service began with The Old Hundredth Psalm, 'All people that on earth do dwell', followed by another favourite, Psalm 24, 'Ye gates lift up your heads'. One of the lessons was read by the fund-raising Dr MacLeod and the Very Reverend Dr David Russell, convener of the Highland and Home Mission Committee, preached the sermon. He gave a heartfelt eulogy of St Columba, involving a distinctly dubious resumé of early Scottish history and praised the generosity of the 8th Duke of Argyll.[40]

All this was very satisfactory, but as usual nothing else could be done until there was more fundraising.[41] So far the cost had been a little under £7,000 but Honeyman advised that at least another £2000 would have to be raised before they could start work on the nave. More than half of the funds already used had come from just thirty subscribers and the response to an appeal to all the Scottish parish ministers had been particularly disappointing. Less than £20 had come in from them, and fewer than twenty of them had even acknowledged the appeal letter. There seemed to be the idea that the church would be of little use once completely restored, but the large congregation at the opening service had proved otherwise. Sunday services would be held again the following summer, and the Trustees intended to plead with the ministers and parishes for more support.[42]

The Trustees' first meeting of 1907, on March 7, began sadly, for both Principal Story and Sir John Cheyne had recently died, and John Honeyman had been forced to resign, because of his increasing blindness. 'I fear my designing days are over,' he had said, 'and that ... I must abandon all hope of seeing even one section of the work ... completely finished.'[43] His plans for a restoration of not only the nave but of all the monastic buildings had been accepted by the Trustees, but it seemed now as if they could never become a reality because of the failure of the recent fundraising campaign. However, the situation suddenly improved. Late the previous year, Helen Campbell of Blythswood had formed a Ladies' Committee to raise money for the restoration, recruiting most of the presidents of the Church's Woman's Guilds as members. By the beginning of July they had £430 in the bank and the many encouraging letters and promises they had received led them to believe that they would soon have £500 – a quarter of the amount currently needed.

Their hopes were fulfilled. By 12 May 1908, £1,250 had been promised. They had appealed first to the Woman's Guilds, 161 of whom had contributed, while others had given assurances of support. Friends of the committee members had sent money and recently the synods and presbyteries of the Church had been approached. Thanks to the efforts of the Reverend Dr Mackie of St Andrew's Church, Kingston, who had visited Iona a few years earlier, Canada had shown the keenest interest and the Honourable Donald Fraser, Lieutenant Governor of Nova Scotia was another powerful friend. India, Australia and New Zealand were supportive too. By 9 February 1909 their fund had risen to £1,500 and the following week Miss Campbell herself lent the Trustees an additional £1,500. In 1920 the Trustees would finally manage to pay her back £500 of this loan, and she generously cancelled the remaining £1,000.[44]

The Trustees, of course, had to find another architect to

replace Honeyman, and they decided on Peter Macgregor Chalmers, a Glasgow man who had been articled to Honeyman and had made his name with his work on ecclesiastical buildings, mostly Romanesque.[45] In March 1908 the Trustees studied his estimate of approximately £1,700 for rebuilding the nave, and asked him for a full report. Considering it on 23 September 1908, they decided to reroof the nave 'imminently'. The Glasgow firm of White & Sons would do it for £2,124, with Mr White senior living on Iona while work was in progress, and Chalmers acting as his own clerk of works. By June 1910 the nave had been completed, and Chalmers was finally able to pronounce the entire building wind and watertight.[46] Invited by the General Assembly on 2 June to make a statement, Dr Donald MacLeod described how the devoted efforts of Helen Campbell and the Dowager Duchess had entirely transformed the previous gloomy situation. The central tower and the chancel still awaited completion, but only the other day Mr Stewart Clark of Dundas Castle had given £1000. Surely the people of Scotland would provide the £2000 or £2500 required to finish the work.[47]

Meanwhile the Dowager Duchess's plans for her husband's memorial were delayed by the lack of heating in the church, until in 1911 five anthracite stoves were installed and in the spring of 1912 the monument itself was ready. It was the work of Sir George Frampton, the highly successful sculptor most famous nowadays for his statue of Peter Pan in Kensington Gardens, London, produced that same year.[48] On 27 May the Trustees considered another letter from the Dowager Duchess asking anxiously if the church was in a fit condition to receive the memorial. Was the heating apparatus working properly? Was a curator going to be appointed to safeguard the building? He would have to live close by so that he could show people round without letting them have the keys, which was what had frequently happened in the past. She had sent plans for a caretaker's house drawn up by Chalmers at her request.

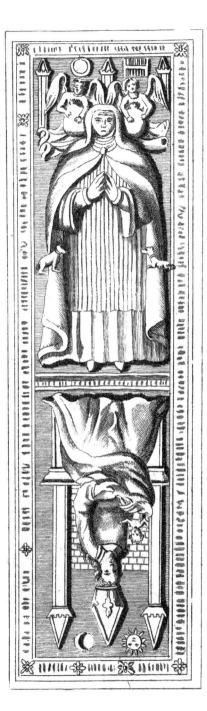

25 Drawing of the grave slab
of Prioress Anna Maclean,
died 1543, taken from T.Pennant,
A Tour of Scotland 1772, i, 254.
Only the top half of the slab
survives (© RCAHMS Licensor
www.rcahms.gov.uk).

26 The ruined Abbey, drawn by William Daniell, about 1815
(© RCAHMS Licensor www.rcahms.gov.uk).

27 George MacLeod (centre) with Bill Amos (left) and others,
outside one of the wooden huts (© Raymond Bailey Archive).

28 The restoration of the refectory, 1941 (© RCAHMS
Licensor www.rcahms.gov.uk).

29 George MacLeod at work in the library of Iona Abbey, 1943 (© The Iona Community Archive).

31 Lady McColl and Dr Warr at the official switching on of electric light
in the Abbey, 1955 (© RCAHMS Licensor www.rcahms.gov.uk).

FACING PAGE, TOP: 30a The Michael Chapel before restoration
(© RCAHMS Licensor www.rcahms.gov.uk).

FACING PAGE, BOTTOM: 30b The Michael Chapel after restoration
(© RCAHMS Licensor www.rcahms.gov.uk).

32 George MacLeod preaching in front of Columba's Shrine at the
opening of the new west range, 1961 (© RCAHMS Licensor www.
rcahms.gov.uk).

The Trustees were able to reply that the architect assured them that the heating system was in good order and working efficiently.[49] The monument duly arrived and was unveiled at a special service on 28 August 1912. So popular was the occasion that when about a hundred passengers disembarked from the steamer they found that all the seats were already occupied. The Moderator of the General Assembly, Dr Marcus Dill, conducted the service along with Dr Wallace Williamson of St Giles' Cathedral, Edinburgh and among those present were the Dowager Duchess herself and her step-daughter Lady Frances. The Dowager Duchess cut the cord of the mantle in the Argyll heraldic colours of gold and black which had covered the monument and it was revealed for the first time. Approximately 274 cms long, 152 cms broad and 122 cms high, its main feature is the life-sized marble effigy of the 8th Duke in his robes as a Knight of the Garter. The Moderator then gave a lengthy address praising the late Duke and the Duchess and attributing the occasion to the enduring influence of St Columba.[50]

The following year, on 17 July 1913, another special service was held, this time to dedicate recent gifts of furnishings. A communion table of Iona marble was to be presented by the Dowager Duchess, but it was not yet ready. When it came, it would be erected by its suppliers, Messrs Galbraith & Winton of Glasgow, at a distance of four feet from the east wall.[51] The oak pulpit, presented by the Bell family of Dundee, was simple in design and had been placed under the tower, 'at a point from which the preacher can best be heard throughout the cathedral.' A number of donors from different parts of Scotland had collaborated in providing the carved oak reading desk. Forty-two stalls, each bearing the initials or the arms of the donors had been presented by the Dowager Duchess and a long list of others and the large and handsome carved stone baptismal font with its Iona marble pillars, base and steps had been given by the widow and daughter of the Very Reverend Theodore Marshall, a former Moderator of the General Assembly. Its

131

oak cover had been made from the sixteenth-century door into the tower. (Plate 19)

These furnishings had all been designed by Chalmers and approved by the Trustees. The font had been made by J. C. Young, the oak items were the work of Messrs McKay & Co, and John Crawford had executed the carvings, these craftsmen all coming from Glasgow. The handsome pulpit Bible had been given by Principal Story's daughters, having been designed by Alexander Ritchie, a local man who had been acting as custodian of the church and who ran a stall where he and his wife sold their high quality craftwork in wood, copper, silver and embroidered cloth, many of the designs inspired by those on the high crosses and grave slabs.[52] The Bible was bound by Mrs Rae Macdonald, the Misses Anderson of Knockderry had presented alms dishes in memory of their mother, while the communion plate was the gift of the Very Reverend Dr J. Mitford Mitchell, commemorating his wife.[53] He was present, and announced the first Psalm, 'How lovely is thy dwelling place'. Dr Wallace Williamson, now Moderator of the General Assembly, performed the various dedications, including that of a bronze tablet in memory of Lady Victoria Campbell, who had died in 1910. He then preached the sermon, recalling the life of St Columba, to whom 'we owed the foundation of the Scottish Church', and the international fame of Iona itself.[54]

After the celebratory service of 1913, little required to be done to the church, apart from the continuing repairs to combat the damp, and from that year onwards it was used by the local Church of Scotland congregation until its dilapidated early nineteenth-century Thomas Telford parish church was renovated in 1939.[55] All expenditure had to be halted during the First World War, however, although necessary repairs were made to the nunnery.[56] The steamship *Grenadier*, which had provided Iona's daily link with Mull, was redeployed to the mine-strewn English Channel and, according to one visitor, with no tourists arriving, peacefulness prevailed and the blessing of St Columba still rested on the island.'[57] Two years after the end of the war, there was a significant development for the Trustees when H.M. Office of Works announced that as from 28 April 1920 the ruins on Iona were now officially listed by the Ancient Monuments Board for Scotland as being of national importance. The Trustees were told that the customary maintenance work did not have to be notified to them, but if any major alterations were planned, they would have to be told.[58]

On 15 March 1922 Peter Macgregor Chalmers 'was called to his rest with startling suddenness', as the Trustees' minutes for their subsequent meeting recorded. He had died of a heart attack, and the Trustees decided that they did not need to look for a replacement, for they could now call upon the services of the Ancient Monuments Board instead.[59] They agreed with the Office of Works architect, J. J. Paterson, that repairs should be made to Reilig Odhráin and St Oran's, to be carried out by the Office of Works but paid for by the Trustees. Luckily, now that the completed church was visible for all to see, subscriptions were flowing in and the work progressed well, with further repairs to the nunnery and attention given to the windows of St Ronan's. The stone for St Oran's was brought from Bunessan on Mull and there were other purchases of stone from Cullaloe, Aberdour. In the summer of 1923 St Ronan's was roofed, C.R. Peers, architect to the Ancient Monuments Board, had made plans for the restoration of the chapter house,[60] and thanks to the continuing generosity of John J. Spencer of Glasgow, the nunnery cloister garth was transformed into an attractive flower garden.[61]

After a long illness, the Dowager Duchess of Argyll died in London on 24 December 1925.[62] Sir George Frampton had duly provided a marble sarcophagus, with her full-length effigy in her peeress's robes, and it had been placed alongside her husband's memorial, giving the impression that they formed one single monument. (Plate 17) Now the marble top was lifted from the sarcophagus in preparation for her funeral. As she had wished, her body was embalmed and brought to Iona, on 30 December, a day of violent gales. Dr Norman Maclean took the service, praising her devotion to the Church of Scotland and, after the committal, the Reverend Angus Macvicar pronounced the benediction in Gaelic. The principal mourner was Lady Frances Balfour, representing Princess Louise, Duchess of Argyll, who sent a wreath, as did Miss Campbell of Blythswood, in her late seventies now and unable to attend. The Dowager Duchess left half of the residue of her estate to the Iona Cathedral Trustees, a sum amounting to £2,876:17:1, to be used to pay the salary of a custodian and the expense of heating the church. The other half was bequeathed to the Argyllshire Nursing Association.[63]

The triumphant restoration now required one final finishing touch. In recent years, an old ship's bell had been rung before services, but that was completely inadequate. David Guthrie Dunn, the 23-year-old owner of Knock Castle, Largs, had inherited a fortune from his tobacco millionaire grandfather and in 1930 he came to the rescue, offering to donate a peal of bells. The Trustees sought the advice of Cleveland Ellis, honorary bell ringer of St Mary's Cathedral in Edinburgh, and it was decided that a single bell would give a richer, deeper toned effect. Various bell founders were invited to tender, and Taylor & Co of Loughborough were successful. They were world famous, having made not only the peal of ten bells for St Mary's but the Great Paul bell of St Paul's Cathedral, London, the largest bell in Britain.

Messrs Morris and Spottiswood, wrights and joiners, undertook various modifications to the church tower, putting in steel beams from which the bell would be hung and it was engraved with the words 'I-Chaluim-Chille' and the date 1931. In the end, the total cost was £452:2:6, significantly more that the £314 which Dunn had offered. The Trustees did not know how to contact him, for he had recently graduated from Cambridge and gone off on a world cruise with two friends on his motor ketch, *The Southern Cross*, but his representatives reported that he was willing to pay the extra amount. On 10 June 1931 over 500 hundred people attended the service of dedication, which was led by the Right Reverend Dr John Graham of Kalimpong, the famous missionary and that year's Moderator of the General Assembly. On 1 December that year Miss Annie Macdonald, a local resident, was employed to be the bell ringer, for which she would be paid £3:10 a year. Sad to say, David Dunn, the generous young benefactor, was accidentally drowned at sea between Cape Town and St Helena on 8 March 1933, on the way back from his world cruise.[64]

Chapter 9

George MacLeod and the Iona Community

With the successful restoration of the entire church, nave as well as chancel, transepts and tower, the Trustees had discharged their most pressing duty. (Plate 16) Services were taking place there, just as the 8th Duke of Argyll had wished, and they could now turn their attention to the difficult problem of raising money for vital future maintenance. However, other people had for some time been pondering the future of the adjacent ruins, not merely from aesthetic considerations, but because these could be put to practical use. In particular, the notion of a retreat centre there was becoming increasingly popular. Indeed, Annie Hunter Small, Principal of the Women's Missionary College in Edinburgh (later to be known as St Colm's College) had been holding regular Iona retreats for her students since at least 1913. Herself a former missionary in India, she was particularly interested in experimenting with models of community living.[1]

The idea of a retreat centre had also been taken up by David Russell, philanthropic head of Tullis Russell and Company, the Fife paper manufacturers. From 1920 onwards, at his own expense, he held a series of annual retreats on Iona for twenty-four students from the four Scottish divinity halls. After the first year at the Argyll Hotel, they stayed even closer to the abbey at the St Columba Hotel, and Russell began to wonder about the possibility of establishing a permanent community on the island. In September 1929 he sought out James Richardson, the Inspector of Ancient Monuments for Scotland who was dealing with the ruins, and discussed with him the possible restoration of the chapter house. That same month, Russell set up the Iona Fellowship for people who had attended his retreats and wished to maintain their connection. They would form small local groups and hold prayer meetings.[2]

Time passed and nothing came of Russell's discussion with Richardson, but he was not about to give up. In 1931 he commissioned the distinguished Roman Catholic architect Reginald Fairlie, who had worked on Russell's own house, to consider what might be done. Fairlie sent a member of his firm, Ian Lindsay, to draw plans of the ruins and then reported back that it would cost around £47,000 to floor and roof the chapter house and dormitory, restore the refectory and create a caretaker's house.[3] However, the country was in the midst of the Great Depression and in 1933, when Russell put his plan to the Trustees, Dr Charles Warr, Minister of St Giles' Cathedral, had to tell him that these were difficult times in which to make a public appeal for funds. It seemed that nothing could be done.[4]

Two years after that, everything suddenly changed when the Trustees received a totally unexpected letter from the American Iona Society, an organisation set up by a group of Highland emigrants to the United States. Inspired by Angus Robertson, President of An Comunn Gàidhealach, the well-known society for the promotion of the Gaelic language and culture, they told the Trustees that if they were given permission to restore the ruins at their own expense, they would transform them into a Celtic College. Their headquarters would have to be on the mainland, for practical reasons, but Robertson believed that the Iona ruins could be restored as a spiritual and educational centre.[5] Astonished, the Trustees were at a loss as to how to respond. The proposal would not, apparently, involve them in any expenditure, but who knew what might happen if they allowed it to go ahead? It was not that they were being unnecessarily timid. They were very conscious that the 8th Duke's Deed of Trust had explicitly forbidden them to burden with debt the properties he was giving, and all he had asked with regard to the other ruins was that they should be carefully preserved. No doubt they also disliked the thought of the disruption around the church which the work would inevitably bring. In the end, the Trustees resolved to meet on 20 November 1935 to consider the American letter, and they invited to attend their meeting the Reverend George MacLeod, a Glasgow minister. He was not a Trustee and never had been, so what was his interest in Iona and why should they be so anxious for him to take part in their confidential discussion?

MacLeod had been born in Glasgow in 1895 into a very distinguished dynasty of Highland ministers who, since the early nineteenth century, had included several Moderators of the General Assembly and Deans of the Chapel Royal. His father, John MacLeod, was a partner in the Glasgow firm of accountants, Kerr, MacLeod and MacFarlan and his mother, Edith Fielden, was the daughter of a very wealthy Yorkshire mill owner. Edith was ambitious for her sons and they were sent to Winchester College, where George was confirmed in the Church of England. Intending to be a lawyer, he had begun his studies at Oxford when the First World War broke out. He enlisted enthusiastically in the Argyll and Sutherland Highlanders, served on the Western Front and in Salonika, reached the rank of captain and was awarded both the Military Cross and the Croix de Guerre. Returning to civilian life, he felt called to study for the ministry, firstly at Edinburgh University and then at the Union Theological Seminary in New York. There he came under the influence of the Reverend Tubby Clayton, founder of Toc H, a soldiers' club which had grown into a charity dedicated to service and friendship within the community.

Back in Scotland in 1922, MacLeod gained a desirable position as assistant at St Giles' Cathedral, thanks in part to his influential father, who had become a Unionist M.P. and would be given a baronetcy in 1924. Four years later MacLeod moved to become collegiate minister of St Cuthbert's, Edinburgh. During his time in Edinburgh he made a reputation as a charismatic preacher and was particularly popular with the city's society ladies, who flocked to hear the handsome and dashing war hero. However, marriage was far from his thoughts. Ever since the camaraderie in the trenches with men from a very different background to his own, he had become deeply committed to bringing back into the Church all those from poorer sections of society who had drifted away. His experiences with people living in poverty in the Edinburgh slums drove him on and when he became minister of Govan Old Parish Church, Glasgow in 1930, he threw himself into trying to relieve the large number of his parishioners who were unemployed and enduring great hardship. By now an outspoken Christian socialist, he organised from the Pearce Institute in Govan an extensive range of activities designed to convince them that the Church could and would help, exhausting even his enormous energy in the process.

As a result, he suffered a lengthy episode of depression, but a recuperative journey to the Holy Land with his father in 1933 revitalised him. Together they attended a service in St Andrew's Church, Jerusalem, where he noted that the communion table was made of Iona marble, and he was deeply moved by an early morning Easter service at the Russian Orthodox Church, which inspired in him a passionate interest in how worship is conducted. Home again in Govan, MacLeod was greatly concerned about the movement of population from city centres to outlying housing estates, for he did not see how the local ministers on the periphery could cope with the sudden influx. Some sort of social experiment was needed, to try out what could be done. Perhaps a community could be set up on Inchcolm, a small island in the Firth of Forth, but then his thoughts turned to Iona, which he had known since his childhood holidays on Mull.[6]

According to his own account, it was Annie Hunter Small who first drew his attention to the possibilities there, although his sister believed that it was she who had put the idea into his head.[7] Whatever the truth of it, his old Professor, William Paterson, had earlier put him in touch with David Russell, and MacLeod had spoken at Russell's 1930 Iona retreat.[8] By the time that his invitation to attend the Trustees' meeting arrived, MacLeod was thirty-seven years old, still single, and not merely an experienced minister, well-known in his parish. A tall and striking figure with a formidable presence, he was at one and the same time difficult but kind-hearted, blunt but with a quick humour, and he had a real gift for communication, not only in the pamphlets that he wrote and the sermons that he preached but on radio programmes too. His broadcast sermons and talks touched the hearts of his listeners and gave him the opportunity of publicising his ideas.

When the Trustees' invitation came, he seized his opportunity and immediately sent off to their clerk a memorandum giving details of the competing plan he had been devising for Iona. It went far further than mere retreats, for what he had in mind was a full-scale social experiment which would point the way towards a solution to the problems of population movement and the Church's apparent inability to deal with them. At the same time, the monastic buildings on Iona would be restored. This was how it would be done. Each summer, a group of young licentiate minister volunteers would go to Iona with a group of volunteer tradesmen to undertake the restoration work, supervised by an architect. The young ministers would divide their time between studying and labouring for the tradesmen. Together the two groups would form a brotherhood, like the brotherhoods attached to the Anglican Church. During their stay on the island they would all live communally in wooden huts and, at the end of two years, the ministers would be sent out to the housing estates to assist the parish ministers there. In this way, people of different backgrounds would come together as a community, the middle-class ministers would learn how to speak to the working-class tradesmen, the Church of Scotland would be saved from disintegration and St Columba's prophecy about Iona's enduring fame would be fulfilled.[9]

So what would really be involved? He was not eager to restore the ruins because of their interest as a historic site. He wanted them in part because of the opportunity they would give for the volunteers to learn by working together and in part because of the use to which they could be put afterwards, as accommodation for retreats and other activities. At any rate, what he was he was proposing was that he should undertake the restoration of two of the cloister buildings: the east range with its large chapter house and dormitory and the north range with its upstairs refectory. There was no thought at that point of doing anything about the west range, since it had never been complete, and of course there was no south range because that was where the abbey church adjoined the cloister. So what he planned was an extensive but not impossibly large project, despite the fact that work could be done only in the summer months.

He was, of course, very interested in the restored church. There was no need for him to do anything about that, for its condition was now excellent, apart from a few minor repairs yet to be completed. What he wanted to do was to make use of it as the place of worship for the retreats and other activities he had in mind. He made a point of referring to it as the abbey church and not as Iona Cathedral, the name by which it was generally known. This might have been because some people disliked the word 'cathedral', which was connected to their aversion to bishops. Whatever its name, he wished to transform the church's interior into something more suitable for the form of worship that he preferred. His experience of the Russian Orthodox service in Jerusalem and his memories of the Anglican services of his schooldays had given him a liking for something more elaborate than the plain interiors of Presbyterian churches and what he regarded as the rather austere services.

Impatient though he was by nature, he knew better than to ask for a full-scale refurbishment of the abbey church, but he followed up his first letter to the Trustees with another on 14 November, asking permission to furnish the small chapel in the south-east corner, known as Lady Victoria's Chapel, since it was where her memorial plaque is situated. He needed this to be done, he said, in time for the retreat he intended to hold at the abbey the following spring. The carved stones kept in the little chapel would have to be moved, of course, and chairs, hassocks, a very simple communion table and some curtains would have to be brought in, but he would pay for everything.[10]

The day of the Trustees' meeting came and MacLeod was invited to sit at the table with them and listen to their deliberations. They began by unanimously agreeing to the restoration of the ruined monastic buildings as a retreat 'for worship, meditation, study and instruction' before moving on to a detailed discussion of the letter from the American Iona Society. They did not really know what to make of it, for although tempted by the financial inducement, they were wary of the implications. The Society wanted the right to invite to Iona people of any denomination or none and to teach all manner of educational subjects. These ideas did not have the Trustees' approval, because their overriding responsibility was to Christianity and they considered that classes in secular subjects would be, at best, irrelevant.

Sir Thomas Holland, the eminent geologist who was Principal of Edinburgh University, questioned the wisdom of setting up a Celtic college anywhere and thought that it would be better if the American society were to establish an Iona Trust to make grants towards the restoration of the ruins and found scholarships for the study of Gaelic language and literature. Dr Warr, minister of St Giles' Cathedral, supported him and the Trustees eventually mentioned MacLeod's memorandum, saying that in general they agreed with his views. He no doubt told them that by now he had received a letter from Angus Robertson of An Comunn Gàidhealach entirely approving of his proposals. The Trustees concluded by setting up a small committee to consider their response to the American Iona Society letter. The members would be Sir Thomas, Dr Warr, the Trustees' clerk and George MacLeod. [11]

Harry Miller, the Principal of St Mary's College, St Andrews warned his fellow trustees later that month to beware of the American plan, for past experience had shown how donors liked to dictate policy. Sure enough, in January 1936 the American Iona Society was indicating that it wished to share in the choice of architect for the project. This was not well received. On 14 December 1935 Reginald Fairlie had sent the Trustees details of the plans and estimate he had drawn up for David Russell and the Trustees had passed these on to the American Iona Society at the end of December.[12] However, as the months went by, it became evident that MacLeod's was the scheme they favoured because it was under the aegis of the Church of Scotland, and the American initiative gradually faded away through lack of encouragement.

Instead, the Trustees would lease the ruins to what would be called the Iona Community free of charge. Of course no one could begin any work until funds were available but in the meantime, MacLeod pressed ahead with his plans for the small south chapel of the abbey church. On 8 March the parish minister, the Reverend Donald MacCuish, was obediently supervising the moving of the carved stones from the small chapel to the north transept and the chancel on rollers used for launching boats. Six days later Alexander Ritchie was exclaiming that he wished that the Reverend George MacLeod would restrain his enthusiasm for private chapels on Iona while Mr MacCuish sighed that if only the stones were not 'so fearfully heavy' the preparations would go more easily.[13] Undeterred, MacLeod arranged different furnishings and

143

lighting for meditation and kneeling, with the aim of creating a suitable atmosphere for services and 'resettling our own souls' compass'. He wanted the Trustees to know everything he was doing, 'however temporary', he told them emphatically,[14] but of course they were suspicious of his intentions. His ideas about how services should be conducted seemed to some people to be positively popish.

In the end, the retreat passed off satisfactorily. Three days were devoted to 'enjoyment of Iona', meeting the islanders and conferring about the work of the ministry, while another three were given over to what was called 'intense retreat'. The student participants' main complaint was that they were not allowed to smoke during the intense retreat phase, and its study of other forms of worship led at least one of those who attended to protest that 'we must hold fast to our Protestant heritage'.[15] For his part, MacLeod was impatient that the Trustees had not yet given their official consent to the restoration of the ruins, although in July they did ask Wilson Paterson, the Office of Works architect, to prepare a sketch of the chapter house and library as these would look if they were restored.[16] It was not until the following year, however, that things began to happen.

On 7 March 1938, the Trustees met, with Dr Warr in the chair. George McLeod was present once more, and he had already submitted to them an extended version of his original memorandum of 1935. Assuring them that his purposes were utterly loyal to the Church of Scotland and that his supreme concern was the preservation of Presbyterianism, he outlined his proposals in greater detail and now suggested that a body of Church of Scotland sponsors should be officially responsible for the Iona experiment, offering himself for the task of being in charge of the day to day arrangements and the recruitment of volunteers.[17] Dr Warr had all along been supportive of MacLeod,[18] and the Trustees received the expanded plan positively, agreeing in principle that he could use the monastic buildings as he suggested, and approving his idea of gathering together sponsors, not as contributors of money but as people of influence who would lend the project authority in the eyes of potential donors. Interestingly, they remarked that, while it would be desirable for the restored buildings to be in harmony with their original appearance, 'the restoration should also express the spirit of the age'. The Trustees would appoint the architect for the restoration, who would be answerable to them, but MacLeod could choose his own architect for the communal huts where he and the volunteers would live.[19]

The sponsors met for the first time on 7 April 1938 in Edinburgh. David Russell was there, as was the acclaimed Scottish artist Sir D.Y. Cameron. A son of the manse, President of the Ecclesiological Society and much involved in beautifying church interiors, he proved to be an enthusiastic supporter of the restoration for the rest of his life and when he died in 1945 he left the Trustees £500 to further their work. The other sponsors included, ex officio, the Chairman of the Trustees, one professor from each Divinity Hall and the parish minister of Iona.[20] The meeting went well and on 26 April MacLeod followed it up by publishing in *The Glasgow Herald* an article describing the intended new Iona Community and declaring again that it would help to fulfil St Columba's prophecy about the island's long-lasting fame. *The Scotsman* at the same time published its own piece about the Iona Brotherhood.[21] The scheme did not please everyone, of course. Niall, 10th Duke of Argyll was wary of what MacLeod was planning, many people disagreed with his socialism and hated the fact that he had become a pacifist, while others were simply jealous of his high profile. When the General Assembly met in May 1938 some of the ministers and elders attending spoke resentfully about how they had first learned of the Iona experiment when they read about it in the newspapers and a new Church committee was set up to keep a watchful eye on what MacLeod and his Brotherhood were doing.[22]

Meanwhile, letters applying to take part in the Iona restoration were beginning to come in from young ministers, and some of these are preserved among George MacLeod's papers. Quite a few of the applicants had been inspired by meeting him or hearing him speak during their student days. Letters arrived from tradesmen too, who had read his articles in the Church of Scotland magazine *Life and Work* and in *The Oban Times*. There was a Newton Mearns blacksmith and woodworker who had been employed for many years in logging camps in Canada; an apprentice joiner from Dundee who was only nineteen but promised to work as hard and as willingly as only those who wish to serve can work; a retired postman who offered to deal with the Iona Community's mail and a builder who had spent four years on the restoration of Glasgow Cathedral.[23]

To the shock of his parishioners, MacLeod now resigned as minister of Govan Old Parish Church, attending his last service there on 22 May 1938 and in June he led to Iona the advance party of workmen, young ministers and divinity students who would start putting up the wooden huts, supervised by his architect, Alastair MacQueen. The men all had to dress alike, in navy blue fishermen's jerseys, trousers and heavy boots. The hut which was to be their dormitory had already been erected and their meals were to be simple but nourishing: porridge, eggs, bread and butter for breakfast, a meat dish and pudding for dinner (i.e. lunch), soup, bread, scones and cake for tea, cocoa and biscuits for supper.[24] It rained almost every day on Iona that summer, but they worked on, for £1 a day and their keep. (Plate 27) It was not exactly the ideal community which MacLeod had imagined, for there were inevitably resentments between the craftsmen and the ministers, coming from very different backgrounds as they did. The craftsmen were of the opinion that the ministers had no conception of what a real day's work meant while, for their part, the ministers were baffled by the men's seemingly ingenuous questions about religion and did not know how to answer them. However, MacLeod was a dominating presence, he kept them together by sheer force of personality and almost military discipline, and nobody left.[25]

One day they were even able to add someone who would be a valuable asset to the Community with the chance arrival of Bill Amos, an Edinburgh master mason who had been on a walking holiday on Mull. His pacifism and socialist principles fitted in well with the Community's ethos and his skills were invaluable.[26] That summer also brought a disturbing piece of news. Like some of the members of the General Assembly, the Office of Works had learned about MacLeod's plans only when they had read about them in the press, and they were angry. They should have been informed. They promptly announced that the ruins were about to be officially scheduled.[27]

Alarmed, the Trustees told MacLeod that he could not go ahead with any of the restoration work until it was approved by the Office of Works. MacLeod was appalled, but Dr Warr managed to effect a compromise and the Office of Works agreed to the scheme in mid-July, on condition that the huts were removed as soon as the work was completed and no archaeological remains were disturbed.[28] The ruins were duly scheduled and MacLeod agreed that work should not start until the summer of 1939. Meanwhile the Trustees, fearing that MacLeod would rush recklessly ahead before the funds came in, insisted that the restoration should proceed in stages, according to an agreed programme approved in advance by themselves.[29] Reginald Fairlie's drawings would be used, but Ian Lindsay, who had produced them, had by this time left Fairlie's firm and set up his own practice. Fairlie generously insisted that Lindsay should be the person to undertake the project and he was appointed as the Trust's official architect the following year.[30]

The question of fund-raising was now more urgent than ever. In November 1936 MacLeod had been saying boldly that he would aim to raise £50,000 from no more than five people, for he was sure that there were enough wealthy Scots to make this possible.[31] He now wrote to three such potential donors, asking them for £5,000 each. The first two did not respond but the third, Sir James Lithgow, the wealthy shipbuilder, made the donation. He had often seen the Iona ruins as he sailed to the Hebrides in his yacht, and wondered why nothing was done about them. According to MacLeod, Sir James asked him if he would give up his pacifism if he made a contribution. 'Not on your life!' MacLeod is said to have replied, whereupon Sir James promptly sent the money.[32] Actually Sir James was very measured in his approach, urging MacLeod in June 1938 to raise the necessary funds quietly and in a manner which would ensure that ultimately the experiment would be welcomed by the majority of Church of Scotland members. For that reason, he asked that his own contribution should be treated anonymously.[33]

At the same time, MacLeod was not forgetting about the abbey church itself. In July 1938 the Trustees gave him permission to put a broad oak table in the chancel, immediately behind the communion table and close to the wall. Vases of flowers would be placed there, and there would be more flowers on the three east windowsills. Wooden sconces for candles would be introduced into the choir stalls and iron candleholders fixed to the wooden beams in the south transept. He also wanted a small pulpit or moveable lectern for services held in the chancel only. He himself was willing to pay for all these additions.[34] He had already made some alterations to the form of worship, much to the annoyance of Donald MacCuish the parish minster who in August 1937 had been described as being 'not enthusiastic' about these 'ritualistic innovations,'[35] and of course MacCuish's congregation were still worshipping in the church while their own building was being repaired. MacLeod declared that because the Duke of Argyll's Deed of Trust had excluded the parish minister from any part in the worship or management of the abbey church, it could become wholly the centre of worship for the Community, adding that the Trustees could continue to invite Mr MacCuish and his flock to services there when they wished.[36]

This high-handed view did not help the situation and one exasperated islander complained that it seemed as if Dr MacLeod and not Mr MacCuish was now minister of Iona,[37] but MacLeod proceeded to act as if he were free to do as he wished in the church in the way of both worship and its setting. His typescript notes for a special service held there on 9 June 1938 included a defence of the saying of the Apostles' Creed at services, the use of responses and the instruction that members of the congregation should be free to assume whichever posture for prayer was most likely to aid to their devotion, standing or kneeling being the most helpful.[38]

In October he published the first issue of *The Coracle*, the Iona Community magazine, in which he outlined the latest developments and encouraged readers to join his new organisation, the Friends of the Iona Community, at a cost of 5 shillings a year. In an effort to reassure his critics, he described the Community as no more than a laboratory for cooperative living, which would operate only during the summer months, and would be a means of showing that Christianity was a faith for the whole world, superior to Communism and Fascism. Iona was a particularly appropriate location for this, he said, with its west door standing in the shadow of St Martin's Cross and with the threat of imminent war against Germany looming over Britain. St Martin had been an army officer who had devoted all his vigour to the expression of Christianity in similarly difficult times.

MacLeod went on to describe how, during the past summer, the wooden huts had been erected by volunteers. Most of the men were complete strangers to each other, he said, but in this isolated place without distractions, working side by side in all weathers, they had soon formed friendships, and despite the inevitable differences of opinion, they had shown time and again that artisans were better men than parsons, not just at their jobs but in grasping the real issues.[39] Of course the very

149

appearance of the huts led to an avalanche of criticisms from both local people and visitors to the island, who considered that they spoiled the look of the ruins. MacLeod brushed these objections aside and heartily denied that the Community involved a return to Rome, supported pacifism, consisted of a set of people trying to play at being Franciscans or was a one-man enterprise.[40]

At the end of the summer, the men all left the island, but by the following May, plans were well advanced for the beginning of the real work. There would be seven young Scottish ministers and one from Prague, who was a skilled choirmaster, five Edinburgh masons, three carpenters, and six other men, including three from the west of Scotland and two from Iona itself. On 16 June 1939, less than a fortnight after they arrived on the island, an article appeared in *The Scotsman* saying that women had been reading with interest the accounts of life in the Iona Community, and wanted to know 'where they come in'.[41] In fact, their exclusion from any form of membership had never been seen as a problem by George MacLeod himself. What he believed he was forming was a brotherhood with a very specific purpose, and at that time women were not eligible to become Church of Scotland ministers or even elders, so there was obviously no part for them to play. His all-male education and his army experience had accustomed him to masculine rather than mixed communities and the fact that he was not yet married himself probably played a part in his attitude. In any case, none of the young ministers taking part initially had a wife, because they were at the very start of their careers and could not afford to marry. The tradesmen were older, but apparently all but two of them were single.

As time went on, this exclusion of women became a source of lingering resentment, not just to those who might have aspired to join the Community but among the families of the increasing number of married men who were forced to leave their wives and children for months at a time. It was not that MacLeod disliked or ignored the opposite gender. His legendary kindness to his parishioners in Govan and his subsequent pastoral letters over the years to the many troubled women who wrote to him, having heard his radio broadcasts, show that he was no misogynist.[42] He probably considered that female members in the Community would be a distraction to his divinity students and ministers and, if they had young families as well, the whole organisation would be in danger of losing its focus. He was now deeply involved in the second part of his plan, which involved sending out young ministers in pairs to the urban housing schemes in Edinburgh, Glasgow, Greenock, Aberdeen and Lanarkshire once their two years of work on Iona had taken place. He himself intended to go to six parishes before Christmas and in the spring, to share their experiences.

In the second edition of *The Coracle* he wrote of the new approach to worship which he believed was needed, the discovery of alternative ways of presenting the faith, perhaps by closer attention to the Christian year and a more dramatic form of worship.[43] He had already put this into practice and when *The Scotsman*'s special correspondent attended an evening service in the abbey church on 15 June 1939, he found the chancel in semi-darkness, with candles flickering as the last rays of evening light filtered through the east window. Earlier in the day, a textile screen had been placed along the east wall behind the communion table.[44] The Trustees had by now agreed that a start could be made on the restoration of the refectory. MacLeod offered to pay Ian Lindsay's fee, and Angus Robertson promised the Trustees a donation of £7,000 for the rebuilding. The Office of Works gave their approval, and Lindsay began to draw up plans for it, the chapter house and the reredorter, the former latrine building which lay just behind it and had been linked to it.[45] Everything seemed to be moving ahead well, but on 1 September 1939 Nazi Germany invaded Poland and two days later Britain declared war on Germany. Could the Iona Community possibly continue in these circumstances?

The Reverend Ronald Selby Wright of the Canongate Church in Edinburgh came to the rescue. Called up to serve in the war as a chaplain to the Royal Scots, he urged MacLeod to try out the Iona Community experiment in his parish and offered his manse as the headquarters.[46] MacLeod gladly accepted, and from that convenient location, he organised the missionary work in the parishes.[47] Everywhere west of Oban now became a restricted area, and everyone was required to have a special pass to enter it.[48] Moreover, non-essential building work was forbidden, but MacLeod was determined that the Iona reconstruction should continue. He had been eager to start with the chapter house rather than the refectory, arguing that by working on it the masons and the others would gain experience of the sort of materials they had to use. The Trustees had agreed, and he was now insistent that it, at least, should be completed. By October 1940, late in the season, Ian Lindsay was away on war service, but the refectory walls were also being re-erected.[49] (Plate 28)

Meanwhile, the Trustees were once more receiving complaints from the Reverend Donald MacCuish about MacLeod's services. Considering the matter on 23 April 1940, the Trustees said firmly that the two men would have to reach a compromise in order to avoid holding competing services, and promised that Mr MacCuish would be told in advance of any alteration to the furnishings.[50] This was because Ian Lindsay, a high church Episcopalian,[51] had sent them a lengthy report with suggestions for interior rearrangements. He had experimentally moved the pulpit from beneath the tower to the north-east corner of the nave, and the lectern from the crossing to the north transept. The chancel had been much improved, he believed, by positioning the stalls three feet further west and he advised that the cold, hard appearance of the holy table should be softened by covering it with a long, coloured cloth. This would be replaced by a white linen one of similar length for communion services.

The holy table should have only a Bible on it, and it would be good to have a cross either on the sill of the east window or hanging above the sanctuary. Once the carved stones had been moved from the north transept, it could become a place for quiet contemplation, ideally with two stained glass windows in the east wall, each representing one significant figure. MacLeod's comments were appended to this document since, he said, furniture impinged on worship and he wished to emphasise the priesthood of all believers. He wanted the pulpit to be in the nave but he did not like the prayer desk being there and he did not want a coloured cloth on the holy table. As to a cross, it could only be justified on medieval grounds which, he said, he hoped to avoid.[52] He was soon to change his mind about that, however, for shortly afterwards David Russell took him to see an exhibition of silver by the late Oscar Ramsden, and there he espied a beautiful silver Celtic cross. When they enquired about it, Mrs Ramsden, seemingly unaware of who MacLeod was, told them that it was not for sale because her husband had always hoped that one day it would go to Iona Abbey. Russell bought it, and it now stands there, immediately behind the communion table.[53] (Plate 18)

The Trustees continued to be more worried about the construction work than the furnishings, and their concerns seem to have been aggravated in September 1940 when, just as lack of timber threatened to halt the rebuilding, a deck cargo of Canadian wood had providentially been washed ashore on Mull. MacLeod had taken possession of it, but had he been allowed to do that? On 24 June 1941 they called him in to their meeting and he explained that he had three times contacted the authorities for permission to use the timber, but had received no reply. Each of the five trustees present that day then appealed to him, individually, to suspend all work in the meantime, because of the war.[54] Angrily, he refused, insisting that he would go ahead with the restoration of the reredorter, guaranteeing its funding in advance. David Russell was among those who wrote to him, supporting his position. The rebuilding was a symbol of spiritual integration in a disintegrating world, Russell said, and it must continue.[55]

In October the Trustees asked the Office of Works for its opinion. The Office supported their view that work should stop, and the following April the Trustees decided that this wrangling could not go on. The time had come to draw up a formal agreement between themselves and George MacLeod.[56] (Plate 29) An interminable series of arguments ensued, complicated by an acrimonious dispute between the Reverend Murdo Macrae, the new parish minister, and MacLeod as to who had the right to hold services in the abbey church.[57] Finally, as the war drew to a close, a deed was drawn up, giving the Trustees the right to terminate the Community's occupation of the abbey buildings at any time and reiterating that, in keeping with the 8th Duke of Argyll's Deed of Trust, all the restored buildings were the property of the Trustees, irrespective of who carried out and paid for the restoration work.[58] By the summer of 1945, the chapter house, library and reredorter had been completely restored, as had the refectory walls. The dormitory above the chapter house was being rebuilt and money had been given towards the restoration of the separate Abbot's House and the Michael Chapel.[59]

Chapter 10

Safeguarding the Future

With the end of World War II, Ian Lindsay returned from his service in the Royal Engineers and George MacLeod set off on energetic fundraising campaigns far beyond Scotland, visiting the United States, South Africa, India, Australia and New Zealand.[1] Wood for the refectory roof was donated by Norwegian timber merchants, in gratitude for the help given to their country by Scotland during the recent conflict,[2] and the floor and ceiling were finally installed in 1949. By then MacLeod had received a donation of £10,000 for the continuing reconstruction of the dormitory and that summer he was able to report that that he was also expecting a gift of New Zealand timber for the east range rooms.[3]

Bill Amos died of lung cancer that autumn, at the early age of forty-six and the general scarcity of expert masons was still causing problems.[4] However, the following year the Trustees were discussing the reroofing of St Oran's Chapel and agreeing to Lindsay's proposal that the north chapel of the nunnery should also be roofed.[5] From time to time restoration of the nunnery would be mentioned, but it remains a ruin to this day. By April 1951 the long awaited caretaker's house, which had been so much desired by Ina, Dowager Duchess of Argyll, was finished at last[6] and in the autumn of 1952 there was a new initiative from David (now Sir David) Russell. Nothing had as yet been done about St Oran's and so he paid for it to be reroofed and for the restoration of St Columba's Shrine.[7]

None of these advances was achieved without the usual

arguments and quarrels, some trivial, some significant. In 1946, for example, the Trustees had been told about a dispute over the nunnery garden. 'Miss Spencer resented Dr MacLeod's manner' when he demanded flowers from the garden for the abbey church, and she told him firmly that they were grown specifically to beautify the nunnery itself (her family, of course, having provided the money for the garden). MacLeod retorted that he knew they were being given away to the local hotels.[8] On a more serious note, the Ministry (formerly Office) of Works remained unhappy about defiance of their rules, threatening in 1948 that unless MacLeod kept exactly to their instructions, made known to him through the Trustees, they would issue a preservation order which would have had the effect of considerably curtailing his activities.[9]

That same year saw a major change in MacLeod's personal life, when he finally married. His bride was his vivacious second cousin, Lorna Macleod, who was twenty-six years younger than he was. His old parish of Govan fell vacant that same year and he was eager to return to it, saying that he would combine his ministry with his leadership of the Iona Community, but Glasgow presbytery refused to allow his appointment. By this time, however, the fiercest opposition to the Iona Community with its pacifism and socialism was beginning to recede, and in 1951 it was formally brought under the aegis of the Church of Scotland, with the establishment of an Iona Community Board. MacLeod was made convener of the new board and was now officially known as Founder of the Iona Community. Although the Board was to report to the General Assembly each year, it would be free to make its own policies and raise its own funds, subject to the Assembly's scrutiny. The committee of sponsors was therefore dissolved.[10]

While all these developments were taking place, life at the abbey continued in the usual way. During the 1950s there were sporadic disputes with the 10th Duke of Argyll's Trustees about MacLeod's use of stones from the south boundary wall[11] and from time to time there were complaints about the behaviour of the Iona Community. In 1952, the Reverend Ivan Cooke was writing to the Iona Cathedral Trustees to allege that Community members were guilty of dancing in the village hall, leaving gates open and engaging in mixed bathing. The Trustees replied austerely that they were responsible only for things that happened on abbey property.[12]

As work progressed on the dormitory, there was a more serious cause for concern, with thoughts beginning to turn to the fate of the famous wooden huts once the project was completed. It had been agreed from the start that they would be taken down as soon as they were no longer required, and MacLeod was anxious to start using them as accommodation for his increasingly popular youth camps. They could not stay where they were, however, and so in 1953 he began prolonged discussions with the Duke of Argyll and the Argyll Trustees about a suitably inconspicuous site for them, for of course they would have to be erected somewhere on Argyll Estates land, preferably out of sight of the abbey. Eventually, an agreement was reached and they were moved across the road.[13]

The restoration work had moved on to another of the freestanding buildings, with the presumed Abbot's House being restored to provide a laundry and additional residential accommodation, and the east range was triumphantly completed in 1956.[14] On 12 August, Queen Elizabeth II, the Duke of Edinburgh and Princess Margaret visited Iona Abbey. They attended the morning service and saw Dr Warr dedicate in the north transept an oak screen which The Queen had gifted when she married the Duke.[15] That same year, MacLeod became a royal chaplain and was elected Moderator of the General Assembly for 1957.[16] As Moderator, he finally became an ex officio member of the Iona Cathedral Trustees, albeit a temporary one.[17]

The royal service was taken to mark the formal ending of the abbey restoration work, and so a new agreement between the Trustees and the Iona Community was required. The latter's

1938 lease of the monastic buildings was extended for a further ten years, as usual without any rent being charged. So what were the Community's intentions for their future on Iona? The focus seemed to some to be shifting away from the island itself to the more readily accessible and thriving Community House in Glasgow, where courses to encourage adolescents and young adults to take part in social and political action were proving popular, as well as the continuing work in disadvantaged urban areas.[18] The young ministers who had acted as labourers had been supposed to leave not only the island but the Community once their service was over, yet many of them were determined to retain their membership even though they were living in their new parishes elsewhere. They accordingly developed into a dispersed, ecumenical community, held together by a shared Rule, the members following an agreed prayer life and meeting together in small groups.[19]

In 1958 fund-raising for electric lighting of the abbey was under way by the Glasgow Women's Electrical Association, led by its president, Lady MacColl. (Plate 31, with small Dr Warr and tall Lady MacColl standing together in the centre of the photograph.) [20] Its installation allowed an extension of the abbey's opening hours, and more and more visitors were arriving both from Britain and from overseas, with the youth camps on Iona and Mull attracting a similar influx. In response to the increasing number of international visitors, more residential accommodation might well have to be built and for the first time, the Trustees and the Community agreed that they would collaborate on a joint appeal. This would mean that they could at least set up a much needed endowment fund to finance future maintenance work. The new Appeal Committee met for the first time in December 1958 and the following year 24,000 Appeal brochures were sent out to British addresses, resulting in donations amounting to £17,000, half of them coming from England. In 1960, the Appeal was extended to the U.S.A., Canada, South Africa and Australia.[21]

The Community continued to lead the services in the abbey itself, and George MacLeod was still interested in beautifying its buildings. In 1955, while on a visit to Texas, he had met Jane Blaffer Owen, a wealthy descendant of Robert Owen, the nineteenth-century socialist and philanthropist. She had been to Iona on several occasions and she had made donations to the Iona Community. She now told MacLeod about an item that she had commissioned from Jacques Lipchitz, the eminent Cubist sculptor. Lipchitz had been approached in 1947 by Father Couturier, of the Modernist Roman Catholic Church of the Dominicans at Assy in Haute Savoie, who wanted a statue of the Virgin Mary. At first Lipchitz had been reluctant to accept the commission, because he came from a Lithuanian Jewish family and the sculpture was to represent a Christian theme. However, he later agreed, believing that true art was universal, and produced a sketch for a bronze sculpture. Entitled 'The Descent of the Spirit', its main features were a dove poised above a representation of the Virgin Mary.

Lipchitz could not afford to have the sculpture cast in bronze, but after seeing a picture of the sketch in a French publication, Mrs Blaffer Owen contacted him and offered to pay for it and for two replicas. Finally completed in 1955, the principal sculpture went to the Dominican church as planned, Mrs Blaffer Owen gave the second to New Harmony, a community founded by Robert Owen in the United States, and Lipchitz kept the third for his daughter. However, Mrs Blaffer Owen now suggested to MacLeod that he purchase that one for Iona, for had not the 8th Duke of Argyll intended people of all Christian denominations to worship there? [22] Although attracted by the ecumenical aspect, when he learned that the price was £7000 MacLeod said that, if the Community had that amount of money, he would be obliged to spend it on the restoration. Mrs Blaffer Owen solved the problem by offering to give £7000 for the restoration work, if MacLeod could find a donor who would pay for the third sculpture.

MacLeod showed photographs of the sculpture to Sir Kenneth Clark, the distinguished art historian, who vouched for its high quality and said that the asking price was reasonable.[23] He also sent photographs to the Trustees. With the exception of Matthew Black, the biblical scholar who was Principal of St Mary's College, St Andrews University and who 'entirely disapproved', they agreed to accept it if a donor could be found.[24] A couple of months later a wealthy builder, Sir John Mactaggart and his wife came forward.[25] According to a note in MacLeod's own papers, on 13 December 1957 the sculpture was shipped on S.S. Dunolly from New York. Landing in Cuba on 28 May, it was transferred to S.S. Venacher, sailed from there on 12 June and finally arrived in Greenock on Christmas Day 1958, having travelled a total distance of 43,370 miles.[26] It was then placed in the centre of the abbey cloister, where it forms a notable feature. (Plate 22)

The following year a request from a Miss Bruce for a statue of Buddha to be put in the abbey was abruptly rejected by the Trustees,[27] but in 1962 Sir David Russell's friend the psychic and author Wellesley Tudor Pole[28] was allowed to present a small statuette of St Michael the Archangel for the Michael Chapel, which had been restored three years earlier.[29] (Plates 30a and b) On the subject of carvings, beginning in 1959 and continuing throughout the 1960s a succession of carvers worked on the capitals of the new cloister pillars. Two of the surviving medieval capitals had been decorated with carved flowers, and this theme was continued, with Iona flora on the north side of the cloister, New Zealand flowers on the south side, American ones on the west and flowers from the Holy Land on the east. As well as an additional thistle and shamrock, there are delicate bird carvings too.[30] (Plates 20a, b, c, d and 21)

The Trustees were particularly concerned about the problem of protecting the highly important carved stones. As we have seen, this had been a longstanding saga, and in 1958 the Carnegie Trust gave a grant of £2,500 towards the reconstruction of the ruins of the free standing monastic infirmary as a museum for them. Even then progress was not easy. Expenditure was higher than Ian Lindsay had estimated, further grants had to be sought from the Carnegie Trust and it was not until 1965 that the building was ready.[31] The final costs of the museum were shared by the Iona Community and the Cathedral Trustees.[32] A later attempt to have the nunnery refectory restored as a more spacious carved stones museum rather grandly called 'a Lapidarium' foundered, largely because of opposition by MacLeod, who feared that fundraising for it would compete with efforts to raise money for other projects.[33]

For some time past there had been thoughts of building a west range to provide more accommodation for the Community's activities and in 1962 work began, to a design by Ian Lindsay. This is the only part of the restored cloister buildings which does not stand on medieval foundations, because of the Benedictine Abbey never having had a complete west range. The new west range is on the site of the monastic kitchen and was ready in 1965, while the nearby ruined bake house was made into a garden.[34] The interior of the abbey church was also improved at this time, with the insertion that year of an important new stained glass window.

In the past, the Trustees had operated a variable policy about stained glass. Sometimes they had agreed that they wanted none at all and when in 1928 Mr A. Campbell Blair had offered them a panel entitled *The Angel Gabriel* by the famous artist Ford Madox Brown, they had rejected it, saying that there was no stained glass in the church.[35] Eight years later Mr Campbell Blair's solicitor wrote to inform them that his client had died and bequeathed the glass panel to them, whereupon Dr Charles Warr told him tersely that, even if a suitable window could be found, it was inconceivable that they would ever desire one characteristic of the Pre-Raphaelite Group of artists. Perhaps he had never liked the beautiful Edward Burne-Jones window in his own cathedral.[36] However, in 1939 Douglas Strachan was commissioned to make a series of clerestory windows donated to the Trustees by several individuals, with depictions of St Columba, St Bride, St Patrick and St Margaret.[37] The new 1965 window is by William Wilson and shows St Columba against a background of doves, a coracle and the isle of Mull. (Plate 23)It is dedicated to the Reverend Kenneth MacLeod, collaborator with Marjory Kennedy-Fraser on their famous collection, *Songs of the Hebrides*.[38]

Ian Lindsay had wished the north transept to have windows with a single image, and that was where it was installed. He died in 1966, having spent twenty-seven years working on the Iona restoration, and the Trustees noted that the night before he passed away he was busy putting the finishing touches to his design for a new guest house.[39] An almost greater shock followed on New Year's Day 1967, when it was announced that George MacLeod, that outspoken socialist, had accepted a life peerage on the nomination of Harold Wilson, the Labour prime minister. He then retired as Leader of the Iona Community, and so did his deputy, Ralph Morton. However, Lord MacLeod continued to be a member, offering his often unwanted advice from then until his death twenty-four years later.[40] Inevitably, as he grew older, his views were seen as being out of date and, although the members shared his dedication to peace campaigning, he was impatient of their endless debates about what they should be doing next. The membership of the Community was changing too, with far more lay people involved in what had originally been very much a clerical brotherhood. In 1969, after a long campaign and despite MacLeod's continuing opposition, the first woman member was accepted: Dr Nancy Brash, a former Church of Scotland medical missionary in India.[41] In 1976, in keeping with the Community's ecumenical commitments, it gained its first Roman Catholic member,[42] and in 2003 the Reverend Kathy Galloway became the first woman leader of the Community.

By this time the Rule of the Iona Community had become

increasingly important as a means of keeping the geographically scattered members together, for some were temporarily working abroad and others lived permanently overseas. The duties they accepted were and are daily prayer and Bible reading, accounting for how they use resources and spend their time, taking action for justice and peace in society and meeting together regularly in groups.[43] The Glasgow Community House moved to Govan in 1977, and developed into an even more active centre for service to disadvantaged areas, as well as becoming the headquarters for the Community's worship resources and other publications. Camas on Mull remained a highly popular outdoor centre, and the guest house on Iona was eventually built. It proved to be a particularly contentious project, for there were fears that any new building of the kind would spoil the look of the abbey, a concern shared by Ian, 11th Duke of Argyll, upon whose lands it would stand. In 1964 the Ministry of Works had initially prohibited its erection but they were later persuaded to agree, provided that it was outside the abbey precincts. There were many arguments and changes of plan along the way, and the building was not finally finished until 1973.[44]

Also in 1973, the 11th Duke of Argyll died. Huge death duties had to be paid and a devastating fire at Inveraray Castle two years later added to the financial problems and led to the sale of the island in 1979. This did not include Iona Abbey, of course, for its properties and the land they stood on are owned by the Trustees. The rest of Iona was purchased by the Hugh Fraser Foundation for £1.5 million and gifted to the nation in memory of Hugh Fraser, 1st Baron Fraser of Allander. The following year, the Secretary of State for Scotland transferred the island into the care of the National Trust for Scotland.[45] Meanwhile, the abbey guest house won a European Architectural Heritage Year Award a year after it was completed and then in 1988 what would be another new award-winning building was opened. This was the MacLeod Centre, planned in celebration of Lord

MacLeod's 90th birthday, three years earlier. Replacing the old youth camps on Iona, it was expressly designed with facilities for young families and for the disabled.[46]

Throughout these years, the Iona Cathedral Trustees continued to struggle with their financial problems, reliant as they still were on fundraising and grants. Maintaining their buildings was an onerous duty which could not be ignored. Only 7% of listed buildings in Scotland were A listed by the Ancient Monuments Commission and the abbey and monastic buildings, St Martin's Cross, St Oran's Chapel and the nunnery all fell into that category, while St Ronan's was B listed. In an attempt to find a solution, the Trustees in 1993 set up a company called Iona Abbey Limited, which was registered as a charity, with the distinguished architect Crichton Lang as chief executive. Its tasks were to maintain, manage and improve the abbey property, raise money, implement the Trustees' policy decisions, appoint professional advisers and liaise with the Iona Community and the National Trust for Scotland.[47]

The new company drew up a business plan, applied for grants and went ahead energetically. In their report for 1997 they were able to declare that 50% of their aims had been achieved. The caphouse of the tower had been very successfully completed, fulfilling one of the 8th Duke of Argyll's ambitions for the abbey church. Repairs to St Ronan's were now finished, preliminary architectural recording work at the nunnery had taken place, there were training courses for young masons and there was a growing sense of partnership with the Iona Community. A temporary problem arose as a result of the number of people trampling over the grass of Reilig Odhráin to visit the grave of John Smith, the Labour Party leader who had been buried there in 1994, but with the permission of the family it was neatly solved by turning the gravestone round so that it could be viewed from the path.

In 1997, there was a memorable occasion when Mary Robinson, the President of Ireland, opened the Cathedral Trust's new

St Columba Exhibition and Welcome Centre at Fionnphort on Mull. It had been funded by large grants from the Heritage Lottery Fund and the European Regional Development Fund Highlands and Islands Objective/Partnership Programme.[48] However, despite all their efforts and despite the previous introduction of mandatory entrance charges to the abbey in June 1994, Iona Abbey Limited was experiencing severe difficulties. The Iona Community still rented the abbey and its buildings free of charge from the Cathedral Trust as they had done from the very start and so it was decided that when the Community's lease was next renewed, it should include a rent for the premises the members used.

A memorandum drawn up at the time noted that the Iona Community provided daily services in the church, including Sunday morning services and evening services, and ran the restored chapter house and library as self-catering accommodation for up to fifty people in shared bedrooms. Their shop was in the north range and their office and enquiry centre in the entirely modern west range, while their coffee house was on the opposite side of the road. As to the Trustees, they did have their own wooden information centre, built in the 1980s, at the entrance to the abbey, but otherwise their occupancy of the buildings was relatively limited. They used part of the Abbot's House as a flat for their workforce and of course there was the museum of carved stones in the infirmary.

In part because of their very visible presence at the abbey, the public have often assumed that it was actually owned by the Iona Community. This misapprehension was no doubt also due to George MacLeod's dominating reputation. He was a very well-known personality and he had done wonderful things for the ruins, his highly successful fundraising making possible the restoration of the east and west ranges and several of the freestanding buildings. However, the donations he raised from the public and indeed the money given by him had not been the sole sources of income and in any case the 8th Duke of

165

Argyll's Trust Deed made it impossible for the ownership to be transferred from the Trustees to anyone else, even if they had wanted to dispose of it. Ensuing discussions about the lease were inevitably complicated and difficult. The Community argued that that it could not possibly afford to pay a commercial rent, and in any case believed that its part in the restoration of the abbey and its buildings gave it the moral right to occupy them free of charge.

The Trustees, for their part, were very conscious that the Community was fulfilling the terms of the 8th Duke of Argyll's Trust Deed by maintaining a living Christian witness on Iona, to the satisfaction and with the support of the Church of Scotland. (Plate 32) However, on their behalf Iona Abbey Limited had to point out that, despite its prodigious efforts, there was a serious financial deficit which could not go on without assured funding support for the vital work of maintenance. The Community, it believed, had various flourishing commercial outlets at the abbey and so surely it could pay.[49] The problem became all too clear when, in 1997, Iona Abbey Limited sent out an appeal to 190 of the top 500 companies in Scotland. Sympathetic replies came in, but only five donations were received, amounting to £2,400.[50]

In August 1998, the Trustees began to explore a new way out of the impasse. On their behalf, Iona Abbey Limited approached Historic Scotland, an executive agency of the government within the Scottish Development Department, to see if it might somehow take over the abbey and the monastic buildings. Iona Abbey Ltd would then be wound up, and Historic Scotland would give a commercial lease to the Iona Community. The Trustees' hopes for the future rested on this possible partnership, with the local Iona people also involved.[51]

Negotiations continued throughout 1999, one of the main stumbling blocks being that, because of the terms of the 1899 Trust Deed, the Trustees were not allowed to dispose of the abbey properties, while Historic Scotland could do nothing unless a formal role for themselves with regard to the abbey and its buildings was legally established. They were worried, too, about the Iona Community's Justice and Peace displays of placards and posters inside and around the abbey because, as a government agency, they could not be seen as being anything other than politically neutral. At the same time, the Community were anxious in case the abbey became nothing more than just another tourist attraction with no spiritual element to it. Finally, on 17 September 1999, a tripartite agreement was in place and Donald Dewar, the Scottish First Minister, was able to announce that Iona Abbey and its buildings had been taken into the care of Historic Scotland, which had been granted by the Iona Cathedral Trust a lease for 175 years. Historic Scotland would, in turn, give a commercial lease to the Iona Community.[52]

The long-running problem of maintenance had at last been solved. After an initial major survey by architects and engineers, Historic Scotland now undertakes an inspection of all the buildings every year and a major condition survey every five years. Their dedicated labour squad of masons, male and female, lives on Iona. Carved stones requiring attention, such as fragments of particularly significant high crosses, can be taken to Edinburgh for specialist conservation. As a result of a conference hosted by the Iona Community in 2012, fresh reassessments of the artefacts emerged and plans were made for a major archaeological research project. A new and much improved display of the carved stones was developed in time for the 2013 anniversary of Columba's arrival on Iona, while information panels based on the latest research were placed throughout the abbey site.

The Iona Community continues to flourish. During the period 2010–12 there were over 200 members and around 1500 Associates, with a similar number of worldwide Friends.[53] Increasingly, it has come to enjoy an international reputation. It is widely known throughout the English-speaking world and beyond as a leading provider of worship resources, with the Reverend John Bell and other popular hymn writers gaining great acclaim. Through its visitors, the Island Centres have important international links too, with churches in Germany, Sweden, the United States, Canada and the Netherlands. The services in the abbey church constantly evolve, for at a time when congregations of all denominations are dwindling, it is important to try out different forms of worship as a way of engaging both new and former churchgoers. An increased emphasis on the environment and on homely, everyday things is attractive to many, including admirers of what is usually termed 'Celtic Christianity',[54] drawn as they are by a desire to get back to a simpler, more spiritual way of life than that which organised religion has sometimes seemed to offer.[55] (Plate 24)

The restored monastic buildings continue to welcome people eager to experience communal life, engage in wide-ranging discussions, take part in craftwork and outdoor activities and, for some, find a sanctuary from their problems, spiritual, psychological or physical. Camas, with its cottages beside a remote bay on the Ross of Mull, provides outdoor and adventure holidays. At one time pilgrims regarded Iona as the climax of their journey, but now the Iona Community thinks of it rather as a place of inspiration where visitors can spend time and then, invigorated by what they have experienced, go back out into the world to work for justice, peace and Christian living. The administrative headquarters, with the Wild Goose publishing and resource centre, are still in Govan, where George MacLeod first developed so many of his ideas, and from there many important urban youth schemes are organised.

So what of Iona Cathedral Trustees? Considering both the effective removal of much of their original purpose and the relevance of their membership for present day needs, the Trust decided to undertake a reorganisation with the advice of OSCR., the Office of the Scottish Charity Regulator. This was effected in 2010 and, as a result, the Trustees added the following significant new purpose to their remit: 'to advance the education of the public in relation to the history, culture and heritage of Iona Cathedral and the island of Iona'. The membership of the Trust was also varied, to make it ecumenical and ensure that each Trustee had a real interest in Iona. As a result, the Trustees appointed at that time included not only, as before, the Moderator, Principal Clerk and Procurator of the Church of Scotland, the Minister of St Giles' Cathedral and the Principal of Aberdeen University, but also the Roman Catholic and Episcopal Bishops of Argyll and the Isles, a member of the Community Council of Iona and an additional appointment from the Church of Scotland. The Leader of the Iona Community and a representative of Historic Scotland attend Trustees' meetings. A good spirit of co-operation is very evident in these meetings, and in the improved relationship with the Iona residents, who had so often in the past felt left out of what was going on. Representatives of all the interested parties were fully involved in the plans for the 1450th anniversary of Columba's arrival and the concurrent 75th anniversary of the founding of the Iona Community.

Would the long history of Iona Abbey still be remembered and celebrated were it not for the recollection of St Columba himself? Almost mysteriously, this charismatic saint's reputation has persisted for almost one and a half thousand years, his monastery surviving rebuilding, collapse, more rebuilding, the changes of the Reformation, neglect, further restoration and what is often described as the secularisation of twenty-first century Britain. Historic Scotland estimates that one third of the 50,000 to 60,000 visitors who come to Iona each year are motivated by faith or at least by an interest in spiritual matters. Likewise, in casual conversation, a surprising number of Scots, both young and old, speak fondly of the island, recalling past visits and proudly mentioning Columba's name.

Perhaps this may be in part because, just as the abbey church and its monastic buildings have adapted to changing circumstances, so has Columba's reputation been transformed throughout the centuries. As we have seen, in his own day and until at least the Reformation he was regarded as a strong protector who, even after death, could actively intervene in worldly affairs. Formidable, even combative, and impressively learned, he was seen as being at the same time perceptive, sympathetic and understanding. Pilgrims from Ireland and Western Europe travelled to his shrine, prayed to him for assistance, and believed that he could bring them victory in battle. Those attitudes could have been expected to end when the Reformers discarded saints, altars and prayers for the dead, but Columba's name was still revered and people still came to Iona, ignoring the dangers of sea crossings in small boats and the discomfort of having to sleep on hay in barns because there was no other accommodation. Some were already familiar with tales of Columba's life and many listened intently as islanders, knowing what tourists like, told them highly-coloured stories of a fierce and severe abbot with a personality akin to that attributed to John Knox in our own time.

Admiring this Irish saint and believing him to have been the first missionary to bring Christianity to Scotland, nineteenth-century Protestants transformed him into a mild, dove-like figure, whose gentle personality would support the troubled and the sick. These differing ideas are neatly epitomised by the two stained glass images of him in Iona Abbey. Douglas Strachan's handwritten notes about his clerestory window say that he wanted to convey Columba's vigour 'as of the sea wind', his severity and his saintliness, while William Wilson's Columba is a slender, contemplative figure who gazes thoughtfully into the distance as he clasps a holy book and holds a cross.

A number of Scottish churches over the years have been dedicated to St Columba and some retain that dedication. To look at just one denomination, *The Church of Scotland Yearbook 2012–13* records that sixteen of its churches in Scotland, mainly in the west, a well-known one in London and another in Jersey are still called St Columba's (or St Colm's).[56] This may seem to be a rather paltry number, but of course many churches in recent years have been deconsecrated, put to other purposes or even demolished. As a result, a further ten are noted in the list of discontinued parishes Moreover, a quick search of the Internet reveals far more existing churches, schools and colleges in Britain, Ireland and the rest of the English-speaking world. Some are undoubtedly nineteenth- or early-twentieth century foundations, and they range from the Cathedral Church of St Columba in Oban, seat of the Roman Catholic Bishop of Argyll and the Isles, to St Columba's Church in Dehli and Adelaide's St Columba College, the first joint Roman Catholic and Anglican educational project in Australia. The many other organisations to use St Columba's name include care homes, retreat centres and a well-known Edinburgh hospice. There is even a waterfall in Tasmania called St Columba's Falls and a Scottish country dance named 'St Columba's Strathspey'.

It can also be instructive to look at personal names. After the introduction of the statutory registration of births, marriages and deaths in Scotland in 1855, the first baby boy to have Columba as a first or middle name was born in 1888 and was a Patrick Columba Hughes, son of the captain's clerk on H.M.S. Ajax. A regular trickle of similar examples followed, reaching a climax in 1955–74 with seventy instances and then tailing off abruptly to none at all in 2009–11. When it was a middle name, the baby's first name was often Irish, suggesting a Roman Catholic family background.

For the most part, 'Columba' was not considered to be appropriate for girls, although in fact a dozen daughters had it registered as a middle name and one was even given it as her first name. Lacking a conventional feminine equivalent, it is also worth considering for a moment the popular name 'Iona'. The first example of that came in 1855, with Iona Mary Caskie, tenth child of an Edinburgh hat manufacturer, while Iona Mary Hutcheson Robertson, daughter of a Glasgow cloth worker, was born in 1863 on a steamboat on the River Clyde between Greenock and Bowling. By the decade from 1995 to 2004 there had been 1,922 examples, with the latest available statistic, for 2009–2011, standing at 621.[57] As a personal name, 'Iona' does not necessarily have any religious connotations, of course. A significant proportion of those who chose it will have had happy memories of a holiday in the area and more than a few will simply think that the name is pretty. However, it seems likely that some have had more than that in mind.

George MacLeod sometimes deprecated the notion that he had chosen Iona as the place for his social experiment because of its spiritual atmosphere, preferring to emphasise the practical motives for its selection. In fact, he once said firmly that the word 'Iona' conjured up for him neither its history nor its abbey but the island itself.[58] Three years after the inception of the Iona Community, he was eager to point out that it had not been created because of some spurious desire to return to the past but to meet the urgent needs of the mainland.[59] However, it was also he who made the famous remark that, on Iona, only a paper as thin as tissue separates the material from the spiritual and this is a feeling shared by a significant number of its visitors. The dramatic scenery is a great attraction but, for believers and non-believers alike, it can be merely one element in their response, for there is often something beyond aesthetic appreciation. The blue green waters, the pebbled shore, the distant blue mountains, the peace of the abbey church and the memory of the saint himself, however he is imagined, fierce warrior or friendly presence, merge in a spiritual experience which draws them back, time and again, to Columba's Iona.

Notes

Chapter 1 – Columba: Fox or Dove?

1 The description comes from Irish verses in The Lebar Brecc, a medieval manuscript in the Royal Irish Academy Library, said to be copied from an earlier manuscript and quoted in A.O. Anderson, *Early Sources of Scottish History AD 500–1286* (Stamford 1990 edn), 27.

2 *Adomnán's Life of Columba*, edd A.O.Anderson and Marjorie Ogilvie Anderson (Oxford, 1991 edn), 239.

3 Máire Herbert, 'Columba (*c.*521–597)', *Oxford Dictionary of National Biography*, Oxford University Press, 2004 [http://www.oxforddnb.com/view/article/6001, accessed 31 January 2012].

4 *Amra Choluimb Chille* ('The Elegy of Colum Cille'), printed in Thomas Owen Clancy and Gilbert Márkus, *Iona: The Earliest Poetry of a Celtic Monastery* (Edinburgh 2003 edn), 96–128; 'The Irish Life of Colum Cille', printed in Máire Herbert, *Iona, Kells and Derry: The History and Hagiography of the Monastic Familia of Columba* (Oxford 1988), 180–202; Bede, *The Ecclesiastical History of the English People* edd Judith McClure and Roger Collins (Oxford 2008), 114–15, 157, 158, 159, 248, 284, 291, 386. See also James Bruce, *Prophecy, Miracles, Angels and Heavenly Light? The Eschatology, Pneumatology and Missiology of Adomnán's Life of Columba* (Milton Keynes, 2004), 1–37, 218–36.

5 Herbert, *Iona, Kells and Derry*, 19–25, 134–42; James Fraser, *From Caledonia to Pictland*, (Edinburgh 2009), 3–6.

6 Herbert, 'Columba', *ODNB*; Cormac Bourke, 'Northern Flames: Remembering Columba and Adomnán' in *History Ireland*, vii, no 3 (Autumn 1999), 13.

7 Fergus Kelly, 'Niall Noígíallach (d. *c.*452)', *Oxford Dictionary of National Biography*, Oxford University Press, 2004 [http:// www.oxforddnb.com/view/article/20074, accessed 9 July 2012]; Brian Lacey,

'The "Amra Coluimb Cille" and the Uí Néill' in *The Journal of the Royal Society of Antiquaries of Ireland*, cxxxiv (2004), 169–72.

8 Herbert, *Iona, Kells and Derry*, 251 n.12; Adomnán, *Life*, xv.

9 Adomnán, *Life*, p. xxix, 7, 239.

10 Ibid., 183–5.

11 Ibid., p.xxix; Fraser, *Caledonia to Pictland*, 69.

12 James MacKillop, *Oxford Dictionary of Celtic Mythology* (Oxford 1998), 111–12; *Mari Elspeth nic Bryan (Kathleen M. O'Brien), 'Index of Names in Irish Annals: Crimthann/Criomthann' at http:// medievalscotland.org/kmo/AnnalsIndex/Masculine/Crimthann.shtml.*

13 *Adomnán of Iona; Life of St Columba* ed Richard Sharpe (Oxford 1995), 10.

14 Adomnán, *Life*, 5.

15 Brian Lacey, 'Constructing Colum Cille' in *Irish Arts Review*, xxi (Autumn 2004), 121.

16 Peter Parkes, 'Celtic Fosterage: Adoptive Kinship and Clientage in Northwest Europe' in *Comparative Studies in Society and History*, xlviii, no.2 (April 2006), 370–4.

17 Adomnán, *Life*, 185.

18 Ibid., p.xxix, 13, 95, 187n.; Herbert, *Iona, Kells and Derry*, 181.

19 Lacey, 'Constructing Colum Cille', 122.

20 Herbert, *Iona, Kells and Derry*, 190, 256 n.35.

21 David Farmer, *Oxford Dictionary of Saints* (Oxford 2011 edn), 294–5; Alison Jones, *The Wordsworth Dictionary of Saints* (Ware, 1992), 172–3; 'St Martin of Tours' in http://www.catholic.org/saints/ saint.php?saint_id=81; Léon Clugnet, 'St Martin of Tours', in *The Catholic Encyclopaedia* (1910), accessed 30 August 2012 from New Advent: http://www.newadvent.org/cathen/09732b.htm; 'St Martin of Tours' in *Catholic Online,* http://www.catholic.org/saints/saint. php?saint_id=81.

22 Adomnán, *Life*, pp.lvii, lxvii.

23 Alfred P. Smyth, *Warlords and Holy Men, Scotland AD 80–1000* (Edinburgh 1989), 94–5, 98–9.

24 Herbert, *Iona, Kells and Derry*, 27–8; Alan Macquarrie, *The Saints of Scotland: Essays in Scottish Church History, AD450–1093* (Edinburgh 1997), 75; Adomnán, *Life*, pp.xxxvi–xxxviii.

25 Adomnán, *Life*, 185.

26 Herbert, *Iona, Kells and Derry*, 27–8; Ian Bradley, *Columba, Pilgrim and Penitent,* (Glasgow 1996), 21.

27 Bede, *Ecclesiastical History*, 115.

Notes

28 Adomnán, *Life*, 7; Herbert, *Iona, Kells and Derry*, 27–8; Gilbert Márkus, 'Iona: monks, pastors and missionaries' in *Spes Scotorum: Hope of the Scots; St Columba, Iona and Scotland* ed. Dauvit Broun and Thomas Owen Clancy (Edinburgh 1999), 132–3.

29 'Amra', in Clancy and Márkus, *Iona: The Earliest Poetry*, 96–128.

30 Adomnán, *Life*, p.xxxi; Herbert, *Iona, Kells and Derry*, 28–9; *c.f.* Ewan Campbell, *Saints and Sea-Kings: The First Kingdom of the Scots* (Edinburgh 1999), 31–2.

31 Nicholas Evans, 'The Calculation of Columba's Arrival in Britain in Bede's *Ecclesiastical History* and the Pictish King-lists' in *The Scottish Historical Review*, lxxxvii, 2, no.224 (October 2008), 183–205.

32 Adomnán, *Life*, p.xxxi.

33 The Royal Commission on the Ancient and Historical Monuments of Scotland, *Argyll: An Inventory of the Monuments, Volume 4, Iona* (Edinburgh 1982; hereafter cited as *RCAHMS Iona*), 1.

34 Anna Ritchie and Ian Fisher, *Iona Abbey and Nunnery* (Historic Scotland 2001), 32.

35 *RCAHMS Iona*, 4.

36 Herbert, *Iona, Kells and Derry*, 261 n.51.

37 See, for example, Jerry O'Sullivan, 'Iona archaeological investigations 1875–1996' in *Spes Scotorum*, 221, 240.

38 *RCAHMS Iona*, 31–4; *Adomnán of Iona*, ed. Sharpe, 70.

39 Finbar McCormick, 'Iona: The View from Ireland', paper given at Iona Conference 2012, http://www.ionahistory.org.uk/researchconference.

40 Adomnán, *Life*, p.xlvi; *RCAHMS Iona*, 37; O'Sullivan, 'Iona archaeological investigations', 237–8; John G. Dunbar and Ian Fisher, *Iona: A Guide to the Monuments* (Edinburgh 1995 edn.), 40.

41 *Adomnán of Iona*, ed. Sharpe, 69.

42 Adomnán, *Life*, 225.

43 Ibid., p. xlvii, 211.

44 Ibid., p. lii.

45 Ibid., 31, 49, 169, 201.

46 Kenneth Veitch, 'The Columban Church in Northern Britain, 664–717: a reassessment', in *Proceedings of the Society of Antiquaries of Scotland*, 127 (1997), 627–47.

47 James Bulloch, *The Life of the Celtic Church* (Edinburgh 1963), 134.

48 Adomnán, *Life*, 199.

49 John A. Duke, *The Columban Church* (Edinburgh 1957 ed.), 126; Carol Farr, *The Book of Kells, its Function and Audience* (London 1997), 41–2.

50 Clancy and Márkus, *Iona: Earliest Poetry*, 39–68; Jane Stevenson, 'Altus Prosator' in *Celtica* 23 (Dublin 1999), 326–68.

51 Bulloch, *Life of the Celtic Church*, 137–8.

52 Duke, *The Columban Church*, 124–6; Bulloch, *Life of the Celtic Church*, 133.

53 Adomnán, *Life*, 63, 109, 139, 201, 203.

54 Ibid., 117, 203.

55 Clancy and Márkus, *Iona: Earliest Poetry*, 39–40, 107; Adomnán, *Life*, 53.

56 Clancy and Márkus, *Iona: Earliest Poetry*, 109.

57 Adomnán, *Life*, 53.

58 Ibid., 51.

59 Ibid., 136–7.

60 Ibid., 197.

61 *RCAHMS Iona* 39–40.

62 Adomnán, *Life*, 27, 53, 61, 79.

63 Fraser, *Caledonia to Pictland*, 76.

64 E.J. Gwynn and W. J. Purton, The Monastery of Tallaght' in *Proceedings of the Royal Irish Academy: Section C: Archaeology, Celtic Studies, History, Linguistics, Literature*, xxix (1911–12), 115–16; Adomnán, *Life*, p.xlix; Campbell, *Saints and Sea-Kings*, 45.

65 Finbar McCormick *et al.*, 'Early Christian metalworking on Iona: excavations under the 'infirmary' in 1990' in *Proceedings of the Society of Antiquaries of Scotland*, cxxii (1992), 207–14.

66 Adomnán, *Life*, pp. li, 137.

67 Donald E. Meek, *The Quest for Celtic Christianity*, (Haddington 2000), 148.

68 Adomnán, *Life*, pp. xlix–l

69 Finbar McCormick 'Iona: the view from Ireland', www.ionahistory. org.uk/iona_fmccormick summary.doc.

70 Pamela O'Neill, 'When Onomastics Met Archaeology: A Tale of Two Hinbas' in *The Scottish Historical Review*, lxxxvii, 1, no.223 (April 2008), 26–41.

71 Adomnán, *Life*, 83, 221.

72 Ibid., 197, 215.

73 Adomnán, *Life*, 83.

74 *RCAHMS Iona*, 45; Adomnán, *Life*, 81.

75 Márkus, 'Iona: monks, pastors and missionaries' in *Spes Scotorum*, 123.

76 *RCAHMS Iona*, 44.

77 Adomnán, *Life*, 69, 221–3.

Notes

Chapter 2 – St Columba's Legacy

1 Adomnán, *Life*, 189–91.
2 *Adomnán of Iona*, ed. Sharpe, 26.
3 Adomnán, *Life*, pp. xvii–xviii; *Adomnán of Iona*, ed Sharpe, 26–7; Herbert, *Iona, Kells and Derry*, 29.
4 Adomnán, *Life*, 125–7.
5 Ibid., 137.
6 Ibid., 165–7.
7 Ibid., 87.
8 e.g., T. O. Clancy, 'The real St Ninian', in *Innes Review*, number 52.1, 1–28.
9 Dauvit Broun, 'Ninian [St Ninian] (*supp. fl.* 5th–6th century)', *Oxford Dictionary of National Biography*, Oxford University Press, 2004 [http://www.oxforddnb.com/view/article/20198, accessed 12 June 2012]; Fraser, *Caledonia to Pictland*, 71; Bede, *Ecclesiastical History*, 114–5, 386 n.115.
10 Adomnán, *Life*, 167.
11 Ibid., 147.
12 Ibid., 133.
13 Ibid., 71; Psalm 44 in the Vulgate, 45 in the King James Bible.
14 Fraser, *Caledonia to Pictland*, 97–105.
15 Ibid., 237, 257–9.
16 Ibid., 79–80; Márkus, 'Iona, Monks, Pastors and Missionaries', 122–3; Adomnán, *Life*, 155–7.
17 Adomnán, *Life*, p. xxxii , 37, 47, 63, 109, 119, 129, 189, 207, 209; Márkus, 'Iona, Monks, Pastors and Missionaries', 132; *Adomnán of Iona*, ed Sharpe, 21–2; Herbert, *Iona, Kells and Derry*, 33.
18 Adomnán, *Life*, p. xxxv.
19 Ibid., 37, 57.
20 Herbert, *Iona, Kells and* Derry, 32–4; Adomnán, *Life*, 57.
21 Adomnán, *Life*, 221–3.
22 Psalm 34 in the King James Bible.
23 Adomnán, *Life*, 221–231.
24 *RCAHMS Iona*, 42; Ritchie and Fisher, *Iona Abbey and Nunnery*, 7.
25 John Bannerman, '*Comarba Coluim Chille* and the Relics of Columba' in *The Innes Review*, xliv, no.1 (1993), 20–1.
26 *Treasures of Heaven: Saints, Relics and Devotion in Medieval Europe* ed Martina Bagnoli *et al.*, (London 2011), 19–22.
27 Anderson, *Early Sources of Scottish History*, i, 263.

28 Bannerman, '*Comarba Coluim Chille*, 20–1.

29 David H Caldwell, 'The Monymusk Reliquary: the *Brecchennach of St Columba*' in *Proceedings of the Society of Antiquaries of Scotland*, cxxxi (2001), 267–82.

30 Herbert, *Iona, Kells and Derry*, 37–40.

31 Meek, *Celtic Christianity*, 165–7.

32 Herbert, *Iona, Kells and Derry*, 24–26, 43; John Bannerman, '*Comarba Coluim Chille*', 23; Fraser, *Caledonia to Pictland*, 98.

33 Henry Mayr-Harting, 'Áedán (*d.* 651)', *Oxford Dictionary of National Biography*, Oxford University Press, 2004 [http://www.oxforddnb.com/view/article/223, accessed 13 Dec 2012]; D. J. Craig, 'Oswald [St Oswald] (603/4–642), *Oxford Dictionary of National Biography*, Oxford University Press, 2004 [http://www.oxforddnb.co/view/article/20916, accessed 31 July 2012]; Bede, *Ecclesiastical History*, 105–114; Fraser, *Caledonia to Pictland*, 116–9.

34 Fraser, *Caledonia to Pictland*, 82; Bede, *Ecclesiastical History*, 103–5; Herbert, *Iona, Kells and Derry*, 40–1.

35 Bede, *Ecclesiastical History*, 153–8; Veitch, 'The Columban Church in northern Britain, 664–717', 628–30; Fraser, *Caledonia to Pictland*, 190–2; Herbert, *Iona, Kells and Derry*, 45–6.

36 Máirín Ní Dhonnchadha, 'Adomnán [St Adomnán] (627/8?–704)', *Oxford Dictionary of National Biography*, Oxford University Press, 2004 [http://www.oxforddnb.com/view/article/110, accessed 26 July 2012].

37 Herbert, *Iona, Kells and Derry*, 48–9.

38 Dhonnchadha, 'Adomnán' in *ODNB*; Herbert, *Iona, Kells and Derry*, 48.

39 Bede, *Ecclesiastical History*, 262–3.

40 Smith, *Warlords and Holy Men*, 131.

41 Herbert, *Iona, Kells and* Derry, 49–50.

42 Thomas O'Loughlin, 'The Library of Iona in the Late Seventh Century: The Evidence from Adomnán's "de Locis Sanctis"' in *Ériu*, xlv (1994), 33–52; Adomnán, *Life*, xl; Fraser, *Caledonia to Pictland*, 338.

43 Bede, *Ecclesiastical History*, 262–6.

44 Dhonnchadha, 'Adomnán' in *ODNB*.

45 Gilbert Márkus, *Adomnán's 'Law of the Innocents'* (Kilmartin, 2008); Herbert, *Iona, Kells and Derry*, 50–2; Adomnán, *Life*, p. xii; Dhonnchadha, 'Adomnán' in *ODNB*; Fraser, *Caledonia to Pictland*, 249, 257; Veitch, 'The Columban Church in northern Britain, 664–717', 634–5.

46 Herbert, *Iona, Kells and Derry*, 53, 138–44.
47 Adomnán, *Life*, 175.
48 O'Sullivan, 'Iona: archaeological investigations', 237–8.
49 Ritchie and Fisher, *Iona Abbey and Nunnery*, 21.
50 Bede, *Ecclesiastical History*, 116, 286–8.
51 Veitch, 'The Columban Church in northern Britain, 664–717', 635–42; Fraser, *Caledonia to Pictland*, 277–82.
52 Fraser, *Caledonia to Pictland*, 368.

Chapter 3 – Visual Arts and Vikings

1 David Stephenson, *Mull and Iona: A Landscape Fashioned by Geology* (Scottish Natural Heritage 2011), 21.
2 M. Macleod Banks, 'A Hebridean Version of Colum Cille and St Oran' in *Folklore*, xlii, no.1 (March 1931), 55–60; *Adomnán of Iona*, ed. Sharpe, 360–2.
3 *RCAHMS* Iona, 17–19; Ritchie and Fisher, *Iona Abbey and Nunnery*, 8–9; Campbell, *Saints and Sea-kings*, 40–3; Bulloch, *Life of the Celtic Church*, 117.
4 See for example Robert B. K. Stevenson, 'The Chronology and Relationship of Some Irish and Scottish Crosses' in *The Journal of the Royal Society of Antiquaries of Ireland*, vol.86, no.1 (1956), 84–96; Isabel Henderson, *The Picts* (London 1967), 134; Roger Stalley, 'European Art and the Irish High Crosses' in *Proceedings of the Royal Irish Academy. Section C: Archaeology, Celtic Studies, History Linguistics, Literature*, vol. 90C (1990), 135–58; McCormick, 'Iona: The View from Ireland', unpaginated; Campbell, *Saints and Sea-kings*, 40.
5 Campbell, *Saints and Sea-kings*, 50–1; Trinity College, Dublin, illuminations from the Book of Durrow: http://www.unc.edu/celtic/catalogue/manuscripts/durrow.html .
6 The Trinity College website, http://www.tcd.ie/about/trinity/bookofkells.
7 Susan Bioletti *et al.*, ' The examination of the Book of Kells using micro-Raman spectroscopy' in *Journal of Raman Spectroscopy* 2009, 40, 1043–49, published online in Wylie Interscience, 11 March 2009, www.interscience.wiley.com; 'Project: The Book of Kells: A New Pigment Study', www.eu-artech.org/files/Book_Report.pdf; 'Analysis of the Book of Kells'; www.tsd.ie/Library/preservation/research/analysis-book-kells.php; Bernard Meehan, *The Book of Kells* (London and Milan 2012), 224–5.

8 Paul Meyvaert, 'The Book of Kells and Iona' in *The Art Bulletin*, vol. lxxi, no1 (March 1989), 6–19; *RCAHMS Iona*, 47; Farr, *The Book of Kells*, 26, 41–3, 140–55; Stalley, 'Investigating the Book of Kells', 94–7; Meehan, *Book of Kells*, 20.

9 Fraser, *Caledonia to Pictland*, 369; Ritchie and Fisher, *Iona Abbey and Nunnery*, 34.

10 Bulloch, *Life of the Celtic Church*, 212.

11 Herbert, *Iona, Kells and Derry*, 68.

12 Fraser, *Caledonia to Pictland*, 369; Smith, *Warlords and Holy Men*, 146–7.

13 Anderson, *Early Sources of Scottish History*, i, 263–5; Bannerman, '*Comarba Coluim Chille*, 20.

14 *Treasures of Heaven*, 22–3; Bannerman, '*Comarba Coluim Chille*', 18.

15 Bannerman, '*Comarba Coluim Chille*', 29.

16 Kenneth Veitch, 'The Alliance between Church and State in Early Medieval Alba' in *Albion: A Quarterly Journal Concerned with British Studies*, xxx, no.2 (1998), 193–8; Smith, *Warlords and Holy Men*, 180–6; John Bannerman, 'The Scottish takeover of Pictland and the relics of Columba' in *Spes Scotorum*, 92.

17 Ritchie and Fisher, *Iona Abbey*, 44–5.

18 Bannerman, '*Comarba Coluim Chille*', 32.

19 Marjorie O. Anderson, 'Kenneth I (*d.* 858)', *Oxford Dictionary of National Biography,* Oxford University Press, 2004 [http:/www.oxforddnb.com/view/article/15398, accessed 20 August 2012].

20 *RCAHMS Iona*, 47; Fraser, *Caledonia to Pictland*, 337.

21 Smith, 'Warlords and Holy Men', 190–1; Bannerman, '*Comarba Coluim Chille*', 33–4.

22 Anderson, *Early Sources of Scottish History*, i, 342–4.

23 *RCAHMS Iona*, 190

24 John Marsden, *Somerled and the Emergence of Gaelic Scotland* (Edinburgh 2008), 20; Meek, *Celtic Christianity*, 183.

25 'Life of St Margaret, Queen of Scotland, by Turgot, Bishop of St Andrews' in Anderson, *Early Sources of Scottish History*, ii, 59–60; Alan Macquarrie, *The Saints of Scotland: Essays in Scottish Church History A.D.450–1093* (Edinburgh 1997), 214–5; Rosalind K. Marshall, *Scottish Queens, 1034–1714*, (East Linton 2003), 8–13; J.O. Prestwich, 'Orderic Vitalis (1075–*c*.1142)', *Oxford Dictionary of National Biography*, Oxford University Press, 2004 [http://www.oxforddnb.com/view/article/20812, accessed 23 March 2012]; *St*

Margaret, Queen of Scotland and her Chapel ed. Charles Robertson (Edinburgh 2012 edn), 29, n.9.

26 Marsden, *Somerled*, 123–4.

27 T. O. Clancy, 'Iona, Scotland and the Céli Dé in *Scotland in Dark Age Britain* ed. Barbara C. Crawford (St Andrews 1996), 111–29.

28 *The Triumph Tree: Scotland's Earliest Poetry* edd T. O. Clancy and Gilbert Márkus (Edinburgh 1998), 185.

29 *RCAHMS Iona*, 49.

30 Marsden, Somerled, 111–3; W. D. H. Sellar, 'Somerled (*d.*1164)', *Oxford Dictionary of National Biography*, Oxford University Press, 2004 [http://www.oxforddnb.com/view/article/26782, accessed 21 August 2012].

31 Marsden, *Somerled*, 117–19.

32 Andrew McDonald, 'Scoto-Norse Kings and the Reformed Religious Orders: Patterns of Monastic Patronage in Twelfth-Century Galloway and Argyll' in *Albion: A Quarterly Journal Concerned with British Studies*, xxvii, no.2 (1995), 206–7.

33 *Oxford Dictionary of Saints*, 42–3; *Wordsworth Dictionary of Saints*, 45–6; H. Ford, 'St Benedict of Nursia' in *The Catholic Encyclopaedia* (New York 1907), accessed from New Advent, [http//www.newadvent.org.cathen/02467b.htm].

34 David Knowles, *The Monastic Order in England* (London 1940, reprinted 1976), 1–15; D. H. Turner, 'This Little Rule for Beginners' in *The Benedictines in Britain*, British Library Series No.3 (London 1980), 10–13; David Knowles, *The Benedictines* (London 1930, reprinted Eugene, USA, 2009), 1–21; for an easily accessible summary of the Rule, see George Cyprian Alston, 'Rule of St. Benedict' in *The Catholic Encyclopaedia.*, vol. 2. (1907), New Advent, accessed. 31 August 2012, [http://www.newadvent.org/cathen/02436a.htm].

35 I. B. Cowan, *The Medieval Church in Scotland* ed. James Kirk, (Edinburgh 1995), 158–60.

36 Marsden, *Somerled,* 126; D. H. Turner, 'Guests, who are never lacking in a Monastery' in *Benedictines in Britain*, 56; Knowles, *Monastic Order*, 475–9.

37 *The Heads of Religious Houses in Scotland from Twelfth to Sixteenth Centuries* ed. D. R. Watt and N. F. Shead (Edinburgh 2001), 111; *Annals of Ulster* ed. B. MacCarthy (1887–94), ii, 240–2.

Chapter 4 – Black Monks and Black Nuns

1 I. B. Cowan and D. E. Easson, *Medieval Religious Houses* (London 1976), 59; Marsden, *Somerled*, 124; Derick S. Thomson, 'Gaelic Learned Orders and Literati in Medieval Scotland' in *Scottish Studies*, xii, part 1 (1968), 66; *Handbook of British Chronology*, ed. F. M. Powicke and E. B. Fryde (London 1961), 294.

2 Marsden, *Somerled*, 124–6; McDonald, 'Scoto-Norse Kings and the Reformed Religious Orders', 208; Bannerman, '*Comarba Coluim Chille*', 45–6.

3 Marsden, *Somerled*, 128.

4 E.g. George Douglas Campbell, 8th Duke of Argyll, *Iona* (London 1870), 84–5.

5 *RCAHMS Iona*, 21.

6 Stephenson, *Mull and Iona: A Landscape Fashioned by Geology*, 2, 3, 19–21.

7 *RCAHMS Iona*, 245–51.

8 Marsden, *Somerled*, 129–30.

9 Ibid., 157 n.17; Smyth, *Warlords and Holy Men*, 85.

10 *RCAHMS Iona*, 22–3, 49–52, 58–62, 143.

11 Ibid., 23, 49; Jerry O'Sullivan, 'Archaeological Investigations 1875–1996' in *Spes Scotorum*, 231.

12 Knowles, *Monastic Order*, 450; Christopher Golden, 'Benedictine Order' (2002), http://www.aedificium.org/MonasticLife/Benedictine-Order.html.

13 Knowles, *Monastic Order*, 411–17. This is Psalm 5 in both the Vulgate and King James translations of the Bible.

14 *RCAHMS Iona*, 130.

15 Ibid., 130–1.

16 Knowles, *Monastic Order*, 456–65; *RCAHMS Iona*, 130–1.

17 *RCAHMS Iona*, 138.

18 Ibid., 21, 131–2.

19 McCormick, 'Early Christian metalworking on Iona', 213; O'Sullivan, 'Archaeological Investigations', 234.

20 *RCAHMS Iona*, 244–5.

21 Cowan, *Medieval Church in Scotland*, 160; R. Andrew McDonald, 'The Foundation and Patronage of Nunneries by Native Elites in Twelfth- and Early Thirteenth-Century Scotland' in *Women in Scotland c.1100-c.1750* (East Linton 1999) 3–15.

22 *Oxford Dictionary of Saints*, 31–2; *Wordsworth Dictionary*

of Saints, 35–6;*The Confessions of St Augustine* transl. Maria Boulding (Guernsey 1999), 9–33; D. Dunford, 'Canoness' and Anthony Allaria, 'Canons and Canonesses Regular' in *The Catholic Encyclopaedia*, accessed 3 June 2012. New Advent, http://www.newadvent.org.cathen/03255b and http://www.newadvent.org/cathen/03288a; Rosalind K. Marshall; *Virgins and Viragos: A History of Women in Scotland from 1080–1980* (London 1983), 56–7.

23 National Library of Scotland, MS 10000; http://digital.nls.uk/50years/1960.html. Psalm 1 begins: 'Blessed is the man who walks not in the counsel of the wicked'.

24 *RCAHMS Iona* 22, 153–72; Dunbar and Fisher, *Iona: A Guide to the Monuments*, 10–11.

25 *RCAHMS Iona,* 172–8.

26 Ibid., 8, 178–9.

27 *RCAHMS Iona*, 251–2; Jerry O'Sullivan 'Excavation of an early church and a women's cemetery at St Ronan's medieval parish church, Iona' in *Proceedings of the Society of Antiquaries of Scotland*, cxxiv (1994), 327–65; *c.f.* 'A Women's Graveyard at Carriockmore, County Tyrone, and the Separate Burial of Women' in *Ulster Journal of Archaeology*, Series 3, xlvi (1983), 41–6; O'Sullivan, *Iona: archaeological investigations*', 232, 236–7.

28 *RCAHMS Iona,* 144.

29 Janet C. MacDonald, 'Iona's Local Associations in Argyll and the Isles *c.*1203–*c.*1575', unpublished Glasgow Ph.D. thesis, 2010, 129–47.

30 Anderson, *Early Sources*, ii, 461; *Handbook of British Chronology*, 294.

31 *RCAHMS Iona*, 143–4.

32 A.A.M Duncan, *Scotland: The Making of the Kingdom* (Edinburgh 1975), 578–82

33 K. A. Steer and J. W. M. Bannerman, *Late Medieval Monumental Sculpture in the West Highlands* (Edinburgh 1977), 101; *Highland Papers* ed. J. R. N. Macphail (Scottish History Society 1914–34), iv, 135–6.

34 *Calendar of Papal Letters to Scotland of Clement VII of Avignon 1378–94*, ed Charles Burns (Scottish History Society 1976), 185.

35 *Calendar of Papal Letters to Scotland of Benedict XIII of Avignon 1394–1419,* ed Francis McGurk, 77.

36 A. Maclean Sinclair, 'The Clan Fingon' in *The Celtic Review,* iv, 13 (July 1907), 33–4.

37 Lizanne Henderson and Edward J. Cowan, *Scottish Fairy Belief* (East Linton 2001), 152; 57–8, 134.

38 *RCAHMS Iona*, 145, 233–4.

39 Ibid., 144; Sinclair, 'The Clan, 33–4.

40 *Papal Letters to Scotland of Benedict XIII*, 51.

41 Ibid., 103.

Chapter 5 – Disaster and Renewal

1 *Papal Letters to Scotland of Benedict XIII*, 194.

2 Ibid., 144–5.

3 Steer and Bannerman, *Late Medieval Monumental Sculpture*, 101–2; *RCAHMS Iona*, 148.

4 *Calendar of Scottish Supplications to Rome 1418–22* ed E. R. Lindsay and A. I. Cameron (Scottish History Society 1934) i, 264.

5 Ranald Nicholson, *The Edinburgh History of Scotland: The Later Middle Ages* (Edinburgh 1974), 298–9.

6 *Acts of the Lords of the Isles 1336–1493* edd. Jean Munro and R. W. Munro (Scottish History Society 1986), p.lvii.

7 *RCAHMS Iona*, 144.

8 Ibid.

9 *Calendar of Entries in the Papal Registers relating to Great Britain and Ireland: Papal Letters* (London 1893–), vii (1417–31), 194, 461–2, 465.

10 *RCAHMS Iona*, 144–5.

11 *Acts of the Lords of the Isles*, p. lvii; *RCAHMS Iona*, 144–5; *Highland Papers* ed. Macphail, i, 82–92.

12 Steer and Bannerman, *Late Medieval Monumental Sculpture*, 108.

13 *RCAHMS Iona*, 52.

14 *RCAHMS Iona*, 24–5, 52, 58, 63–74, 110–11, 140; Ritchie and Fisher, *Iona Abbey and Nunnery*, 11–13.

15 *RCAHMS Iona*, 52, 114, 123–30.

16 Ibid., 22, 152–75.

17 *Highland Papers* ed. Macphail, iv, 175–6; *RCAHMS Iona*, 178.

18 *RCAHMS Iona*, 52, 58, 102–7.

19 Ibid., 237.

20 Ibid., 231–2; Steer and Bannerman *Late Medieval Monumental Sculpture*, 30, 108.

21 *RCAHMS Iona*, 148.

Notes

22 Sinclair, 'The Clan Fingon', 33–4; Steer and Bannerman, *Late Medieval Monumental Sculpture*, 101.

23 *RCAHMS Iona*, 237–8; Steer and Bannerman, *Late Medieval Monumental Sculpture*, 38.

24 *RCAHMS Iona*, 232; 223.

25 *RCAHMS Iona*, 231–2.

26 Michael A. Penman, 'Campbell, Colin, first earl of Argyll (*d*.1493)', *Oxford Dictionary of National Biography, Oxford University Press,* 2004; online edn, May 2005 [http://www.oxforddnb.com/view/article/4481, accessed 17 Sept 2012]; Michael A. Penman, 'Campbell, Archibald, second earl of Argyll (d.1513)', *Oxford Dictionary of National Biography*, Oxford University Press, 2004; online edn, May 2005 [http://www.oxforddnbcom/view/article/4468, accessed 17 September 2012].

27 Nicholson, *Scotland: The Later Middle Ages*, 542–4; Raymond Campbell Paterson, *The Lords of the Isles: A History of the Clan Donald* (Edinburgh 2008), 55.

28 *Fasti Ecclesiae Scoticanae Medii Aevi Ad Annum* 1638, ed. D. E. R. Watt and A. L. Murray (Edinburgh 2003), 257–69; *The Handbook of British Chronology*, 254–5, 293–4; Cowan, *Medieval Church in* Scotland, 81, 129–32.

29 Cowan, *Medieval Church in Scotland*, 81, 131.

30 Steer and Bannerman, *Late Medieval Monumental Sculpture*, 116.

31 Ibid., 116; *RCAHMS Iona*, 148

32 *RCAHMS Iona*, 148.

33 *Handbook of British Chronology*, 294–5; Steer and Bannerman, *Late Medieval Monumental Sculpture*, 116.

34 Steer and Bannerman, *Late Medieval Monumental Sculpture*, 115–116; *RCAHMS Iona*, 227–8.

35 *RCAHMS Iona*, 149.

36 Steer and Bannerman, *Late Medieval Monumental Sculpture*, 131; *Adomnán of Iona*, Sharpe, 92.

37 Donald Munro [*sic*], *A Description of the Hybrides* (Edinburgh 1774), no. 88, Columkill, text published on http://www.undiscoveredscot-land.co.uk/usebooks/monro-westernisles; *Fasti Ecclesiae Scoticanae Medii Aevi ad Annum 1638* ed. D. E. R. Watt and A. L .Murray (Edinburgh 2003), 270, 274.

38 *RCAHMS Iona*, 13; Marsden, *Somerled*, 115–16.

39 *RCAHMS Iona*, 141.

40 Steer and Bannerman, *Late Medieval Monumental Sculpture*, 102;

Kimm Curran, 'Quhat say ye now, my lady priores? How have ye usit your office, can ye ges? Power and Realities of the office of Prioress in Late Medieval Scotland' in *Monasteries and Society in the British Isles in the Later Middle Ages* edd J. Burton and K. Stöeber (Woodbridge 2008), 124–41.

41 Both are illustrated in Steer and Bannerman, *Late Medieval Monumental Sculpture*, plate 27.

42 C. Cessford, 'The Pictish Mirror Symbol and Archaeological Evidence for Mirrors in Scotland' in *Oxford Journal of Archaeology*. xvi (1) (1997), 99–119.

43 *RCAHMS Iona*, 233.

44 Margaret Sanderson, *A Kindly Place: Living in Sixteenth-Century Scotland* (East Linton 2002), 145–9; Marshall, *Virgins and Viragos*, 56–7; but see also Kimm Curran, 'Death, Removal and Resignation. The succession to the office of Prioress in Late Medieval Scotland' in *Twisted Sisters: Women, Crime and Deviance in Scotland since 1400*, ed R. Ferguson and Y. Brown (East Linton 2002), 35–53.

45 National Library of Scotland, MS 16499, *Hours of Our Lady*, from Iona.

46 Eileen Power, *Medieval English Nunneries c.1275–1535* (Cambridge 1922), 42, 59–60, 69–73.

47 *RCAHMS Iona,* 179.

48 Cowan and Easson, 151.

49 *RCAHMS Iona,* 226–7.

50 Steer and Bannerman, *Late Medieval Monumental Sculpture*, 114–15; *RCAHMS Iona, 226–7,* 229.

Chapter 6 – A Romantic Ruin

1 Gordon Donaldson, *The Scottish Reformation* (Cambridge 1960), 74.

2 Gordon Donaldson, *Reformed by Bishops* (Edinburgh 1987), pp. ix–x; Donaldson, *Scottish Reformation*), 71–5.

3 Domhnall Uilleam Stiùbhart, 'John Carswell (*c.*1522–1572)', *Oxford Dictionary of National Biography,* Oxford University Press, 2004 [http://www.oxforddnb.com/view/article/4773, accessed 25 Sept 2012]; Meek, *Celtic Christianity*, 214–5; James Kirk, *Patterns of Reform: Continuity and Change in the Reformation Kirk* (Edinburgh 1989), 280–304.

4 Donaldson, *Scottish Reformation*, 74–5; Gordon Donaldson, *Scottish Church History* (Edinburgh 1985), 80–1; Rosalind K. Marshall, *Ruin*

    and Restoration: St Mary's Church, Haddington (Haddington 2001), 23.

5 *RCAHMS* Iona, 149.

6 *Registrum Secreti Sigilli Regum Scotorum, the Register of the Privy Seal of Scotland* ed M. Livingstone *et al.*, (Edinburgh 1908–82), iii, no. 2861; v, no. 3255

7 Donaldson, *Scottish Historical Documents,* 170; *RCAHMS Iona,* 179.

8 Donaldson, *Scottish Historical Documents,* 156–7.

9 James Kirk, 'Knox, Andrew (d.1633), *Oxford Dictionary of National Biography*, Oxford University Press, 2004 [http://www.oxforddnb.com/view/article/15780, accessed 4 April 2012]; Donaldson, *Scottish Historical Documents,* 168–9.

10 Cathaldus Giblin, *Irish Franciscan Mission to Scotland 1619–1646* (Dublin 1964), 81–2.

11 Rosalind K. Marshall, *St Giles': The Dramatic Story of a Great Church and its People* (Edinburgh 2009), 80–1.

12 *RCAHMS Iona,* 149.

13 William Sacheverell, *A Voyage to I-Columb-Kill* in William Sacheverell, *An Account of the Isle of Man* (Douglas 1859), 101.

14 *RCAHMS Iona,* 52, 78, 94.

15 Thomas Ross and G. Baldwin Brown, 'The Magdalen Chapel, Cowgate, Edinburgh' in *The Book of the Old Edinburgh Club,* viii (Edinburgh 1916), 36–7; Marshall, *St Giles',* 78.

16 *RCAHMS Iona,* 141–2.

17 Gordon Donaldson, *The Making of the Scottish Prayer Book of 1637* (Edinburgh University Press), 1954, *passim.*

18 *RCAHMS Iona,* 150.

19 J. R. N. Macphail, 'The Cleansing of I-colum-cille' in *The Scottish Historical Review*, xxii, no.85 (October 1924), 14–19.

20 Allan I. Macinnes, *The British Confederate* (Edinburgh 2011), 1–129; David Stevenson, 'Campbell, Archibald, marquess of Argyll (1605x7-1661)', *Oxford Dictionary of National Biography*, Oxford University Press, 2004; online edn, May 2006 [http://www.oxforddnb.com/view/article/4472, accessed 24 September 2012].

21 Macphail, 'The Cleansing of I-colum-cille', 19–24.

22 *RCAHMS Iona,* 150.

23 *The Scots Peerage*, ed. James Balfour Paul (1846–1931), i, 368–70; John S. Shaw, 'Campbell, Archibald, first duke of Argyll (*d.* 1703)', *Oxford Dictionary of National Biography*, Oxford University Press,

2004 [http://www.oxforddnb.com/view/article/4474, accessed 2 Oct 2012].

24 Sacheverell, *Voyage to I-Columb-kill, 98*–107.

25 Martin Martin, *A Description of the Western Isles of Scotland* (Edinburgh 1999), 156–62.

26 *The Letters of Sir Joseph Banks: A Selection, 1768–1820*, ed. Neil Chambers (London 2000), 34.

27 John Gascoigne, *Joseph Banks and the English Enlightenment: Useful Knowledge and Polite Culture* (Cambridge 2003), 90–8.

28 Thomas Pennant, *A Tour in Scotland and Voyage to the Hebrides, 1772* (Memphis, U.S.A. reprint of 1776 publication), 142–52.

29 *To The Hebrides – Samuel Johnson's Journey to the Western Islands of Scotland and James Boswell's Journal of a tour to the Hebrides*, ed. Ronald Black, (Edinburgh 2001, 2nd edn), 378–96.

30 John Gibson Lockhart, *Memoirs of the Life of Sir Walter Scott W.S.* (Edinburgh 1837), iii, 243–6.

31 *The Poetical Remains of the late Dr John Leyden, with memoirs of his Life* (Edinburgh 1819), 24.

32 Nicholas Roe, *John Keats: A New Life* (Yale 2012), 256–7.

33 *The Poetical Works of William Wordsworth* (London 1837), v, 238–41.

34 *RCAHMS Iona*, 151.

35 *The Scots Peerage*, i, 388.

36 *Memoirs of the Life of Sir Walter Scott*, 244; *RCAHMS Iona*, 151.

37 Argyll Papers, Inveraray Castle, Bundle 1528.

38 *RCAHMS Iona*, 151.

Chapter 7 – George, 8th Duke of Argyll

1 *The Scots Peerage*, i, 388–9; *George Douglas, 8th Duke of Argyll KG, KT, Autobiography and Memoirs* ed. The Dowager Duchess of Argyll (London 1906), i, 12–60.

2 *Autobiography and Memoirs*, i, 61–129.

3 Ibid., i, 129–32.

4 Ibid., i, 132–255, 263–4, 414.

5 H. C. G. Matthew, 'Campbell, George Douglas, eighth duke of Argyll in the peerage of Scotland, and first duke of Argyll in the peerage of the United Kingdom (1823–1900)', *Oxford Dictionary of National Biography*, Oxford University Press, 2004; online edn, May 2009, [http://www.oxforddnb.com/view/article/4500, accessed 25 Feb 2012].

Notes

6 *Autobiography and Memoirs*, i, 98; Matthew, 'Campbell, George Douglas, eighth duke of Argyll'.

7 *Autobiography and Memoirs*, i, 307, 311; *The Scots Peerage*, i, 390–1.

8 Campbell, 'George Douglas, eighth duke of Argyll'.

9 *Autobiography and Memoirs*, i, 229, 320–1.

10 Ibid., i, 485; Matthew, 'Campbell, George Douglas, eighth duke of Argyll'.

11 Ibid., ii, 245, 252.

12 Joanna Soden, 'Stanley, Montague (1809–1844)', *Oxford Dictionary of National Biography*, Oxford University Press, 2004 [http://www.oxforddnb.com/view/article/26277, accessed 12 Oct 2012].

13 *Autobiography and Memoirs*, i, 181.

14 8ᵗʰ Duke of Argyll, *Iona*, 1–58.

15 Ibid., 59–130.

16 Argyll Papers, Inveraray Castle, Bundle 523, letter of John Campbell to the 8ᵗʰ Duke of Argyll, 30 June 1855.

17 Ibid., 'Estimate of Proposed Repairs to Iona Cathedral' [*c*.1855–8].

18 *RCAHMS Iona,* 232.

19 Ibid., 232.

20 Argyll Papers, Inveraray Castle, Bundle 523, letter of John Campbell to the 8ᵗʰ Duke of Argyll, 25 August 1858.

21 Ibid., Bundle 1763, letter of John Stuart to Lord Stanhope, 5 October 1867.

22 Ibid., Bundle 1528, letter of James Ferguson to the 8ᵗʰ Duke of Argyll, 7 June 1873.

23 *Dictionary of Scottish Architects*, (Sir) Robert Rowand Anderson, http://www.scottisharchitects.org.uk; Sam McKinstry, *Rowand Anderson: 'The Premier Architect of Scotland'* (Edinburgh 1991), 20–88.

24 A. J. G. Mackay, 'Skene, William Forbes (1809–1892)', rev. W. D. H. Sellar, *Oxford Dictionary of National Biography*, Oxford University Press, 2004; online edn, Oct 2006 [http://www.oxforddnb.com/view/article/25671, accessed 16 Oct 2012].

25 Edinburgh University Library, Special Collections Department, La. IV 17, folios 208–15.

26 Argyll Papers, Bundle 1528, 'List of articles found in making the excavations and repairing the ruins on the island of Iona from 10 August to 5 Sept. 1874'.

27 Edinburgh University Library, Special Collections Department, La. IV 17, folios 208–15.

28 Brian Dix, 'Dryden, Sir Henry Edward Leigh, fourth baronet and

seventh baronet (1818–1899)', *Oxford Dictionary of National Biography*, Oxford University Press, 2004 [http://www.oxforddnb.com/view/article/60772, accessed 16 Oct 2012].

29 Royal Commission on the Ancient and Historical Monuments of Scotland, MS28/40/10, Sir Henry Dryden notebooks and letters, including letter of J. H. Plowes to Sir Henry Dryden, 29 August 1871.

30 Argyll Papers, Inveraray Castle, Bundle 1528, letter of Robert Rowand Anderson to the Duke of Argyll, 16 February 1875.

31 Argyll Papers, Inveraray Castle, Bundle 1583, Letters of the 8th Duke of Argyll to [his chamberlain], 22 February–12 March 1875.

32 *RCAHMS Iona*, 151–2.

33 Iona Cathedral Trust newspaper cuttings book, 1899–1916, letter in a journal named *St Andrew*, 30 April 1903.

34 e.g. Argyll Papers, Inveraray Castle, Bundle 523, Expenses of soup kitchen for poor people at Ardfinary, 5 February 1852.

35 P. B. Waite, 'Campbell, John George Edward Henry Douglas Sutherland, marquess of Lorne and ninth duke of Argyll (1845–1914)', *Oxford Dictionary of National Biography*, Oxford University Press, 2004; online edn, Oct 2005 [http://www.oxforddnb.com/view/article/32269, accessed 17 Oct 2012].

36 Mark Stocker, 'Louise, Princess, duchess of Argyll (1848–1939)', *Oxford Dictionary of National Biography*, Oxford University Press, 2004; online edn, Jan 2008 [http://www.oxforddnb.com/view/article/34601, accessed 17 Oct 2012].

37 *The Scots Peerage*, i, 390; Matthew, 'Campbell, George Douglas, eighth duke of Argyll'.

38 *The Scots Peerage*, i, 392.

39 *Dictionary of Scottish Architects,* http://www.scottisharchitects.org.uk , John Honeyman.

40 E. Mairi MacArthur, 'Celebrating Columba on Iona 1897 and 997' in *Spes Scotorum: Hope of the Scots*, 245–9.

41 Lady Frances Balfour, *Lady Victoria Campbell: A Memoir* (London, 3rd edition, n.d.), 280.

42 *RCAHMS Iona,* 152.

43 Balfour, *Lady Victoria Campbell*, 280.

44 *The Scotsman,* Notices, 24 May 1897 and 12 June 1897, The Scotsman Publications Ltd.; MacArthur, 'Celebrating Columba' in *Spes Scotorum*, 245–9; *Edinburgh Evening News*, 9 June 1897, The British Newspaper Archive (www.britishnewspaperarchive.co.uk).

45 Balfour, *Lady Victoria Campbell*, 282–3.

46 'Sketches of Iona, etc.' and 'Iona Monuments', with Argyll Papers, Inveraray Castle.

47 Balfour, *Lady Victoria Campbell*, 8–30, 279, 283; Joan B. Huffman, 'Campbell, Lady Victoria (1854–1910)', *Oxford Dictionary of National Biography*, Oxford University Press, 2004; online edn, May 2006 [http://www.oxforddnb.com/view/article/48786, accessed 18 Oct 2012].

48 Balfour, *Lady Victoria Campbell*, 277–8.

49 *The Scots Peerage*, i, 392.

50 Ibid.; National Records of Scotland, Register of Births, 19 October 1847, http://www.scotlandspeople.gov.uk.

51 *The New York Times*, 31 July 1895; *Scots Peerage* i, 389; *The Scotsman,* 31 July 1895, The Scotsman Publications Ltd.

52 National Records of Scotland, 1871 Census, http://www.scotlandspeople.gov.uk.

53 National Records of Scotland, Register of Deaths, 3 August 1886, http://www.scotlandspeople.gov.uk.; National Records of Scotland, Edinburgh Sheriff Court Wills, 12 April 1882, registered 8 November 1886, http://www.scotlandspeople.gov.uk.

54 List of Ladies in waiting etc to Queen Victoria, http://boards.ancestry.co.uk /topics.royalty.links202.1.1.1.1/mb.ashx

55 *The Scotsman,* 31 July 1895, The Scotsman Publications Ltd.

56 Sermon of the Reverend Dr Norman Maclean at the funeral of Duchess Ina, *The Scotsman*, 31 December 1925, The Scotsman Publications Ltd.

57 Donald MacKechnie, *A History of the Parish Church of Glenaray and Inveraray*, http://www.inveraraychurch.org.uk/history.html.

58 Waite, 'Marquess of Lorne and ninth duke of Argyll'.

59 Balfour, *Lady Victoria Campbell*, 284.

Chapter 8 – The Trustees' Restoration

1 Iona Cathedral Trust, Iona Abbey Ltd Company Papers, 12, 13a;*The Scotsman*, 30 September 1899, The Scotsman Publications Ltd; *The Glasgow Herald*, 30 September 1899, The British Newspaper Archive (www.britishnewspaperarchive.co.uk).

2 Ibid.; *The Scotsman*, 28 January 1892 and 5 October 1899, The Scotsman Publications Ltd.; Ferguson, *George MacLeod*, 143; MacArthur, *Columba's Isle*, 77, 86.

3 William Ferguson, *Scotland: 1689 to the Present* (Edinburgh 1968),

324–5; *Practice and Procedure of The Church of Scotland* ed. James T. Cox (Edinburgh and London 1948), 419–21; *The Constitution and Laws of the Church of Scotland* ed James Weatherhead, (Edinburgh 1997), 20; J. H .S. Burleigh, *A Church History of Scotland* (Oxford 1960), 404–5.

4 *The Scotsman*, 30 September 1899, The Scotsman Publications Ltd.

5 Balfour, *Lady Victoria Campbell*, 283–4.

6 *The Scotsman*, 30 September 1899, The Scotsman Publications Ltd.

7 Ibid., 5 October 1899.

8 T. W. Bayne, 'Story, Robert Herbert (1835–1907)', rev. A. T. B. McGowan, *Oxford Dictionary of National Biography*, Oxford University Press, 2004; online edn, May 2010 [http://www.oxforddnb.com/view/article/36327, accessed 20 Oct 2012].

9 Norman Maclean, *The Life of James Cameron Lees* (Glasgow 1922), 435–6, 439–40, 443–4; Marshall, *St Giles'*, 127–46.

10 Iona Cathedral Trustees Minutes, 1899–1922, 6.

11 Ibid., 6–9.

12 *Dictionary of Scottish Architects*, http://www.scottisharchitects.org.uk, John Honeyman.

13 *The Scotsman*, 5 June 1905, The Scotsman Publications Ltd.

14 Ibid., letter of Lady Frances Balfour, 15 July 1902.

15 Iona Cathedral Trustees Minutes, 1899–1922, 11–16.

16 Ibid., 18.

17 *The Scotsman*, 24, 25, 27, 30 April, 3 May, 12 May, 21 June 1900, The Scotsman Publications Ltd; *Evening Telegraph*, 26 April and 21 June 1900, The British Newspaper Archive (www.britishnewspaperarchive.co.uk); *The Glasgow Herald,* 30 April 1900, The British Newspaper Archive (www.britishnewspaperarchive.co.uk).

18 Iona Cathedral Trustees Minutes, Minutes, 1899–1922, 19–33, with report by Mr Menzies inserted between pages 38–9.

19 Iona Cathedral Trustees Minutes, 1899–1922, 34.

20 Ibid., 34–6.

21 Ibid., 34–5, 40.

22 Ibid., 3, 34; 5.

23 Ibid., 39–40.

24 *The Scotsman*, 15 July 1902, The Scotsman Publications Ltd.

25 *Ibid.*, 17, 21, 29 July 1902.

26 Iona Cathedral Trustees Minutes, Minutes 1899–1922, 53.

27 Ibid., 118–22.

28 Ibid., 60.

29 Ibid., 66.

30 Ibid., 118–22.

31 Ibid., 120–2.

32 Ibid., 74, 138.

33 Ibid., 77.

34 W. Fulton, 'Cooper, James (1846–1922)', rev. D. M. Murray, *Oxford Dictionary of National Biography*, Oxford University Press, 2004; online edn, Jan 2010 [http://www.oxforddnb.com/view/article/32551, accessed 2 Nov 2012]; 25 March 1903, *The Scotsman*.

35 *The Scotsman*, 29 May 1903, The Scotsman Publications Ltd.

36 Iona Cathedral Trustees Minutes, 1899–1922, 82–90.

37 Ibid., 99, 102, 105–7, 112.

38 Ibid., 102, 138.

39 *The Scotsman*, 7 July 1905, The Scotsman Publications Ltd; Iona Cathedral Trustees Minutes, Minutes, 1899–1922, 116.

40 *The Scotsman*, 15 July 1905, The Scotsman Publications Ltd.

41 Iona Cathedral Trustees Minutes, 1899–1922, 115.

42 Ibid., 128–30

43 Ibid., 146.

44 Ibid., 150–1, 164, 170–2, 181, 191, 246.

45 Ibid., 162–3; The Reverend Tom A. Davidson Kelly, 'Three Responses to the Eucharistic Teaching and Practice of the Scottish Church Society: George Bell, Peter Macgregor Chalmers and Nevill Davidson Kelly' in *Scottish Church Society Report*, 2009, 33–5; Dictionary of Scottish Architects, http://www.scottisharchitects. org.uk; *The Scotsman* obituary, 17 March 1922, The Scotsman Publications Ltd.

46 Iona Cathedral Trustees Minutes, 1899–1922, 163–4, 166, 173, 180, 182–4, 201.

47 *The Scotsman*, 3 June 1911, The Scotsman Publications Ltd.

48 Tancred Borenius, 'Frampton, Sir George James (1860–1928)', rev. Andrew Jezzard, *Oxford Dictionary of National Biography*, Oxford University Press, 2004; online edn, Oct 2007 [http://www.oxforddnb. com/view/article/33242, accessed 24 Oct 2012].

49 Iona Cathedral Trustees Minutes, 1899–1922, 211–4.

50 *The Scotsman*, 29 August 1912, The Scotsman Publications Ltd.

51 Iona Cathedral Trustees Minutes, 1899–1922, 196–7, 182, 215, printed list between pages 232–3 ; ibid., 1923–37, 50, 94, 194, 220.

52 MacArthur, *Columba's Isle*, 90–2.

53 Iona Cathedral Trustees Minutes, 1899–1922, 208, 217–20, printed

list between pages 232–3; Iona Cathedral Trust Papers, Box 8/12, Memorandum of Restoration.

54 *The Scotsman*, 16, 18 July 1913, The Scotsman Publications Ltd; *The Glasgow Herald*, 18 July 1913, The British Newspaper Archive (www.britishnewspaperarchive.co.uk); Lord Sands (Christopher N. Johnston), *Life of Andrew Wallace Williamson K.C.V.O., D.D.* (Edinburgh 1929), 232; Iona Cathedral Trustees Minutes, 1899–1922, 204, 219.

55 *RCAHMS Iona*, 243–4; Dunbar and Fisher, *Iona: A Guide to the Monuments*, 7, 13.

56 Iona Cathedral Trustees Minutes, 1899–1922, 222.

57 *The Scotsman*, 21 July 1921, The Scotsman Publications Ltd.

58 Iona Cathedral Trustees Minutes, 1899–1922, 247–8.

59 *The Scotsman*, 17 March 1922, The Scotsman Publications Ltd.

60 Iona Cathedral Trust Papers, H.M. Office of Work Account Book for Iona and Dirleton Castle and Iona Cash Accounts, 1922–9; Iona Cathedral Trustees Minutes, 1899–1922, 232; ibid., 1923–37, 1, 14, 16.

61 Iona Cathedral Trustees Minutes, 1899–1922, 234–5, 242, 244–5, 251–2; ibid., 1923–37, 2.

62 Ibid., 1899–1922, 232.

63 *The Scotsman*, 28, 30, 31 December 1925, The Scotsman Publications Ltd; *The Western Morning News* (www.britishnewspaperarchive.co.uk), 28 December 1925; Iona Cathedral Trustees Minute Book, 1923–37, 11–14, 71–9, 86; Iona Cathedral Trust Papers, Box 8/2, The Duchess of Argyll's Trust Disposition and Settlement; National Records of Scotland, death certificate of Miss Helen Campbell, 24 June 1927, http://www.scotlandspeople.gov.uk.

64 Iona Cathedral Trustees Minutes, 1923–37, 110–19, 123, 151–4, 161, 166, 193–4; *The Scotsman*, 11 June 1931, The Scotsman Publications Ltd; and obituary notice, ibid., 18 March 1933.

Chapter 9 – George MacLeod and the Iona Community

1 St Colm's College Archive, summarised on Mundus: Gateway to missionary collections in the United Kingdom http://www.mundus.ac.uk/cats/48/1015.htm; Ronald Ferguson, *George MacLeod: Founder of the Iona Community* (London 1990), 144.

2 Lorn Macintyre, *Sir David Russell: A Biography* (Edinburgh 1994), 105–9; NLS. MacLeod of Fuinary and Iona Community Papers, Acc.9084/268, notes on foundation of Iona Fellowship.

Notes

3 Macintyre, *Russell*, 111–12.

4 Ibid., 193.

5 *The Scotsman*, 12 March 1927, The Scotsman Publications Ltd; Ferguson, *MacLeod*, 14; Macintyre, *Russell*, 193.

6 NLS, MacLeod Papers, Acc.9084, 29, 34, 36–57, 199–200; Ferguson, *MacLeod*, 1–133.

7 Ferguson, *MacLeod*, 144; private information.

8 Macintyre, *Russell*, 109, 193; Ferguson, *MacLeod*, 56.

9 NLS, MacLeod Papers, Acc.9084/289 i, 1–8, an expanded version of his 1935 memorandum.

10 Iona Cathedral Trust Correspondence File, 1935–40, n/p, 14 November 1935.

11 Iona Cathedral Trustees Minutes, 1923–37, 224–6; Iona Cathedral Trust Correspondence File, 1935–40, n/p, 14 and 18 November 1935; Ferguson, *MacLeod*, 147–8.

12 Iona Cathedral Trust Correspondence File, 1935–40, 14 December 1935; 23 December 1935.

13 Ibid., 1935–40, n/p, 8, 14 and 27 March 1937.

14 Ibid., n/p, 9 March 1937.

15 NLS., MacLeod Papers, Acc.9084/268, press cutting from *The Evening Citizen* entitled 'A Student's Impression and Criticisms' by John Heron.

16 Iona Cathedral Trust Correspondence File, 1935–40, n/p, 22 July 1937.

17 NLS., MacLeod Papers, Acc 9084/289 i, documents relating to the foundation of the Iona Community.

18 Macintyre, *Russell*, 194.

19 Iona Cathedral Trustees Minutes, 1937–50, 4–6; Ferguson, *MacLeod*, 149–51.

20 Macintyre, *Russell*, 198; NLS, MacLeod Papers, Acc.9084/294, Sponsors' File, 1938–49; NLS, ibid., undated list of sponsors, and letters of D.Y. Cameron; W. N. Smith, 'Cameron, Sir David Young (1865–1945)', *Oxford Dictionary of National Biography*, Oxford University Press, 2004; online edn, Jan 2008 [http://www.oxforddnb.com/view/article/32256, accessed 6 Nov 2012]; Iona Cathedral Trustees Minutes, 1937–50, 241.

21 NLS, MacLeod Papers, Acc 9084/289 i, *Glasgow Herald* press cutting; *The Scotsman*, 26 May 1938, The Scotsman Publications Ltd.

22 Ferguson, *MacLeod*, 154–5.

23 NLS., MacLeod Papers, Acc 9084/293, letters from applicant volunteers, 1938–9.

24 NLS., MacLeod Papers, Acc 9084/289 i, Scheme of Meals (and clothes), *c*.1937.

25 Ferguson, *MacLeod*, 152–3; *The Coracle: Rebuilding the Common Life: Foundation Documents of the Iona Community* 1ˢᵗ issue (reprinted Glasgow 1988), 1–12; Anne Muir, *Outside the Safe Place* (Glasgow 2011), *passim*.

26 Ferguson, *MacLeod*, 163, 342.

27 Iona Cathedral Trust Correspondence File, 1935–40, n/p, 4 and 5 July 1938; Iona Cathedral Trustees Minutes 1937–40, 5 July 1938, 10–13.

28 Ibid., 1937–40, 25 October 1938, 13–18.

29 Ibid., 10–18, 29.

30 Macintyre, *Russell*, 198; Iona Cathedral Trust Correspondence File, 1935–40, n/p, 16 May 1939; Iona Cathedral Trust, Box 8/12, 15 April 1939.

31 Macintyre, *Russell*, 196, quoting letter of George MacLeod to David Russell, November 1936.

32 Ferguson, *MacLeod*, 155–6.

33 NLS, MacLeod Papers, Acc 9084/292, letters of Sir James Lithgow to George MacLeod, 23 June and 30 July 1938; Anthony Slaven, 'Lithgow family (*per.c.*1870–1952), *Oxford Dictionary of National Biography* Oxford University Press, 2004; online edn. May 2006 [http://www.oxforddnb.com/view/article/51878, accessed 17 May 012].

34 Iona Cathedral Trustees Minutes, 1937–50, 31.

35 Iona Cathedral Trust Correspondence File, 1935–40, n/p, 7 August 1937.

36 NLS, MacLeod Papers, Acc 9084/289 ii.

37 Iona Cathedral Trust Correspondence File, 1935–40, n/p, 20 June 1939.

38 NLS, MacLeod Papers, Acc 9084/29.

39 *The Coracle,* i (October 1938), 1–12.

40 Ibid., ii (May 1939), 18.

41 'An Iona for Women', *The Scotsman* 16 June 1939, The Scotsman Publications Ltd.

42 NLS, MacLeod Papers, Acc 9084/317, 318.

43 *The Coracle,* ii, 1–24; George MacLeod, 'Progress of the Iona Community: Its Purpose becoming Better Understood', *The Scotsman* 30 May 1939, The Scotsman Publications Ltd.

44 'The Iona Community, ii, The Life of the Members' by A Special Correspondent, *The Scotsman*, 15 June 1939, The Scotsman Publications Ltd.

45 Iona Cathedral Trust Correspondence File 1935–40, 25 April, 15 May, 30 June 1939; NLS, MacLeod Papers, Acc 9084/310 iii.

46 David George Coulter, 'Wright, Ronald William Vernon Selby (1908–1995)', *Oxford Dictionary of National Biography*, Oxford University Press, 2004 [http://www.oxforddnb.com/view/article/60417, accessed 10 Jan 2013].

47 *The Coracle*, iii (November 1939), 3–12; *The Scotsman*, 8 January 1940, The Scotsman Publications Ltd.

48 T. Ralph Morton, *The Iona Community: Personal Impressions of the Early Years* (Edinburgh 1977), 49.

49 Iona Cathedral Trust Correspondence File 1935–40, 22 October 1940.

50 Iona Cathedral Trustees Minutes, 1937–50, 23 April 1940.

51 *Dictionary of Scottish Architects*, Ian Lindsay, http://www.scottisharchitects.org.uk/architect_full.php?id=202407.

52 Iona Cathedral Trustees Minutes, 1937–50, 64–81.

53 Macintyre, *Russell*, 202; Ferguson, *MacLeod*, 185.

54 Iona Cathedral Trustees Minutes, 1937–50, 24 June 1941, 102–11.

55 NLS, MacLeod Papers, Acc 9084/294, Sponsors' File.

56 Iona Cathedral Trustees Minutes, 1937–50, 28 October 1941; 28 April 1942.

57 Ibid., 1937–50, 140, 165–78, 186, 200, 202–18, 224–30.

58 Ibid., 208; Ferguson, *MacLeod*, 207.

59 Ferguson, *MacLeod*, 207.

Chapter 10 – Safeguarding the Future

1 Iona Cathedral Trustees Minutes, 1937–50, 243, 263; ibid., 1951–66, 22; Ferguson, *MacLeod*, 212, 219, 252, 261.

2 Iona Cathedral Trustees Minutes, 1937–50, 263, 320; Ferguson, *MacLeod*, 212–3; *The Scotsman*, 11 February and 10 June 1947, The Scotsman Publications Ltd.

3 Iona Cathedral Trustees Minutes, 1937–50, 317, 320, 321.

4 Ibid., 330; National Records of Scotland, Register of Deaths, 26 October 1949, http://www.scotlandspeople.gov.uk.

5 Iona Cathedral Trustees Minutes, 1937–50, 384; 355.

6 Ibid., 9.

7 Ibid., Macintyre, *Russell*, 247.

8 Ibid., 1937–50, 260–1.

9 Ibid., 301.

10 Ferguson, *MacLeod*, 250.

11 Iona Cathedral Trustees Minutes, 1951–64, 45–6, 51–3.

12 Ibid., 29–30.

13 Ibid., 39, 54.

14 *RCAHMS Iona*, 130–1.

15 Ferguson, *MacLeod*, 278.

16 Ibid., 280.

17 Iona Cathedral Trustees Minutes, 1951–64, 145.

18 Morton, *The Iona Community: Personal Impressions*, 74–8.

19 Ibid., 43–5.

20 Iona Cathedral Trustees Minutes, 1951–64, 177.

21 Ibid., 66, 108–9, 145–7; Iona Cathedral Trust Papers, Appeal Folder, 1958–63; NLS, MacLeod Papers, Acc.9084/324, 325; Iona Appeal Trust 1959–62, 1970.

22 Jacques Lipchitz with H. H. Arnason, *My Life in Sculpture* (London 1972), 172–6.

23 NLS MacLeod Papers, Acc.9084/334, MacLeod Papers, a somewhat inaccurate typescript memorandum on the subject by George MacLeod.

24 Iona Cathedral Trustees Minutes, 1951–66, 91–2.

25 Ibid., 115.

26 NLS. MacLeod Papers, Acc.9084/334, typescript memorandum by George MacLeod.

27 Iona Cathedral Trustees Minutes, 1951–66, 217–8.

28 Macintyre, *Russell*, p. xi, 124; Iona Cathedral Trustees Minutes 1951–64, 262–3.

29 *RCAHMS Iona,* 131–2; Morton, *The Iona Community*, 95.

30 Iona Cathedral Trustees Minutes, 1951–66, 216, 254; unbound typescript Iona Cathedral Trustees Minutes, 7 November 1966, 9 December 1969; *RCAHMS Iona*, 125.

31 Iona Cathedral Trust Papers, Box 8/10, Infirmary Museum Correspondence, 1958, 1962, 1963, 1965; Iona Cathedral Trust Minutes, 1951–64, 187, 198–201, 213–4, 253–4, 283–4.

32 Iona Cathedral Trustees Minutes, 1951–64, 283–4.

33 Iona Cathedral Trust Papers, Box 8/10, 22, correspondence relating to the proposed lapidarium, 1971–3.

34 *RCAHMS Iona,* 137–8.

35 Iona Cathedral Trustees Minutes, 1923–37, 101.

36 Iona Cathedral Trust Correspondence File, 1935–40, 5 and 11 May 1936; Marshall, *St Giles'*, 143, 158, 159.

37 Iona Cathedral Trust Correspondence File, 1935–40, 24 September 1936, 17 June, 15 July 1939; *The Scotsman*, 26 September 1939, The Scotsman Publications Ltd.

38 Iona Cathedral Trustees Minutes, 1951–64, 242; Iona Cathedral Trust Correspondence File 1935–40, 15 July 1939; Iona Cathedral Trust Papers, Box 11/34a, March 1965; J. L. Campbell, 'MacLeod, Kenneth (1871–1955)', *Oxford Dictionary of National Biography*, Oxford University Press, 2004 [http://www.oxforddnb.com/view/article/53025, accessed 27 Nov 2012].

39 Iona Cathedral Trustees unbound typescript Minutes, 4 October 1966.

40 Ferguson, *MacLeod*, 351; Iona Cathedral Trustees unbound typescript Minutes, 23 April 1968.

41 Ronald Ferguson, *Chasing the Wild Goose* (Glasgow 1998), 112; Ferguson, *MacLeod*, 372.

42 Ferguson, *Chasing the Wild Goose,* 117.

43 Ibid, 104–7; *What is the Iona Community?* (Glasgow 1996 edn), 2–10; Kathy Galloway, *Living by the Rule* (Glasgow 2010), *passim*.

44 Iona Cathedral Trust Papers, Box 3/1, 1963–72; Box 8/4, 1966; Box 9/2, 1965–6; Iona Cathedral Trustees unbound typescript Minutes, 1964 ff.

45 Iona Cathedral Trust Papers, Box 7/16; Anne Pimlott Baker, 'Fraser, Sir Hugh, second baronet (1936–1987)', *Oxford Dictionary of National Biography*, Oxford University Press, 2004 [http://www.oxforddnb.com/view/article/40113, accessed 1 June 2012].

46 http://www.iona.org.uk/macleod_home.php.

47 Iona Cathedral Trust Papers, Box 5/9b, Iona Abbey Ltd papers.

48 *Iona Abbey Ltd. Annual Report and Accounts to 1994; to 1995, to 1996, to 1997.*

49 Iona Abbey Ltd Company Papers, 1994–7, 49; Iona Cathedral Trust Papers, Box 5/9b.

50 Iona Cathedral Trust Papers, Box 7/10, 1997 Financial Appeal Papers.

51 Iona Cathedral Trust Papers, Box 5/9b, 27–8 February 1999.

52 Scottish Government Press Release, 17 September 1999; Extract Deed of Variation from the Books of Council and Session, 12 November 2004.

53 Ferguson, *Chasing the Wild Goose,* 131; *What is the Iona Community?*, 1–2; Galloway, *Living by the Rule*, 11; *Reports of the Iona Community Board,* Proposed deliverances to the General Assembly of the Church of Scotland, 2010, 2011, 2012.

54 Meek, *Celtic Christianity*; Donald McKinney, *Walking the Mist* (London 2005); Ian Bradley, *Celtic Christianity: Making Myths and Chasing Dreams* (Edinburgh 1999); J. Philip Newell, *Christ of the Celts: The Healing of Creation* (Glasgow 2008).

55 E.g. Mary C. Earle, *Celtic Christian Spirituality* (London 2012), 95–9.

56 *The Church of Scotland Yearbook 2012–13*, ed. Douglas Galbraith (Edinburgh 2012), 108–272, 377–97.

57 National Records of Scotland, Register of Births, 1855–2011, http://www.scotlandspeople.gov.uk.

58 Ferguson, *MacLeod*, 241–2.

59 NLS, MacLeod Papers, Acc.9084/360, typescript draft article.

Index

201

Index

Index

209